GETTING PAID

Small Business Management Series
Rick Stephan Hayes, Editor

Simplified Accounting for Non-Accountants
  by Rick Stephan Hayes and C. Richard Baker

Accounting for Small Manufacturers
  by C. Richard Baker and Rick Stephan Hayes

Simplified Accounting for Engineering and Technical Consultants
  by Rick Stephan Hayes and C. Richard Baker

Simplified Accounting for the Computer Industry
  by Rick Stephan Hayes and C. Richard Baker

The Complete Legal Guide for Your Small Business
  by Paul Adams

Running Your Own Show: Mastering Basics of Small Business
  by Richard T. Curtin

Up Front Financing: The Entrepreneur's Guide
  by A. David Silver

*How to Finance Your Small Business with Government Money:
SBA and Other Loans, Second Edition*
  by Rick Stephan Hayes and John Cotton Howell

The Entrepreneurial Life: How To Go For It and Get It
  by A. David Silver

The Complete Guide to Buying and Selling a Business
  by Arnold S. Goldstein

Getting Paid: Building Your Powerful Credit and Collection Strategy
  by Arnold S. Goldstein

GETTING PAID

Building Your Powerful
Credit and Collection
Strategy

Arnold S. Goldstein

A Ronald Press Publication

JOHN WILEY & SONS

New York   Chichester   Brisbane   Toronto   Singapore

This publication is designed to provide accurate and
authoritative information in regard to the subject
matter covered. It is sold with the understanding that
the publisher is not engaged in rendering legal, accounting,
or other professional service. If legal advice or other
expert assistance is required, the services of a competent
professional person should be sought. *From a Declaration
of Principles jointly adopted by a Committee of the
American Bar Association and a Committee of Publishers.*

Library of Congress Cataloging in Publication Data:

Goldstein, Arnold S.
  Getting paid.

  (Small business management series)
  "A Ronald Press publication."
  Includes index.
  1. Collecting of accounts—Handbooks, manuals, etc.
2. Credit management—Handbooks, manuals, etc.
I. Title. II. Series.

HG3752.5.G64 1984   658.5′8   83-16704
ISBN 0-471-88989-X

Printed in the United States of America

10 9 8 7 6 5 4 3 2 1

PREFACE

At a local university several years ago, I heard a flamboyant professor lecture his business administration students on the dynamics of credit.

Waving a single dollar bill in his right hand, he asked, "See this dollar? It represents a typical business' profit." Magically, two crisp single dollar bills materialized in his left hand, "See these?" he said. "They represent that same business' bad debts." Immediately heads snapped to attention. The professor continued, "Imagine waving a magic wand to turn these left-hand losses into right-hand profits:

"Profits would triple.

"Struggling companies would turn into thriving enterprises.

"Business failures would shrink by 50%.

"Investment dollars would return threefold earnings.

"Prices on every product and service could fall dramatically."

Peering over his horn-rimmed glasses, the professor added, "Unfortunately, you will find no magic wand in the real world. But to succeed in any business you must find ways to transform credit losses into profits. Sure, you can build a better product or provide superior service, but real success ultimately depends on mastering the art of *Getting Paid!*" I never forgot that lecture.

In this book I will give you more than a guide to credit and collections. *Getting Paid* offers a total step-by-step strategy to achieve increased profits using a proven two-pronged program to slash credit losses while maintaining or even increasing sales.

Consider the story of an enterprising drug wholesaler who outflanked his competitors by doubling sales while slashing credit losses 80%. How did he do it? Through an effective two-step program offering customers even more credit in return for a conditional assignment of the customer's most valued but commonly overlooked asset—its lease—as collateral security.

And you'll see how an appliance distributor obtains verification of debt from his troublemaker accounts by having his accountant send out a routine audit acknowledgment for their unwitting signature.

What can you learn from a tight-fisted medical clinic? They'll show you how to use attorneys to collect over 40% of your overdue bills with absolutely no legal fees. How? Their attorneys agreed to send out a collection letter without charge, in return for handling the case if the letter didn't produce results.

Perhaps you can benefit from the experiences of a novelty manufacturer who routinely lost over $100,000 annually in unpaid bills. With an easy-to-use consignment agreement his losses dwindled last year to a paltry $387. And the best part? Sales were up 30%.

In the following pages you will see more practical, "no-nonsense" methods that can turn wishful thinking to hard reality. You'll find out why you end up with slow-paying or deadbeat accounts, and you'll learn what you can do about them, including effective techniques to collect from even the most stubborn customer and detailed tactics to actually improve goodwill and customer loyalty while establishing a tough credit program.

Getting Paid offers:

Precise checklists to help you implement your successful program.

Effective forms and agreements needed to protect you.

Costly pitfalls you must avoid.

Powerful, but little known ways to combat chronic credit problems.

Case histories and examples illustrating how others conquered the same problems you face.

A complete credit/collection policy you can easily adapt to your business.

Whether you own a small retail business or manage credit for a large company, you'll find in this book profitable answers to troublesome credit questions. Even doctors, bankers, accountants, and attorneys will benefit from the secrets of improved collections. This book will be an excellent investment for anyone and everyone who extends credit to businesses or consumers and is sincerely interested in *Getting Paid*.

Take a fresh look at your own credit and collection program. During these turbulent financial times many businesses are falling victim to their own credit sins. Don't let it happen to you. The secrets of *Getting Paid* can build your first-line defense and help you survive and prosper.

ARNOLD S. GOLDSTEIN

Chestnut Hill, Massachusetts
December 1983

$\equiv$ ACKNOWLEDGMENTS $\equiv$

Every book has its architects. I am grateful to Barry R. Levine, my law associate, for his candid comments; Robert Sammarco, for his technical assistance, and particularly to my wife, Marlene, for her tireless clerical efforts in preparing the manuscript.

I am most indebted, however, to the true architects of this book—the countless creditors and debtors who have proven there is a correct path to *Getting Paid*.

A. S. G.

CONTENTS

═══ LIST OF EXTRACTS ═══

1

GETTING PAID: NEW RULES FOR AN OLD GAME

WHATEVER HAPPENED TO THE GOOD OLD DAYS?

In a frame on Harry Truman's Presidential desk a bold sign proclaimed "The Buck Stops Here!"

Archie Kurtzman, the feisty president of Kurtzman Textiles, adorns his oversized mahogany desk with his own sign, "Will the Buck Ever Get Here?" Born of truth and humor, it's Archie's constant reminder that getting paid frequently eludes Kurtzman Textiles.

"Whatever happened to the good old days when creditors ruled with iron fists?" asks Archie. Leaning back with hands folded behind his head, Archie begins to dream of those good old days. His imagination transports him back over the eons of time, when Archie the frustrated creditor could play by different rules.

Click: Archie is in ancient Rome and with flowing toga parades his droves of deadbeats to the slave market. Justice is swift. Justice is sweet.

Click: Returning to merry old England, Archie is armed with a whip and wry smile. "Kurtzman Textiles wasn't paid," he snarls. The lash of the whip extracts its revenge. Poverty was painful.

Click: Grabbing his tricornered hat, Archie pictures himself in Colonial America. Smiling, Archie is consoled by the vision of his delinquent debtors languishing in a dark, dank debtors' prison, contemplating the sins of stiffing Kurtzman Textiles.

Snapping back to reality, Archie contrasts the plight of a creditor in modern America.

"It's no contest," admits Archie. Reaching for a swollen file he waves it as his symbol of futility. "This file is my most recent fiasco. This deadbeat Mel calls in a $16,000 order for my new fabric line. Before I can run a credit check, Mel's back on the phone screaming for the goods or he'll cancel the order. I decided to gamble and ship. One, two, three months went by without a check. Mel's secretary ran interference when I phoned. When I dropped in on Mel he pulled the vanishing act. After five months of chasing I turned the account over to my attorney, who hit me up for a $1,000 retainer. Mel's next move was to tie the case up in court with an invented story that the goods were defective. Last week Mel's business went belly-up under a bank foreclosure. I'm out $16,000 for my goods, $1,000 in legal fees, and eight months of running around like a donkey trying to collect. Mel? He's living like a king sporting his new Mercedes around town." Crushing his tired cigar in quiet desperation, Archie complains, "Stiffed again! What does it take to find their check in the mailbox? Magic? Miracles?"

NO MAGIC—NO MIRACLES

Put away your magic wand. Don't pray for miracles. You need *new* rules to win the credit game, rules that can once again give you the winning edge over customers who can't or won't pay. That's why I wrote this book. I want to show you how others are winning the credit game. And how you can also.

In a large sense I'm a traitor to my own cause. I'm a debtor's attorney, a consultant to the distressed, distraught, and defunct business. I call creditors the enemy. They refer to me as the rogue. My job is to make sure creditors are paid as little as possible, as late as possible. It's an interesting line of work. You meet some fascinating people.

Pouring through my doors are the troubled businesspeople. Over 4000 during the past twenty years, to be more precise. They come from every size and type of business. Real people, they were the debtors in Disneyland sharing the common problem of too many bills and too little cash.

The pirates sat across my desk with every known scheme to grab more credit, and every imaginable ploy to escape payment. Staying legally and profitably in debt was their line of work. Through my doors came the professional deadbeats. They'd skip from business to business, always leaving behind a mountain of debt created by their chronic incompetence. In larger droves came the sincere, honest, well-intentioned businesspeople with homes mortgaged to the hilt and butts worked to the bone, seeing their dreams vanishing as they handed me a bushel basket of unpaid bills to tackle. Whoever they were, wherever they came from, they either couldn't pay or wouldn't pay. Sharing their twilight world gave me the perspective for this book.

It was their creditors who provided the inspiration. I met the enemy. Over 500,000 creditors owed over two billion dollars came clamoring for payment. They were a pathetic lot. Most tried to collect using the tired, shopworn, and predictable rules. For all their effort, waving the magic wand or kneeling down and praying for miracles would provide the same empty mailbox. Others never even tried. Living in their own apathetic fantasy land, their laughable overdue notices merrily arrived month after endless month. As Archie said, it was no contest. The creditors were the predictable losers. Passing through the cookie cutter's mold the creditors were shaped to be uninformed, unimaginative, and unpaid.

The cookie cutter however bypassed some creditors. They were the few, the select few who knew how to play the game. They were more than a match. Imaginative and resourceful, they were playing by the *new* rules. They always got paid. They are the architects of this book.

CREATIVE CREDIT FOR THE CHALLENGE AHEAD

How powerful is your present credit and collection strategy? Be honest. Are you the victim of every deadbeat who knocks on your door, or do you consider yourself a pretty shrewd operator only occasionally clipped by the few small inevitable losses even the best credit manager faces?

In reality, the answer is meaningless. The fact is that whether your program is successful or unsuccessful, it must undergo radical change if it is to remain—or become—successful in these rapidly changing times.

"It's back to the drawing board," says Robert Sammarco, credit manager of New England Wholesale Drug. "The credit and collection rules of the 1970s no longer work in the 1980s and will be totally obsolete by 1990. The economy, competitive pressures, and how accounts perceive credit require us to take a fresh look at the credit picture."

Bob's right. You'll need your own blueprint for success, but plan it with the reality your customers will:

1. Demand *more* credit.
2. Default at a *faster* rate.
3. Be *slower* in making payment.
4. Be *tougher* in dealing with you.

Let's take a closer look at each.

1. *Your Customers Will Demand More Credit.* Credit will become the number one sales tool for the 1980s. Accounts will demand more credit and get it. Competition will force you to agree.

There are several reasons for this. Most products and services have multiple sources. In the past competition was based primarily on price or service. Credit was only the byproduct of the sale created by a price or service advantage. Price and service already have been finely honed. Suppliers, for their part, can no longer look to price or service alone to close a sale. Credit increasingly is the new weapon in their sales arsenal. Bill Humphrey, sales manager for East Bay Wholesale Grocers, explains it: "We have twelve competitors in our area pushing for retail accounts. We all carry the same lines and have to work within a 2 to 3% price spread of each other to survive. Prices were already slashed to the bone in the 1960s. In the 1970s we shifted to service to gain a competitive edge. So we offered daily deliveries. When our competitors followed, our competitive advantage was again neutralized. Where else could we turn but to liberalized credit to attract and retain customers?" East Bay doesn't stand alone. Suppliers in every industry have discovered the same. Suppliers stand in line "auctioning" their credit.

Customers, of course, are the beneficiaries of this credit largesse. It encouraged the hottest growth industry—the undercapitalized firm. Whether it's to start or expand their business, owners have happily discovered lines of anxious creditors to provide inventory, equipment, and services with their newly aggressive and liberalized credit policies. It proved a convenient alternative to invested or borrowed capital.

Amy Kaplan, a Boston homemaker turned entrepreneur, proves the point. Her goal was a ladies' apparel shop. With $40,000 saved to buy an opening inventory, she no sooner signed the lease when New York garment suppliers began to ply her with credit terms too good to pass up. "I didn't have to invest a dime," says Amy. "My credit terms were fantastic. They gave me two years to pay for the opening inventory and thirty-day terms on subsequent orders. The best part was I negotiated for no interest charges." The creditor-capitalized rather than owner-capitalized firm is so common today that I even wrote a book about it— *Starting on a Shoestring* (Wiley). It's another sign of the times.

Are you prepared to *intelligently* use credit as a sales tool?

2. *Failure Will Skyrocket.*   Pick up any newspaper or business journal and you'll see it in black and white. Five hundred thousand businesses collapsed in 1982. That's double the 1979 rate of 250,000. The economy is partly to blame. The liberalized credit picture also played its role.

Total credit losses in the business sector are fast approaching 5% of sales, a sharp increase over the 2 to 3% of only a few years ago. Economists predict that losses—paralleling business failure— may jump to 8% or even 10% by 1990. Think about it. If the forecast is accurate, you'll lose ten cents on every sales dollar to defunct accounts.

Marginal accounts, the smaller and recently established firm, will remain the primary culprit. But that was always the case.

The big surprise will be the coming collapse of many rated NYSE- or AMEX-listed conglomerates and the other biggies whose credit was never before questioned. They present a double threat. As a primary account, their loss can easily topple a small supplier. What's worse is the chances they'll catch you off guard.

When W.T. Grant went under, it came as a shock to over 500 suppliers. Reportedly 100 of those suppliers, like dominoes, collapsed under the cash-flow strain of the lost receivables. Pick up the *Wall Street Journal*. Every day seems to bring a new surprise— Braniff Airlines, Penn Central, Johns-Manville, and hundreds more all heading for the bankruptcy court. Strip away the facade of size and you'll see other high flyers as shaky as a house of cards. What does it all prove? There is no sure bet when it comes to credit.

Can you afford any more losses?

3. *Payments Will Be Slower.*   Accounts will play longer with your money. In 1970 the average business collection period was 43 days. In 1980 it approached 60 days. But even these statistics can be deceptive as they include the triple-A accounts.

Break the numbers down and you'll find marginal accounts— the small and new companies holding out for 90 to 120 days with alarming frequency. In some hard-hit industries, accounts struggling with cash-flow problems are now commonly 120 to 180 days in arrears.

There's a jumble of reasons for the "pay later—much later" phenomenon. The economy is part of it. Firms routinely discounting their bills in the past are now 30 to 60 days. In most cases the reason isn't externally caused, but due to the constant cash-flow problems created by undercapitalization, rapid expansion, or poor financial planning.

Cash flow has always been the excuse cited by the slow-paying account. However, today, many managers say they plan their cash flow with the idea they can get away with 60- to 90-day payments. A hobby shop operator stated, "Five years ago I'd enter an order in January, planning on payment by March 10. Today, I'll buy in January, planning on either an April payment or perhaps splitting the payments over 2 to 3 months. It's not that I can't pay faster, but more that the creditors are lenient in letting me go the extra 30 to 60 days."

Fast collections were always a headache with the small firm. The larger rated firms, however, are falling into the same pattern for other reasons. One accounts payable manager for a giant industrial coating firm confided a philosophy shared by many of his colleagues. "We'd rather play with trade credit at 18% interest rather than borrow at 20 to 22% and exhaust our credit line with the banks," he admits. "Besides," he adds, "with our smaller suppliers we may be their major account. They wouldn't dare shut us off and jeopardize our good will. So we shoot for 90-day payments for our smaller suppliers, and even then try to knock off the interest charges."

The domino effect is also hard at work. Many firms justify their late payments, pointing the finger at their own slow receivables. Some accounts, with a "do unto others" philosophy, argue they must reciprocate with their own suppliers to stabilize cash flow.

Even the healthy, cash-rich firms have a deliberate hold on check writing. And who could be richer than a bank? Still one bank president in one concise statement seems to be saying it for all debtors. "When everyone else is stalling for 60 to 90 days, why should we pay any faster?

Can you hang on with *slower* paying accounts?

4. *Expect Tougher Customer Attitudes.* A few years ago a book appeared on the market, *Your Check Is in the Mail* (Warner Books), crammed with hundreds of tactics to connive, outfox, and generally commit mayhem on creditors, and it sold like hotcakes. It was a sign of the times.

The sad truth, Mr. or Ms. Creditor, is that debtors are indeed playing the credit game with a new perception and even morality. The sugar-coated terms "trust" and "honor" have gone the way of the handshake deal and the two-cent candy bar.

Earlier in this chapter I pointed out the unhappy statistic that my own clients, through a variety of devices, waved good-bye to over $2 billion in debts. It was a pile of money owed to a pile of creditors. God-fearing, church-going as they are, my clients still looked at it as nothing more than an unfortunate statistic. We came a long way from the Calvinistic morality of the past.

Why? One reason is that creditors are faceless. The relationship is more often based on pieces of paper than personal relationships.

One retailer who recently eliminated $180,000 in debt under a Chapter 11 reorganization points out it's hard to have empathy for a Los Angeles–based conglomerate when you're a little guy in Hartford.

Organizational size is still another answer. With the one- or two-man firm, accountability was precise. Hiding behind a corporate structure and staff, today's entrepreneur looks at credit loss as a corporate not personal responsibility.

"Dog eat dog" is what one credit manager calls it. "It cuts across every aspect of creditor–debtor relationship. Customers buy, but do they worry about whether they can pay from *your* perspective? They go into Chapter 11 reorganization to save *their* business. Do they lose sleep over *your* losses? An account decides to drop you as a supplier but owes $4,000. Will he hesitate to knuckle you to accept $2,000?" You know the answers. That's why you're reading this book.

Textbooks define credit as "man's confidence in man." Baloney! If it worked so well we wouldn't have credit managers tearing their hair our or courts loaded to the rafters with claims. So let's forget the textbook nonsense. Credit is the exquisite art of making damn sure you'll be getting paid.

STANDING OUT FROM THE CROWD

Now for some good news. As tight-fisted and nasty as your customers are, or are likely to become, they are not your primary adversary. A powerful collection strategy is knowing how to out-flank his other creditors. They're the true enemy.

Why not? You're all after:

1. Healthy customers.
2. Fast collections.
3. No losses.

In reality, the customer is the target of your mutual efforts. Although customers may create their own brand of aggravation, success seldom is based on how shrewd you are in tackling the debtors, but whether you know how to block and outflank competitive creditors.

Several years ago I conducted a seminar for credit managers. About forty credit chieftains showed up searching for the secrets to their customers' checkbooks. I went into the spiel to explain the point.

"Suppose I owed each of you $100, or a total of $4,000. Now I have a problem. I only have $1,000, represented by these ten $100 checks. So here it is, folks," I announced throwing the ten checks in the air. "Go get it." What a sight it was. They were knocking over chairs, pushing, shoving, and ready to throw each other out the window to be one of the ten lucky ones with the prized paper in their hands.

When the charade was over I asked the participants with the checks in their hands to standup. "Congratulations. You didn't beat me. You were successful because you beat the other creditors."

Admittedly it's not a novel thought. It's only a restatement of the "squeaky wheel" theory. You remember it—it's the one that got the oil. But now for the good news. While most creditors agree with it, few know how to practice it effectively. And that gives you a world of opportunity to be truly creative. You have to stand out from the crowd.

Reflecting on the 500,000 creditors unfortunate enough to cross my clients' paths, that singular point always divided the successful from the unsuccessful. In one imaginative way or another the successful creditor somehow managed to stand out from the crowd.

Following a potpourri of strategies, they were inevitably craftier at either *motivating* my clients to pay with a smart incentive, or *forcing* my clients to pay with a tougher collection approach. They didn't simply wave a carrot and a stick, but a *larger* carrot and stick than competing creditors.

"In building a better mousetrap," says Dave Wyatt, a credit consultant, "you do it on the basis of relativity. You can't expect favorable results by copying your competitors. You have to do better. It's no different with credit management. The place to start is by investigating collection strategies and standards within your market and industry. Next you design a program with more powerful motivators. You can't play by everyone else's rules and expect to do better."

The good news continues. Credit and collection strategies have not changed much in the past few decades, despite rapid changes in every other phase of business. The mousetrap, or carrot and stick if you prefer, have remained about the same. It's not difficult to stand out from the crowd.

PLAYING BY NEW RULES

Change never comes easy. This is particularly true when the change is both dramatic and contrary to your own past practices and the fuzzy thinking of the credit industry as a whole. Getting paid means being a contrary thinker, a pioneer, and a maverick.

Wake up Charlie in credit, Sam in sales, and Millie in legal. The changes will shake and wrack your organization and be felt in every nook and cranny.

Expect competitors to question your sanity. But plan on their playing a fast game of catch up once they find the new rules do work.

You'll start with a fear of what can be lost and only a vision of what can be gained. That, too, is part of the process of change and the reality of getting paid.

What are these new rules? It's not a simplistic formula or recipe you can bake in the oven at 350°, cool, and serve. Rather, its a combination of ingredients—ideas that must be molded into a powerful and workable program to increase profits.

For the moment take a bird's-eye view of the significant new rules. They'll unfold in detail as you pass through later chapters, but for now buckle up your seatbelt for a quick spin.

1. *Credit Effectiveness Will Be Measured By a New Yard-stick.*   Traditional formulas to determine the effectiveness of the credit function will disappear, or at least take a back seat to a new formula—profit contribution. The credit department will no longer isolate itself from the responsibility of direct accountability for bottom-line results.

2. *Plan to Unify Sales and Credit.*   It's a logical next step. Rather than clinging to the disjointed sales/credit activities of

the past, customers will be handled under a "total account" strategy. The credit function will remain important, but it will be more closely intergrated with sales, under the responsibility of an account manager.

3. *Credit Will Become Your Hottest Sales Tool.* It was a point made earlier but it will increasingly happen and has proven remarkably successful. As a sales tool it will demand close co-ordination with the sales, advertising, and promotion activity.

4. *Your Credit Will Be Strategically Redeployed.* Total outstanding credit won't necessarily increase for your firm—and in fact may decrease, even with a more aggressive credit/sales approach. But it will necessitate a harder look at who's obtaining credit and why? This, too, will require a new yardstick based on account contribution to your firm's profitability.

5. *Marginal Accounts Will Become Your Best Growth Area.* Not because they suddenly become more credit-worthy, but because you'll analyze their economic value in a new light, coupled with better ways to protect yourself against defaults. Your competitors' rejects will become your welcome and profitable customers—once you learn how to handle them.

6. *Prices and Service Policies Will Be Reworked.* As credit becomes a more visible and important sales tool, the customer will reciprocally be *less* interested or conscious of increased prices or reduced service. This trend will require analytic correlation between credit–price and service to maximize profits.

7. *Credit Will Become Your Major Weapon for Customer Retention.* The indebted account will turn into the captive account. Playing by the new rules will prevent supplier shift unless you're fully paid. Customer loyalty, albeit forced, will help ensure continued sales.

8. *Say Good-bye to Conventional Credit Reporting.* At the very least it will be only a secondary resource for checking out accounts. Comprehensive computerized reporting will play its role, but it will be augmented by other, more reliable indicators and an investigation process more proportionate to risk.

9. *Look for New Credit Criteria.* Present-day methods are the Achilles' heel of credit. They just don't work. Galloping on

the inside track is a fast-growth credit criterion based on two factors: profit contributions and security.

10. *Incentives and Penalties Will Go Through Their Own Quiet Revolution.* Stronger incentives for quick pay, or COD shipments, and stiffer interest for late payers are on the horizon. Again, it's all part of the *bigger* carrot and stick. Expect to pay a premium to motivate fast payments. Expect customers to pay a premium if they don't. Anemic incentives used today don't fit today's economy or credit picture.

11. *Collateral Security Will Become Your Credit Back-bone.* It's certainly true for major suppliers who may have more at risk than the owner and all other creditors combined. Not only will collateral be a more widespread practice but it will be used more creatively, justifying new credit terms.

12. *Credit Monitoring Will Be on the Upswing.* And that goes far beyond monitoring credit limits. It means flexibility, ability to anticipate problems, and closer coordination with your customer.

13. *Quicker Action on Overdues.* This will be part of your total strategy. You'll move faster, much faster, to collect and you'll use a broader range of incentives and collection tools. In-house collections will increase, collection-agency participation will decrease, and legal action, where required, will be more aggressive.

14. *Customer Workouts and Turnarounds.* These will demand very active creditor involvement, particularly among the larger creditors. And it will come sooner and be far less adversarial as creditor and debtor work for mutually beneficial solutions.

THE EMPHASIS IS ON INDIVIDUALITY

One rule stands out above all others—*individuality*. It's the cornerstone of every successful credit strategy.

Let's start with *your* firm's individuality. It's unique. No two companies are quite alike. As you go through this book you'll see many new ideas. The key question is, Can they work for your firm? Some will, some won't. Your industry will be one factor. The competitive situation another. Then you'll have to ask yourself the hard questions about size, organization, cash flow, capital resources, and even operational and growth philosophy—what are you now and what do you want to become?

Next, turn to the individuality of your *customers*. If you have 1000 accounts you won't have one fixed policy for all—not if you want to succeed. Their business is as unique as yours. Each has its own value to you, operating characteristics, and problems. And each offers its own best opportunity and approach when credit problems arise. Effective credit management is having the flexibility to deal with each account on its own best terms.

Third, you're dealing not only with the individuality of the account as an abstract entity—or pile of inventory and equipment—but with the individuality of its *people*. Credit is a "people" game. It's people who decide which checks will be written. So in reality you'll end up with an approach to the entity for what it represents in financial terms, and to its people as you try to psyche out what will motivate them in human terms.

Finally, you come to the individuality of the *situation*. And no two are ever quite alike. A problem may have its sibling but never its precise twin. How can they be when you consider all the variables? So once again you'll be back to the drawing board trying to figure out the one right solution to that one existing problem.

The need for individuality is easy to write about. It's very difficult to put into practice. But you can do it. The place to start is by throwing out your 90-page credit policy loaded with fixed, archaic, and counterproductive regulations. It makes interesting reading, but it doesn't solve credit problems, for it goes contrary to the essential ingredient of individuality.

What you do want is someone, perhaps it's yourself, who can and will make credit decisions with his or her thinking cap on. And what will be under that thinking cap? A rare blend of ingredients that goes far beyond the financial, accounting, and legal skills representing credit management of the past. No, it's not magic, nor a miracle. It will take a dash of salesmanship, a pinch of psychology, a small dose of chutzpah, and the creativity to get out there and see problems for what they are and deal with them. A rare breed? You bet. But it always takes a rare breed to pry the check loose from those who can't or won't pay.

2

CREDIT INFORMATION THAT TELLS THE STORY

ARE YOU ROLLING THE DICE?

You have a choice. You can spend thousands of dollars and countless man hours running thorough credit investigations, or you can make credit decisions on a roll of the dice. Sometimes you can do better with the dice.

A California wine distributor thinks so. Back in 1974 the company had staggering 6% credit losses on sales of two million dollars, while spending over $75,000 on credit checks. By 1975 some changes were made. Credit-check costs were slashed to $9,000, as management began to roll the dice, shipping without extensive investigation. Losses came in under 4%. Don't tell this firm that credit is a science. They'll laugh you out of California.

There's no easy formula to tell you who will pay and who won't. But shooting snake eyes isn't the answer either. Not for the typical firm. If it was I'd refer you to a good book on gambling instead of writing this chapter. But I will tell you this—many firms *think* they have a first-rate credit investigation program—but would come out ahead shaking the dice.

Your firm may be among them. Credit experts agree that 60 to 70% of all firms clear credit while wearing dark glasses. They're charitable. The figure 90 to 95% comes closer to the mark. Few firms do the job right.

The right credit *decisions* depend on the right credit *information.* Obtaining that information is what this chapter will show you, and in the next chapter you'll see how to convert it into winning credit decisions. No, it's not a simple process, and you'll still have your credit losses, but the odds will improve.

TRIPLE-TEST YOUR INFORMATION

How do you measure the value of credit information? You need a three-part test. The information in your files has little or no value unless it's:

1. Accurate.
2. Complete.
3. Current.

Two out of three don't count, because the validity of the whole is dependent on the validity of each. So making certain your files are accurate, complete, *and* current is the first objective.

Let's take a close look at your credit files to see whether they pass the test.

Is the Information Accurate?

Face facts. You don't know how accurate the information is, because you can't filter the facts from fiction. And if your files are typical, you'll have more fiction at your fingertips than you can find at a local bookstore or library.

You can't accept information at face value. Customers have creative pens. They can paint just the right picture to convince you to ship. What will it take? A dash of distortion, an inch of illusion, a dram of deception, a touch of trickery, or an ounce of outright fraud. Even "honest" customers can shade matters to brighten an otherwise bleak financial picture, Ask the IRS. They see it in reverse.

Pick up any one of your files. The customer tells you the company sales are $300,000, but perhaps they are $250,000. The $25,000 profit may be a $35,000 loss. A few assets are swollen, some liabilities shrink, and it all looks so rosy. How can you really tell what's real and what's phony? What you do know is you assumed it to be accurate, so you shipped. Trust can be troublesome.

If you still think you can believe everything you read, you should read the Dun and Bradstreet report on a certain furniture store. It shows sales of $1,200,000 and an owner who graduated the Harvard Business School. Someday creditors may discover the business never grossed more than $250,000 and its owner barely made it through reform school. Don't blame Dun and Bradstreet. They hear it, so they reported it. You're the one who has to dig deep and really investigate. After all, it's your money on the line. So take another glance at your files. What makes you think you have the *true story*?

Is Your Information Complete?

It may be by your standards, but you may be using the wrong standards. Many suppliers do. They rely on one or two credit indicators where they need several more to get the total picture.

Credit resources are like chapter in a book. Each tells part of the story, but you have to read them all to see the entire story. And it's not only a matter of relying on too few credit indicators, you may be relying on the least valuable while ignoring the best and easiest to obtain.

I see it all the time. One creditor uses only financial statements and credit references. Another bases it on a D & B report and a bank reference. Still another believes credit interchanges are enough to do the job. It's all nonsense, and it's nonsense because every credit source is both good and bad. The strength of one is the weakness of another. What one source won't tell you, another one will. Each is a piece of the total puzzle.

In this chapter you'll learn how to effectively use seven credit sources, to reach all the information possible, put them in priority, and cross-reference what they tell you so you have the *complete story*.

Is Your Information Current?

Stale credit information is the same as yesterday's newpaper. It doesn't tell you what's happening today. But remember—you're still shipping today.

A credit picture is never static. No company is in precisely the same financial condition as it was one year ago—or even three months ago. For some, change is gradual, for others, rapid. And the changes can be hardly noticeable unless you make it your business to notice. That requires constant information updates.

Suppliers sometimes don't consider it important. They have historical performance to go on. As long as the checks keep coming in, the goods keep going out. However, without constant monitoring, you never know when the checks will stop arriving, leaving you with an unexpected loss.

Take one last look at your files. Eyeball the dates on your most recent information. Can you honestly say that what you have from 1976 is the *current story?*

MORE INFORMATION AT LESS COST

Information costs money. There always comes a point of diminishing returns where the cost outstrips the risk. How much can you logically spend to credit-check a new customer and his $1,200 order?

Many firms classify new accounts and run them through a credit check proportionate to the size of the order or anticipated credit line. R & R Distributing Co., a soft-drink jobber, follows a rather typical approach. Orders under $500 are automatically shipped without any credit check. Orders between $500 and 1,500 go through a D & B check and one or two reference checks. Between $1,500 and 5,000, a TRW credit check and bank references are added. Once orders (or a credit line) go beyond $5,000, the account gets the full treatment and is required to add current financial statements and go through a credit association or interchange club check.

Although this almost universal practice of structuring the credit check to order size makes sense, with a little added effort it can double your protection.

1. *Credit-Check* Every *Shipment.* The trouble with an automatic-ship policy on orders under $300 or $500 is that customers know the policy. Deadbeats always throw in small orders, knowing they'll escape a credit check. Some divide, for example, a $1,000 order into two $500 orders spaced weeks apart. Even the smallest order should go through a D & B or TRW check.

2. *Change Your Priorities.* The most common device used for checking small or even mid-sized orders are credit references. With a $2,000 order you check the given references and ship. But the references don't mean a thing, as you'll later see. Instead, start with a credit service report for the smallest orders and add bank references, if you want to dig a bit deeper. Credit reports are as easily obtained as references and I consider them a more accurate guide.

3. *Monitor Losses by Category.* For example, you may have a 7% loss rate in the under $500 automatic-ship category. But you may have a 9% loss rate in the $500 to 1,500 category (or whatever classification you use). It points out that you're too lenient in this category. Tighten it up. Demand more information with these orders.

4. *Understand the Economics.* The reason most firms don't go after more information is because they don't think it's cost-justified in relation to the order. It's faulty thinking. You can triple your protection with usually no added cost or slow-down. For example, you may spend one-half hour checking credit references. How much longer does it take to pull one or two credit reports and perhaps a bank check?

5. *Spread the Work.* You can add to your information by making the job of gathering information also a sales responsibility. Some of the best input can come from your sales staff. And it doesn't cost any more to get them involved.

Try this experiment. Whatever your current policy is, take a select number of new accounts from each category and *double* the amount of information you use in making the credit decision. Calculate how much more it will cost you to obtain that added information and profile it against reduced losses. You may see some interesting results. Remember this: It's far cheaper to spend the few extra dollars before you ship than trying to collect afterwards.

FINDING THE BEST CREDIT SOURCES

Probably the most common question in the entire field of credit and collection is, "What's the one best credit source or guide?" You should already know the answer. There is no one "best" source. You need as many as you can reasonably use.

To an extent, I rank priority or value based on the particular industry. For example, I consider Dun and Bradstreet excellent in checking large firms, but give it low marks with the smaller firm. Sales representatives' reports are vital with retail accounts but of little importance with manufacturing or service firms. Every size and type business offers its own best clues.

You should know—and be able to utilize instantly—at least these sources of credit information:

1. Customer-provided information (financial statements, history, and background).
2. Bank references.
3. Credit reporting agencies.
4. Credit associations and interchange clubs.
5. Sales staff.
6. Creditor references.
7. General sources.

The value of your information will depend on the mix of sources, how you cross-reference what each tells you, and whether you know how to extract the information you need. Let's move on and you'll see how to land that information.

WHAT YOUR CUSTOMER CAN TELL YOU

Start with your customer. He/she should provide the preliminary information used as a springboard for further checking.

Direct person-to-person meetings should be a top priority, particularly if the new account will or might become a large customer. The direct meeting accomplishes several objectives. First, you get to know your customer as an individual. Credit reports and pieces of paper are sterile. You have numbers and words, but it's people who pay bills. You want to meet them, size them up, test, probe, and develop a relationship. Customers have a better payment record with suppliers they know than those they never met. It's basic psychology. It's another lesson to be learned from the banks. They seldom make loans on a "mail order" basis. They want their borrower evaluated as an individual.

Communication is also helped through a direct meeting. If the customer is large and suggests a long relationship, then it's important to set the tone for the relationship by reviewing the terms, anticipating and resolving future problems, and generally allowing you and the customer to know what's expected. It goes beyond a credit objective. You can land a new account only to lose it because you didn't understand its needs or problems. The lost customer is not only lost profits but a tough customer to collect from.

With the large account you'll want substantial credit information. It's awkward to handle it by mail, as it creates an almost antagonistic air right from the beginning. With a direct meeting, the information can be casually obtained through general conversation. Imagine your own reaction if you opened an envelope to find a form loaded with questions or financial statements. It creates resistance. If that same supplier wined and dined you over a steak dinner, you'd tell that person twice as much and never even realize it. It's all part of sales technique.

Speaking of sales technique, that points out the fourth—and most important—reason for a direct meeting. You're not there just to check credit; it is a unique opportunity to sell. Build a new, small account into a larger one. Explore the customer's potential. Estimate what he can be worth to your bottom line. Isn't that also part of the credit equation?

A New Jersey brush manufacturer selling to wholesalers and chain accounts believes in the direct meeting. Whenever the company receives an order in excess of $5,000 from a new account it quickly checks out the customer for size and sales potential. "We don't send a sales representative to do the spadework," says its vice-president. "Either the president or I will grab a plane, even if it's to Seattle. We want to meet that customer, walk through his operation, see what he's all about, and kick a few tires. We talk sales but are alert for credit signs. It pays big dividends. In many cases we'll turn a $10,000 customer into a $100,000 customer and we walk away with plenty of credit information. In one case it saved our neck. Visiting a large hardware chain which was already cleared for a $30,000 shipment we noticed a stack of overdue and dunning notices on their comptroller's desk."

Always arrange the meeting at your customer's business. Don't expect that person to sit across your desk and be cross-examined. Let the customer give you the grand tour of the operation, let him or her open up, and think that the account is important. The customer will talk. Your job is to listen.

It's not always practical or possible to arrange a direct meeting. When you can't handle it, delegate it to a sales representative in the area. He or she is your goodwill missionary and the eyes and ears you can't provide. Whether your sales rep should attempt to obtain credit information depends on this person's normal duties and the division of responsibility with the credit department. At the very least the rep should supplement the information. Later in this chapter I'll show you how.

Letter requests, of course, have their own limitations. The best approach is to:

1. *Request Only the Most Essential Information.* Lengthy applications and financial statements discourage response and accuracy.

2. *Sell the Benefit.*   Let the customer know the information will help him obtain the *maximum* credit line.

3. *Make the Request Seem Routine.*   And it should be routine. A preprinted or form letter works well here.

4. *Assure Confidentiality.*   A customer has the right to expect it.

5. *Let the Customer Know the Order Is on Hold.*   Specify the shipment is held pending receipt and acceptance of the credit information.

An effective letter may take this form:

Gentlemen:

   Thank you for your interest in our company and your recent order. So that we may ship your order, would you please complete the enclosed credit application and provide us with your most recent financial statements. It will help us grant the most favorable credit terms. This information will be held in strict confidence.

Sincerely,

Ten Questions to Ask Your Customer

Whether you use credit applications, personal meetings, or phone calls, try to obtain the following information:

1. Age of company.
2. State of incorporation.
3. Names of officers.
4. Names of owners or stockholders (if a small firm).
5. Bank.
6. Present supplier (selling your brand merchandise).
7. Reason for switching suppliers.
8. Estimated annual purchases from your firm.

9. Expansion plans.

10. Prior firms at same location (if retail).

Each question has its purpose. Age of company shows stability. The state of incorporation is useful if it becomes necessary to commence suit. The names of the officers and owners can help you cross-reference them to other firms who may have burned you. The bank is where you'll be heading next for a credit reference. The present supplier and reasons for switching can help you uncover whether it was for credit or other reasons. It's also a good marketing tool. Estimated purchases and expansion plans help define the profit potential from the account. Prior firms at the location also shed light on the stability of the location and can be used to determine whether you've dealt with those firms.

A final point. Find out every trade and business name used by the firm, including its affiliates, divisions, and parent firms. Make sure you know who you're dealing with, so you can put the entire corporate family to the credit test.

Obtaining Financial Statements

Customer-completed financial statements are usually a waste of time, particularly if your customer is a small firm. Better than half of your smaller customers don't know how to complete a statement accurately. Those that do may either fudge or outright fake it. I've seen hundreds of those statements. I pity the creditors who rely on them.

Another reason to stay away from customer-furnished financial statements is because customers are inclined not to complete them. Some are scared by them, and others don't have the time. So it means a lost order.

A number of suppliers believe the value of financial statements is to discourage bad credit risks. An insolvent firm, for example, won't complete the statement (realizing its futility) or risk faking it (realizing its consequences). But how can you be sure?

If you do want to go with customer-supplied finances, then keep it basic. Just the essentials will give you a good idea, and a complicated one, nevertheless, loses accuracy. Print a warning on the bottom. Let the customer sign under oath, and a reference to the mail-fraud statutes doesn't hurt either. It may keep their pens a bit less creative.

The best way to land financial statements is either to request tax returns or accountant-prepared statements. Tax returns are already on hand; no work is needed. And, if anything, they'll portray the worst possible financial situation. So you have a built-in hedge.

Accountant-prepared financial statements, unless certified, may not be much better than the information provided the accountant by management. However, it's likely to be more accurate than customer-completed financials.

Try to obtain financials directly from the accountant. The approach may allow you to obtain new financials from the accountant on an annual basis, without further customer authorization. One firm successfully uses this customer authorization form:

To: (Accountant)

You are authorized to provide my supplier,

XYZ Company
10 Elm Street
Anytown, U.S.A.

copies of our most recent financial statements, including balance sheet and income statement, upon our supplier's request and until notified to the contrary.

_____
Customer

It's not a farfetched idea. This simple bypass speeds up and simplifies credit processing in dozens of ways and to everybody's benefit.

TALKED TO A BANKER LATELY?

Your own banker can be the most reliable source of credit information. The objective is to use him or her as a credit emissary in talking to your customer's bank.

You, of course, can call a customer's bank for a reference, but bankers being a cautious, conservative bunch seldom say much unless you're part of the pinstripe fraternity. That's why you want your banker to intercede.

Naturally, you can't go running to your banker to check every new account. Your banker is running a bank, not your credit department. But your banker can be used sparingly for some of your large accounts, or when your credit decision is on the fence.

What can your banker find out about your customer?

1. The average cash balance on account.
2. History of returned (bounced) checks.
3. Outstanding loans with the bank.
4. Status of bank loans.
5. Other liens or encumbrances against customer assets.
6. Growth and future prospects for customer.
7. Problems experienced by the firm.
8. General condition and stability.

This is precisely the information you too should look for from a customer's bank. When making direct contact, the information may be "guarded," but most banks cooperate.

The president of a large Chicago firm says that bank credit information is among the most important credit tools he uses. "In countless cases," he adds, "we have been able to accept orders from customers where favorable bank information was able to offset or refute unfavorable facts developed through other sources. In countless other cases direct and frank comments from banks have enabled us to avoid major losses."

When using a bank to clear initial credit, say so. If you need bank information because you suspect the account is in trouble, then be candid about it. You want the customer's bank to respond to your specific concern. Above all, retain the information as confidential. If your customer believes the bank talked too much, it will get back to your own banker. Remember, you want him or her on your side.

RATING THE CREDIT RATINGS

Dun and Bradstreet (D & B) has been synonymous with credit for so long that it seems redundant to advise any businessperson today to look for this foremost credit agency for credit information.

What few suppliers realize is the full range of D & B services. The reference books offer justification enough for approving small orders to well-rated firms. For large orders, turn to D & B's Key Accounts' reports with periodic follow-up reports, put together by D & B's best investigators.

Besides the reference book and the Key Account report, there are many other reports and services geared to specific industries. The only way to find out about all the available services and costs is to phone D & B. Their representative can design an information system to suit your needs and at the best cost.

Many D & B subscribers don't fully utilize what they're paying for. For example, they may look only to the ratings and ignore the specialized information available in the reference books. The rating books show the organization structure of the listed firm, its age, and length of time at that rating. The reference books go far beyond this and provide a narrative about the company, its sales, profitability, reports from other suppliers, encumbrances of record, some basic financial-statement information, and the background of its principals.

How do I rate D & B? I give it top grade when it comes to rating the large firms (sales of several million dollars or over), but poor grade with the smaller firms.

The reason for the poor rating with small firms is due to their inability to separate the fact from fiction. They essentially write up and report what the owner tells them, or what they can quickly gather from several other sources.

For this reason, I highly recommend D & B as a quick tool for shipping small orders to large, well-rated firms, and only as a third or fourth place backup in evaluating the small firm.

Some of the limitations of D & B can be answered by *TRW Credit, Inc.* It fills a void in the credit-reporting system. Started several years ago, TRW has suppliers from around the country feed in the payment histories of their respective customers. This information is then collated and reported out by customer name. For example, if you order a report on X Company, the report may show the payment history with 10 to 15 suppliers.

The effectiveness of the TRW system is its random reporting. Unlike customer-furnished references, a TRW report picks up the history with any firm tied in to the system.

TRW Credit, although an excellent and vital service, has its own intentional limitations. It won't tell you much more about a customer than its payment history with select suppliers. To the extent that information is valuable, the service is valuable.

There are weaknesses even with the TRW system, beyond its limited purpose. One problem is that a particular customer may not do business with many TRW firms. One, two, or even three references don't mean much. Another problem is that a clever customer can rig the system. By identifying the reporting suppliers it can pay them, while remaining a "slow pay" with nonparticipating suppliers.

TRW coupled with a D & B report provide a good cross-reference. A customer may get by one service, but it's not likely it will fool both.

While D & B and TRW are the dominant national reporting agencies, many industries rely on agencies that specialize within their industry. For example, the Jewelers Board of Trade, the Paper and Allied Trades Mercantile Agency, and the Lyons Furniture Mercantile Agency are a few.

These specialized agencies are somewhat of a cross between a reporting agency and an interchange club, as they have characteristics of both.

There are several advantages and disadvantages with these firms. The one major advantage is that specialization tends to generate better investigation and information. At least that's what a subscriber would assume. Some agencies do fulfill that goal exceptionally well. Others do a poor job and are markedly less accurate than the national agencies. This inconsistency of quality is their main disadvantage and could put you at a distinct disadvantage unless you know just how good the particular agency is.

The second disadvantage with the specialized agency is that it depends chiefly on information provided by major suppliers within the industry. This doesn't provide assurance the customer is prompt with secondary suppliers from outside the "core" industry. Unless you are a primary supplier in that industry, step carefully.

Suppliers focusing on a particular industry should subscribe to these specialized services. The cost is nominal and depending on the scope of the report and strength of the agency, it may replace either D & B or TRW Credit as a reference. It's never a good idea to rely *only* on a specialized agency. You need a backup.

HOW TO "INTERCHANGE" INFORMATION

You can directly "interchange" information with other suppliers through a wide assortment of credit interchange associations and clubs.

The National Association of Credit Management, for example, operates credit interchange bureaus on a closely coordinated basis. Each bureau, although locally owned or controlled, obtains information from its members, and in turn provides the information to other bureaus through the National Association.

The reporting system is not complicated. Members agree to:

1. Notify the bureau of all customers.
2. Provide the names of all known creditors when making an inquiry.
3. Respond promptly and in complete detail to all requests for information on a customer.

With bureaus all over the country maintaining this type information, it follows that members can receive quick and accurate information on a prospective customer.

The National Association of Credit Management recommends that you order an interchange report:

1. To investigate any first order.
2. When you receive an unusually large order.
3. When a customer changes payment habits.
4. To increase a credit line.
5. To stay abreast of marginal accounts.

Local Credit Interchange Groups

These groups are essentially small business clubs organized in an informal basis. Membership is open to suppliers within the particular industry.

The members get together several times a month to discuss their experiences with specific customers or group of customers. Typically, advance notice is given of the accounts to be discussed at the next meeting, so the needed information will be available.

As each customer's name is called, each member who has dealt with the account states his experience. In a two- or three-hour meeting, you can obtain substantial information on a wide number of accounts.

Interchange groups are excellent for monitoring accounts, but they, too, have their restrictions.

Since the clubs are organized on a local and industry basis, they are primarily used by wholesalers and jobbers servicing the industry within the localized area. As with specialized credit agencies, they don't answer the needs of secondary suppliers servicing the industry, since the club generally consists of primary (major) suppliers. For example, New England has an interchange club of ten to twelve drug wholesalers. If a particular pharmacy decides to switch suppliers, its credit history is immediately known to any prospective wholesaler. But it may not mean much to a cosmetic firm as a pharmacy may pay a primary supplier more promptly than a secondary or "one-shot" supplier.

If you are a major supplier, servicing a local area, an interchange club is a good bet. Write to the National Association of Credit Managers. They can tell you about clubs in your area.

TURN YOUR SALESPERSON INTO A BLOODHOUND

In lines where salespeople are assigned specific customers, they can and should be part-time credit investigators. And it shouldn't be as a favor to the credit department. Spell it out in their job description.

Sales representatives have top notch investigative capabilities for many reasons.

1.   They may be the first representatives of your firm to reach the customer. Sales reps are the people closest to the account and the ones who have—or will develop—a personal on-going relationship with the customer. I've seen good salespeople get more credit information in twenty minutes than a credit department could obtain in a week.

2.   The salesperson can scan inventory and pick up the names of other suppliers. This provides you a long list of references beyond what the customer furnishes.

3.   The sales rep is your "eyes and ears." He or she can report the physical condition of the business, and except for the benign "neat and orderly" notation in a D & B report, it's the only way to find out what the customer's business "looks like."

4.   Monitoring a customer's condition is easier with a salesperson on the job. The rep can detect signs of decline and deteriorating condition.

5.   The salesperson is a mediator. For example, a customer may request a $20,000 credit line. You may not feel comfortable with a $20,000 credit line but be willing to go with $10,000. Who knows better whether the customer will go along with a $10,000 credit line than your sales representative. Credit is part of sales. The salesperson knows your respective bargaining positions.

Let me show you just how effective all this can be. A Baltimore food wholesaler has his salespeople sit in once a month with the credit manager to review accounts. The salespeople report any observed problems—or even positive changes experienced by a customer.

If an account begins to fall behind in payments, the salespeople first try to work it out, and in any case report back the reasons.

But that's only their monitoring function. Their real credit contribution is in reconnaissance—scouting out all there is to know about a prospective customer, using this sales report form:

SALES REPORT ON NEW ACCOUNTS

Name: Address:

Principal's Name: Tel. No.:

Years at Location: Size (sq. ft.):

Affiliated or Parent Firm:

Estimated Sales Volume: $

Describe Physical Appearance:

Describe Area or Locality:

Estimated Inventory Level: $

Prior Supplier:

Reason for Change:

Is Previous Supplier Paid:

Estimated Purchases from Our Firm:

Credit Line/Terms Requested:

Bank References:

Customer-Furnished References:

Other Suppliers:

Recommended Credit:

           (Use Reverse for General Comments)

You can modify that same form to fit your needs, but consider the scope of information the sales personnel can feed back to the credit department.

Make your salespeople accountable for bad debts if they share responsibility for the loss. And oftentimes they do. About two years ago I sat in at a meeting with a client, his credit manager, and salesperson trying to figure out how to salvage a $70,000 receivable due from a small department store that suddenly went belly-up into bankruptcy. The credit manager was surprised because the store had a $100,000 credit line and was behind only 45 days when it collapsed. The sales rep piped up, "I'm not surprised. A large discount store opened up across the street about a year ago and you could see the account beginning to fall apart." The salesperson could see it—but the credit manager couldn't because he was 1200 miles away. After the old "I didn't tell you because you didn't ask me" routine, the salesperson was fired.

Your salespeople want to get paid. Make sure they help you get paid.

PROSPECTING WITH CREDIT REFERENCES

Credit references are fool's gold. When the references are furnished by the customer they don't mean a blessed thing, so put the dime back in your pocket and don't even make the phone call.

The reason for this statement should be obvious. Any customer can find three suppliers to vouch for him, while 230 other creditors are out chasing him. Of course, you don't know about the 230 who are in various stages of being stiffed. You're too busy listening to platitudes.

I have seen plenty of troubled, debt-ridden, and defunct businesses in my time. I have yet to see one who didn't have at least three good references on standby. Some of these references are new suppliers who are fortunate enough to be current but will soon join the ranks of the less fortunate. Sometimes a reference is a major supplier who keeps the customer on a short credit leash. More times than not it's a supplier who has payment promised if only he'll say all those nice things. And in a few cases the reference is your customer's uncle or father-in-law hiding behind a business name.

However, these references come about and, whoever they are, your customer knows they'll say the right things. Do you suppose he'll refer you to someone who won't?

So don't waste time with customer-furnished references. If you're still tempted, then at least scatter your shots. Ask the customer for six or seven references. Don't make it easy by limiting it to three. Tell the customer you want his primary and next largest supplier, then ask for two or three secondary suppliers in diverse lines. Round it out with a utility, the landlord, and perhaps the company's insurance agency. If you obtain favorable reports from all (or most) of these sources, you have a reasonable chance.

Try to locate the suppliers on your own. This is where your salespeople come back on the scene. Have them check out the merchandise lines. If they know their business they can figure out 10 to 15 probable suppliers in 10 minutes. Now you have a list to work with.

Some suppliers without a sales staff simply call a list of probable major suppliers in the area. If one doesn't sell the account they probably know who does. The primary supplier in turn usually can refer you to several smaller suppliers. It only takes a few phone calls to get the ball rolling.

Asking the Right Questions

Once you find reliable credit references, ask the right questions:

1. How long have you sold on credit to this customer?
2. What are the terms?
3. What is the customer's credit line?
4. What was the account's highest balance during the prior year?
5. What is the present balance owed?
6. What part of his current account is overdue? For how long? Why?
7. What are the company's general paying habits?
8. Is there any general information about the account that will be useful in basing credit?

Obtaining fast and honest answers to those questions is another matter, Identify yourself and explain the purpose of the call. Speak directly to the credit manager. Of greatest importance, promise to reciprocate the favor.

A reputation for reciprocating is the key to a direct interchange system. Other credit managers will only cooperate if they have your cooperation in return. And it doesn't hurt to do a little more than is expected to cement the interchange relationship. One credit manager makes it a point to follow up telephoned reports with a mailgram. It's an added touch.

Your own honesty is another ingredient. To obtain truthful responses, other credit people must have confidence in your own reports. The quickest way to be frozen out of the referral system is to be caught in a few less-than-honest reports.

Mail inquiries are never as productive as telephone references. With a quick phone conversation you have the answers in minutes and it will tell you more than the sketchy information on a written form.

Place customer-furnished references at the bottom of your list. However, if you can randomly call four or five suppliers with diverse lines, it has about the same value as a TRW Credit report.

How to Get Information from Competitors

The one supplier you'll probably be inclined to ignore is a competitor. It stands to reason. Why should a competitor help you out?

This situation requires tactful handling, because the response will depend on three factors:

1.   Whether the competitor *really* thinks of you as a competitor or whether the competitor is resigned to the fact the account is lost.
2.   The competitor's prior relationship with you.
3.   Whether the competitor thinks you'll reciprocate.

The competitiveness of the situation is usually the major obstacle. If the customer is committed to dropping the competitor, then let the client first cut his relationship *before* you call. Don't call and take the competitor by surprise. It won't help you in obtaining a reference and can only hurt your prospective customer.

It can happen that a customer plans to buy only selected lines from you, while retaining your competitor for other lines. Your competitor should also be forewarned of this division.

The most common case is when a customer won't terminate your competitor until it starts its relationship with you, which in turn depends on a credit extension. So you're back where you started. In these situations, use a two-pronged approach:

1. *Check the Customer's Invoices.*   It's the simplest and easiest way to get around the problem. Assume your customer uses ABC Company as its supplier. Ask to review his invoices from ABC for the prior six months or so. The statements and invoices will tell the story in five minutes. It's not necessary to tell the customer you want the statements for credit purposes. Let the customer think you want to run a price comparison check.

2. *Try for a "Phantom" Reference.*   Don't call for yourself. You have other contacts in the industry so ask a noncompetitive supplier to call for a reference. Your competitor may be more candid with him than he will with you.

He may also be more honest with him. A pet supply firm found that out. It called an existing but competitive supplier for a reference and was told, "The account is no good. We have him on COD and even then his checks bounce." Since the pet shop appeared successful, the prospective supplier took the added two steps. It had a "noncompetitive" supplier phone and it was told the pet shop was a terrific account. The pet shop's statements from this major supplier proved it.

Past suppliers are less of a problem because you don't represent a threat. The objective here should be to find out "why" the relationship came to an end. See if it matches your customer's story. Plenty of customers will tell you they dropped X Company because its "prices were too high" or "deliveries too slow." Talk to the supplier. You may find out that X Company is owed $10,000 and was dropped only when it shut the credit spigot.

When it comes to credit, you can't have a better ally than a competitor.

FOUR MORE COMMONLY OVERLOOKED SOURCES

There are hundreds of other places to go if you want to pick up bits and pieces of credit information. Some are time-consuming and probably not worth the effort unless you're dealing with a large account; however, others don't take much effort at all and can produce interesting information.

Use this checklist:

1. *Public Records.* Check out whether there are mortgages (security interests), tax liens, or attachments against the customer. These will be on file in the state recording office and city (or county) office where the customer is located. Your attorney can show you how to check. For distant accounts you can have a check conducted by several firms at nominal cost. Data-File Services, Inc., Santa Monica Boulevard, Los Angeles, California, is a firm I have used with good results.

Dun and Bradstreet reports and some other agency reports show mortgages; however, the report may be stale and not disclose recent encumbrances. If prior mortgages are an important credit factor, do your own search.

2. *Court Records.* One of my clients, a small gift store chain, had a reasonably good D & B report and TRW Credit report and yet had twelve collection lawsuits against it. Sure it happens. A check of court dockets could have picked it up.

Court records are usually not checked because it is time-consuming and you wouldn't think you need it once you use all the other sources. But it can be quite effective, particularly if you deal with local accounts. A practical procedure is to give the list of new accounts to your attorney on a weekly or biweekly basis. He can check them by batch during his next trip to the courthouse. Courts increasingly computerize defendants by name. Any one account can be checked in two or three minutes.

3. *Check Your Customer's Customers.* It's not a common reference source, and it must be handled right. If your customer has a long-standing relationship with two or three major customers, they're in a position to supply useful information. The two items to focus on are (1) the stability of the relationship and (2) whether your customer is functioning smoothly.

TYPE OF BUSINESS JOBBER/DEALER PRODUCTS SPECIAL INSTRUCTIONS LIMIT DATE AUTHORIZED

Corporation
Partnership
Proprietorship

Successor To

Terms
Regular
C.I.A.
C.O.D
Special

Owners		Salesman	In Business Since	References	Date	Account Opened	H.C	Pays		Year	Sales	H.C	Payments
Phone												
Bank												
Address												
Loan $	Security	Av. Bal. $										

DUN & BRADSTREET, INC.

| Last Report | Rating |
| Service Exp | Date |

		Date of Statement
RECORD OF SUITS, JUDGMENTS, BAD CHECKS, ETC.		Cash
DATE	ITEM AMT.	Receivables
		Inventory
		Current Assets
		Current Liabilities
		Working Capital
		Deferred Debt
		Net Worth

Year	Sales	Bal.	Paid
Month	Sales	Bal.	Paid
Jan.			
Feb.			
Mar.			
April			
May			
June			
July			
Aug.			
Sept.			
Oct.			
Nov.			
Dec.			
Total			

Agency Trade Payments
Date
H.C
Disc.
Prompt
Slow
Notes
C.O.D
Atty

Exhibit 1. Customer Credit Information Form.

Late deliveries, out-of-stock situations, and obvious shifting of suppliers are frequent customer complaints. And it can signal the need for further investigation.

4. *Ask Your Own Attorney or Accountant.* You may be a fortunate supplier represented by an attorney or accountant who specializes in your industry. These specialists know what's what, and who's who within the local industry. And if they don't know a customer they can easily find out about him.

Our own law firm is quite active representing the drug industry. One of our clients is a wholesale drug firm. If it needs information about a particular drugstore we can help. Other accountants or attorneys specialize in the liquor, restaurant, and nursing-home industry and just about any other significant industry you can name. These are good people to have on your side.

PUT IT ALL TOGETHER

Compile all the information pouring in from the various sources. Reduce it to writing so you can see the total picture. Use this Customer Credit Information Form (Exhibit 1) as your guide.

Attach to the Customer Credit Information Form the back-up data. Your thick file will contain:

Credit agency reports.

Sales rep's reports.

Interchange reports.

References.

Bank references.

Financial statements.

Credit applications.

Now you can begin to make "thinking cap" decisions, as you begin to analyze what it all tells you. And if you've done the job right it will tell you plenty.

3

CREDIT DECISIONS WITHOUT GUESSWORK

There's a standard axiom in credit circles that customers can be divided into three distinct groups:

1. The top 10%—the cream of the market—representing very little credit risk.
2. The bottom 10% representing obviously hopeless credit risks.
3. The "middle" 80%. The questionable group—some sound, some unsound, and all mixed up together with no ready means to tell them apart.

The axiom is wrong. If you closely followed the previous chapter, you have the means right at your fingertips. Now all you have to do is start using the information to arrive at some decisions.

ANSWER TWO QUESTIONS

Just about every credit and collection book starts out with a discussion of the 3 Cs of every credit decision—*character*, *credit history*, and *capital*. Some wisely add the fourth—*collateral*. I certainly agree with collateral; I devote an entire chapter to it.

The alphabet-soup approach, like parenthood and apple pie, is difficult to attack. But there's a simpler way to say it:

1. Has the customer paid in the *past*?
2. Will the customer pay in the *future*?

A positive answer to one question doesn't necessarily ensure a positive answer to the other. Two short examples explain the point:

As I write this book I have about 10 to 12 business clients with an excellent track record on bill paying. Their D & B and TRW Credit ratings are superb. So are these credit references. They have no trouble lining up new credit despite the fact that most of these firms *won't* be alive one year from today. One firm, a gourmet shop, was capitalized with $200,000 coming from the pocket of a rich father-in-law. The business has lost $40,000 to 50,000 a year since it opened. Suppliers have been paid because the money *was* there.

Here's an example of the opposite problem. A young woman opened a clothing store with limited capital. It was tough sledding for the first year or two, and then business and profits picked up. She has her share of old, unpaid bills and a spotty credit history to prove it. But her business is catching up the bills, and with her projected $30,000 to $40,000 annual profits it won't take long to be out of the woods. The sad part is that she can't get credit. All her new suppliers have their own limited vocabulary—"COD."

It's the number one error haunting the credit field. Suppliers tend to attach too much importance to the *past* and not enough emphasis on the *future* when making credit decisions.

One reason is its relative simplicity. It doesn't take a genius to evaluate a credit reference, an interchange recommendation, or TRW Credit report. It takes more work to roll up your sleeves and ask "Where's the customer heading?" For many suppliers it's the unanswered question.

You want it answered for more than credit reasons. Risk is only a small part of the equation. The potential benefit—what your prospective customer may become—is the other.

Did you ever hear of Radio Shack? With over 5000 stores, the name would only escape a hermit. I know one of its smaller suppliers who sells over one million dollars a year to the chain. But he started years ago when Radio Shack was a small, one-store shoestring startup in downtown Boston. Competitive suppliers with their blinders on didn't see the potential and didn't extend the credit. This supplier did, gambling with a healthy $50,000 credit line. It paid big dividends.

PAYMENT PERFORMANCE: LOOK CLOSER

No suggestion is made that you should ignore payment history. It is an important indicator for the future. Of greater importance than the payment record are the reasons behind it. There can be many reasons why a business may have a spotty or even chronically poor credit record and still be a worthwhile risk. Look for certain patterns:

1.   A pattern of paying certain suppliers on time and not others has several possibilities. The most common is the priority the customer attaches to the supplier. "Lifeline," or primary, suppliers selling essential goods will be paid on time because the customer needs the product. Secondary, or "one-shot," suppliers are dispensable. When cash flow is tight, cash availability is channeled to the primary suppliers and away from the secondary.

This common condition shouldn't in itself disqualify the customer. Your first step should be to assess the cash-flow or profitability prognosis. Is the customer's financial condition improving or not? The second question is whether you'll be a primary or secondary supplier? Your own anticipated payments should be comparable to other suppliers selling goods of equal demand.

2.   Chronic delinquencies are another matter. An account with only poor references has either a serious cash-flow situation or poor payment habits. But don't be quick to throw this prospective customer away either. As with my friend with the clothing store, the cash position may straighten itself out and turn into a prompt account. The only way to handle this type account is with a very

small credit line, or a slightly larger line if adequately secured, if you have confidence in improvement. If the problem is attitude or habits, the situation will never correct itself. COD is all that's justified.

3.   The "stand-out" delinquency is where a customer has a good payment history with seven or eight suppliers, but a poor record with one or perhaps two others. When "slow pay" is the exception not the rule, the problem may not be financial. Usually it's a dispute with the supplier. Your best strategy is to ask for more references to make certain it is the exception and confirm with both the supplier and customer that a dispute exists.

4.   Don't overlook seasonal or cyclical problems. Cape Cod businesses, for example, who have payables unpaid at the end of the summer season, won't pay those bills until the next summer rolls around. A Vermont business, dependent on the winter ski business, can only pay during its season. Check into the payment pattern to see whether it's fast or slow in relation to its cyclical cash flow.

5.   As a final step, check to see whether a poor credit history resulted from a casualty, business interruption, or other one-time mishap. Not long ago I reviewed a TRW Credit report on a Dallas firm. It was dismal. Fifteen suppliers listed accounts over 120 days old. It took a phone call from his accountant to explain the firm was shut down for three months due to a labor strike. Checking further we found this same firm promptly paid for twelve years prior to the strike, and is again back on track.

What it comes down to is the references can only tell you "how they pay." It's not enough. You have to find out "why."

EVALUATING YOUR PROSPECTIVE CUSTOMER

Good credit managers don't know what they're missing. They should say good-bye to their $35,000-a-year job, put on a pinstripe suit, and become six-figure investment advisors or stock speculators. Why not? The *credit* decision takes the same skill and analysis as the *investment* decision. Perhaps the only real difference between creditors and investors is that creditors oftentimes have more invested in the business than do the investors.

That brings me to my present plight. If I had a sure formula for evaluating a company to show you who would and would not make the grade, I wouldn't be writing this book. I'd be too busy playing the stock market. Don't bother reaching for another book. It won't give you any guaranteed formulas either.

The best you can hope for is to improve your chances for separating the winners from the losers by pulling out a pocket calculator and adding some common sense to the pile of information in your file.

Divide your analysis into two broad categories:

Nonfinancial
1. Background of the company.
2. Management.
3. Market position.

Financial
4. Solvency.
5. Profitability.
6. Liquidity.

EVERY COMPANY HAS A PEDIGREE

Starting with a history of the company requires you to know every name the business operated under since its inception. The credit application should disclose this. While you're at it, pull together the names on all divisions, affiliates, subsidiaries, and its parent firm, if any. Your analysis should review the entire corporate family.

Move on to the age of the firm. It's an arbitrary statistic, but firms under five years old require a more thorough analysis than older, well-established firms. The critical years are years 2 to 4 of a business life. That's when most fail. With the embryonic firm, your analysis will center on the financial strength of the firm since there's so little history to go on.

Credit reports refer to the term "antecedents." These are reported business failures, insolvency proceedings, lawsuits, and casualties. These usually stand out as "blotches" on the D & B report.

Insolvency proceedings are the most common. Chapter 11 reorganizations and prior composition or extension agreements are the usual entries to contend with. If the firm is still under a Chapter 11 proceeding, immediately disqualify it for anything but COD terms. It's too risky for new suppliers. A good rule-of-thumb is to extend only COD or short credit terms to any firm who has gone through a reorganization within the prior three years. Ninety percent of the firms that make it through a Chapter 11 fail a year or two later.

An insolvency proceeding three or more years earlier shouldn't disqualify reasonable credit. Many firms stumble early in their life due to undercapitalization. The creditors essentially capitalize the business by assenting to the debt cancellation, putting the firm back on its feet. As with a new firm, the firm with an insolvency record requires increased reliance on the financials to test current solvency and profitability.

If a prior bankruptcy is of concern, obtain the details. A call to the counsel for the creditors' committee or trustee will tell you the causes, the settlement, and the prognosis. Avoid credit for the firm with two or more insolvency proceedings. Check predecessor firms owned by the same people. I have several clients who have failed three or four times under separate corporate names. They won't do any better the next time around either. For this reason, it's critical to trace the prior affiliations of the owner.

Casualty losses are usually less of a problem. These too may appear on a D & B report. Fire losses, however, can be a problem because a pattern can point to arson or inability to insure the business. The only remedy is to determine whether the business has adequate insurance. Check into it if you will be a large creditor.

Lawsuits are inevitable in any business. Be on the lookout for a pattern of collection lawsuits or any one lawsuit that can cripple the company. Several collection lawsuits, even if for small amounts, highlight a payment problem. Even then you have to look at it in relative terms. For example, two or three collection suits against a firm with hundreds of suppliers are probably contested claims. Several more suits against a small firm defy the conclusion that all the creditors are wrong.

The one larger lawsuit can be a business killer. Sometimes it temporarily helps a business by cleaning up its balance sheet. How? Before the lawsuit, the business records the debt as a liability on its balance sheet. Once suit is commenced, and defended, the debt is removed as a liability and is treated as a contingent liability which may not be picked up in the financials.

A large import firm ran into that situation. It had $800,000 in liabilities, with one supplier owed $600,000. When this primary supplier started suit, the liabilities shrank to $200,000 while the lawsuit appeared as a buried footnote. New suppliers never noticed it and based on the "solvency" of the firm extended another $300,000 in credit. Eventually the $600,000 creditor put the firm out of business.

Always look for the "hidden lawsuit." If the potential judgment is large enough to impair the business, restrict credit until it's resolved.

MEASURE THE MANAGEMENT ABILITY

You know the statistic. Over 90% of all business failures are caused by mismanagement. And of all the items to analyze, nothing defies evaluation quite like management ability.

Experience is a common criteria but even that can be illusive. Points to consider are experience in that type business and experience within the firm.

The age of the firm is meaningless unless matched by the experience of its management. New management can play havoc with a fifty-year-old enterprise. How many times have you seen a successful father, for instance, turn a healthy business over to a wayward son or daughter? I always diary it ahead a year or two as a probable bankruptcy case. Of course, the reverse can also be true. There are plenty of tired owners falling by the wayside under archaic management who see their business saved with young blood. But it always comes back to one adage—You're gambling on *people*.

Experience must also be measured by prior responsibility. A person can have twenty years' experience in the industry but not have the balance or span of experience to run the entire show. Ask not only "how long" but "what did you do."

The most challenging type is the budding entrepreneur right out of college, planning to set the world on fire. They have plenty of ideas, no experience, and the chutzpah to ask for an outlandish credit line. They also have the remarkable ability to attract investors and suppliers alike. Enthusiasm can be contagious. Don't fall victim to the disease. Let them show you either a track record or collateral.

Inevitably, it all comes down to a subjective test. As Syd Parlow, a management consultant, says, "You can't assess management by reading a book or a financial statement. You have to talk to the people, find out what they know, what they have done, what they plan to do, and why. Throw out the questions. Listen to the answers. Within an hour you can tell if you're talking to a turkey or the goose who will lay a few golden eggs."

If the account is large enough, do some background checks. Pull a personal credit report on the principals. How do they run their personal life? What is their personal financial condition? They'll never run a business better than their own personal affairs.

The D & B report identifies the officers and their backgrounds, education, and experience. It also tells you how long they have been with the company and their capacity. Sometimes you have to check further, if the credit line warrants it.

In small corporations an owner with a poor credit background can easily use a "straw" to act as an officer. It happens more often than you may think. From my own observations, I'd say that at least 5% of all small businesses are owned or controlled by people who never appear on credit reports or corporate papers. There are many reasons. Social Security disqualification, divorce settlements, and even job conflicts explain some. The professional deadbeats or "bust-out" artists are hiding behind the rest. They never find it difficult to find a "straw" to "front" the operation for them. There's always a girlfriend, relative, dumb friend, or naïve employee willing to put his or her name on the corporate papers. You never know who you're dealing with. Not with a small business.

How can you check it out? There is no easy way. And when you can, it's time-consuming. Your best bet is to ask its bank one more question—"Who signs the checks?" These characters seldom give up quite that much control. Your salespeople can also help. They should be able to walk into a small business and find out "who is who."

Unlike any other credit indicator, management assessment requires direct contact. You don't have that opportunity when you receive an order from a new account 1000 miles away. It's only a name. If you have a sales rep in the area let that person check out the business and report in. Ask about management when checking credit references from local or major suppliers. It's as important a question as payment history.

SIX WAYS TO CHECK MARKET POSITION

Market position is a "catch-all" phrase. It includes analysis of growth, industry, competition, customers, and several other points not disclosed under financial analysis.

Here's a checklist to follow:

1. *Is the Business Growing?*   You can use any of three sources. The D & B report comments on growth by showing sales changes, and in the narrative on the history of the company. Salespeople should also comment on it. Finally, the comparative sales in the customer's income statement will show the growth rate.

Many credit people look at growth as a positive credit indicator. I disagree. It, too, needs a closer look. Rapid expansion, for example, is a major cause of business failure. And many companies grow, not by retained earnings or fresh investor capital, but by leveraging with credit. Look at all the discount store chains who grew rapidly with creditors' money only to slash debt with a Chapter 11.

Properly funded growth can, however, be a positive credit sign, because it represents active management or strong market acceptance. But it's in assessment of account profitability that growth becomes tremendously important. Recall the case of my acquaintance who is now a primary supplier to the 5000-store Radio Shack chain? He played it right. He could see the potential and the expansion plans and what it would all mean to his own sales. That's how businesses are built. They "piggy-back" onto customers who are going places.

2. *How Strong Is the Industry?* Every industry has its cyclical problems. Ask the domestic auto-makers. Years ago small Mom and Pop food stores were in trouble. Today they're strong as franchised units. Independents in the drug, liquor, and hardware business face tough sledding. Few are in good condition. The garment industry is always in trouble. On New York's Seventh Avenue, they don't talk in terms of "if they go bust." It's only a matter of "when."

If you're constantly selling to a particular industry, you should know what's happening with it and to it. It doesn't answer the question of whether to ship or not, but it can help mold an intelligent liberal or conservative credit policy.

3. *Who Are the Customers?* This is high on my list when I analyze a company. I'm on the lookout for firms that have a small customer base or high customer vulnerability. Here's what I mean.

A small baby goods distributor in our area did 60% of its business with one discount store chain. Suddenly the chain dropped him and switched to direct buying. With the lion's share of its volume gone, the distributor collapsed with $275,000 in unpaid debts. We have all seen other failures brought about by a customer's customer going bankrupt, starting the domino effect.

The real question is not whether this type customer will pay you, but instead whether the customer's customer will continue to buy—and pay *him.*

Accounts who sell or deal with governmental agencies are always suspect. They have the highest vulnerability of all. No customer can put a supplier out of business faster than the government. Maybe you don't know quite what it's like to deal with the government: today you have a contract—tomorrow you don't. When you do sell them they take their sweet time paying. After they pay (nine months later) they audit to make sure they didn't overpay. And they say they always overpaid. You can't fight city hall.

A governmentally dependent customer requires a short credit leash. Anything else is a bad gamble.

4. *How Does the Competition Stack Up?*   This is of secondary importance. The customer's own growth adequately answers it.

The one danger is in selling to the firm facing a "sudden" competitor. That's when yesterday's financials don't mean much in forecasting the future.

Harley-Davidson, the famous motorcycle manufacturer, for example, had the heavy-duty motorcycle market all to themselves, while the Japanese cornered the lightweight market. Just some months ago Yamaha and several other Japanese producers decided to upgrade to the heavy-duty models in direct competition with Davidson. Who can really say how healthy they'll be next year?

Retailers have their own competitive problems. Around the block from my home a small fast-food restaurant thrived for years. In two months, a new McDonald's siphoned off 70% of its business. The small restaurant will never survive. Suppliers may be the last to know.

What can you do to check competitive influences?

1. If the account is an existing customer, then monitor purchases. A buying slowdown may be an indicator of competitive pressures.

2. Keep your salespeople on their toes. They should report back new competitors who may threaten a customer's position.

3. Ask about competition when checking credit references on new accounts. Existing suppliers usually can detect competition problems.

5. *What About the Physical Plant?*   If you or a sales representative can inspect the customer's business, you'll have an excellent credit indicator. It pulls together not only your assessment of management but the accuracy of the financials.

Keep your eyes open. Look over inventory levels, merchandising (if a retailer), mix, and condition. Does the customer buy direct from manufacturers (a sign of credit strength), or is it a "hand-to-mouth" operator buying small quantities from wholesalers and jobbers?

What about overbuying problems? The woods are full of retailers who are loaded with unpaid inventory. Focus in on the payables on the balance sheet and you can see if this fits your customer.

What is the condition of the equipment and fixtures? Old equipment means anticipated major expenditures to replace. Excessively expensive fixtures point to waste.

Standing alone, physical appearance of the business means little. Textbooks say a clean, orderly, well-organized operation is a good credit sign. It's nonsense. Those generalizations are dangerous. Scanning the 2000 businesses I represented in bankruptcy, I found no correlation between appearance and credit-worthiness.

What it does do is send you in the right direction in checking the financials.

6. *Is the Location Stable?*   This is a consideration only when dealing with retailers. Even then it's of secondary importance but still worth considering.

Slum or ghetto area stores can be remarkably profitable. What makes them risky is their lack of stability. Plenty of declining neighborhoods have seen a mass exodus or closing of retail outlets. Sometimes it happens unexpectedly.

About three weeks ago we closed up a liquor retailer who survived for years in a ghetto area. The owner, peering at the wrong end of a Colt .45 for the third time that year, said, "Enough is enough" and dropped the keys to the business on the lap of its major creditor.

D & B usually mentions area when reporting on retailers. It's worth spotting in forming a credit policy.

USING SIMPLE ARITHMETIC AS A CREDIT GUIDE

Let's turn to the financial criteria. You can get to the meat of a customer's financial statements rather quickly if you know what to look for. Then it's only a matter of simple arithmetic. Financial geniuses need not apply.

A batch of financial statements can be intimidating to nonfinancial types, and that includes 80% of all businesspeople who have trouble enough understanding their own financial statements without worrying about their customers'.

The financial types, on the other hand, can have a picnic with a set of financials. Dun and Bradstreet and the Graduate School of Credit Management offer intensive courses in financial analysis. D & B backs it up with instructional manuals weighing over eight pounds. Some firms do it all by computer, much like the IRS selects returns for audits. They get the computer whirling, plug in the few dozen financial entries, and a few seconds later it spits out an analysis. One model computer reportedly even tells you the recommended credit line. It makes credit work fun. When the customer doesn't pay, just kick the computer.

Most of this technology and sophistry is nonsense. Sure, if you're asked to extend $200,000 in credit to a questionable conglomerate you may want to burn the midnight oil pouring over financial statements. But how much time can you spend when a customer wants a $5,000 credit line? That's when you need fast answers.

No two people analyze financial statements the same way. The approach is always different, and the conclusions also differ. D & B, for example, recommends use of fourteen finanacial ratios for analysis. Robert Morris Associates recommends at least twenty. There are some good books on the market that can show you 40 to 50 financial ratios to consider. One book, outbidding the others has 80 ratios. It shouldn't take more than two days to dissect your customer's statements. And when you're through you'll know more about his business than your own.

So let's forget the nonsense. Your objective is to scan the financials as *rapidly* as possible to answer one question—Do you ship or don't you?

I have my own technique and have successfully used it for years. It's simple and 95% as accurate as the long, complex methods.

SEVEN FAST STEPS FOR CREDIT SCORING

Your analysis has three objectives. You need to know (1) How things stand now, (2) How things got the way they are, and (3) Where things are going.

Take two initial steps before you even start. Try to obtain two or preferably three years' financial statements. You can't learn much from a single statement because it doesn't tell you the trend of the business.

Next, obtain industry figures. Acceptable or average ratios differ from business to business, so you need a basis for comparison. Robert Morris Associates, a leading collection firm, can help you here. They compile average financial statements for every size business, dividing them into small, medium, and large companies. The Bank of America, San Francisco, California, publishes their own sets. Write them for a copy, specifying the type business.

Now you're ready to start, checking out the company for:

1.   Solvency.
2.   Profitability.
3.   Liquidity.

How Solvent Is the Business?

Solvency is the foundation for credit. It's the first factor to consider, since it makes no sense to investigate profitability or liquidity if the firm is insolvent. You want your bills paid. Only the solvent firm can pay these bills.

Test solvency with these three steps:

Step 1.   Accounts Payable Aging.   Your primary objective is to see how the account will pay you. What better way to find out than to see how they're paying existing suppliers? That's what an account payable aging will show you.

The balance sheet will tell you the total accounts payable outstanding. For example, payables may be $60,000. Next, calculate the average monthly purchases. To do this, divide the annual cost of goods sold by twelve (months). If the business has a cost of goods sold of $360,000, it buys, on average $30,000 a month. You have your answer. The average aging of its payables is 60 days.

If normal trade terms are 30 days, the 60-day aging shows considerable overdue bills. It may be that one major supplier is in arrears 90 to 120 days, while smaller suppliers are current, just the reverse, or that the business is reasonably uniform on its arrearage with all suppliers. Only the customer can give you this information, and if it's interested in credit it should.

A few days ago a hardware store requested a $15,000 credit line from a wholesaler client. Its payables were $85,000 and had a $350,000 cost of goods sold on sales of about $500,000. Since the business buys about $30,000 a month, its creditors, on average, were waiting about 90 days for payment. The wholesaler shipped on COD. Why check further?

Step 2. *The Current Ratio.* Bankers love this ratio. It gives you the measure of short-term solvency, and the adequacy of working capital to meet current obligations.

To calculate the ratio, divide the total current assets by the total current liabilities as follows:

$$\text{Current Ratio} = \frac{\text{Total Current Assets}}{\text{Total Current Liabilities}}$$

The major difficulty with this ratio is determining the acceptable number. As a very rough rule-of-thumb, nonservice firms should have at least a 2:1 ratio. Only an industry comparison can tell you the appropriate ratio for your customer. Drugstores, for example, show an average 2.5:1 ratio. Liquor stores are about 3:1. A service business without inventory may be in good shape with a 1:1 ratio.

A current ratio on the low side by 25% or more (compared to similar businesses) is a warning of a pending solvency crisis. If the current ratio is low, credit should be restricted until it improves.

New startups usually have an anemic current ratio, particularly if they are pooly capitalized. The ratio generally improves as the business generates retained profits. An established business with a poor ratio represents a greater risk because it is usually the result of accrued operating losses. Trend comparisons are particularly needed with the current ratio. A poor and still deteriorating ratio highlights a very poor credit risk.

Step 3. *Total Debt to Net Worth.* This ratio measures the overall debt against owner's equity. If the total debt exceeds the owner's equity, it means the creditors have a greater investment in the business than the owners.

The ratio is calculated as:

$$\text{Ratio} = \frac{\text{Total Debt}}{\text{Total Net Worth (Owner's Equity)}}$$

Finance books recommend a ratio of less than 1:1. That is, the equity should exceed the debt. That's too simplistic a statement. Many businesses are started on a shoestring (minimum owner's investment) and survive because they can generate profits fast enough to retire debt.

As with the current ratio, trend analysis is needed. A poor but rapidly improving debt/net worth ratio may justify a reasonable credit line, whereas a presently acceptable but rapidly declining ratio signals future solvency problems.

How Profitable Is the Business?

Profitability of the enterprise is only important to the extent that it shapes the future solvency (or insolvency) of the business, and reciprocally its ability to pay bills. The most solvent firm will eventually turn insolvent after years of chronic losses. Conversely, the insolvent firm who begins to generate profit may clear its hurdles, provided its creditors are sufficiently patient.

Consider these profitability ratios:

Step 4. Net Profit on Sales. This ratio measures the profitability of the business as a percentage of sales. For example, if the business has sales of $800,000 and before tax profits of $24,000, the percentile profit is 3%.

$$\text{Net Profit on Sales} = \frac{\text{Net Profit}}{\text{Net Sales}}$$

Don't expect profits in the new startup operation. It typically takes a new business a year or two to reach its breakeven point. Understandably, this is the same time period when credit need is most intensive. The creditors end up gambling the new business will reach its profitability goal, but ships without adequate evidence that it will reach the profit point.

Assume you are asked to extend credit to a new firm in business for six months. You can obtain a balance sheet to check solvency, but no income statement will yet be available. Request your customer to provide monthly sales and a break-even calculation. For example, if the break-even point is $300,000 a year, how close is it to the $25,000 a month mark? Can the business someday reach profitability? Don't ship on blind hope and faith.

The established business has its income statement to convince you of profitability. However, with the small firm the chances are you'll end up with noncertified financials. This also means you won't see much in the way of profits. Small-business owners have a way of hiding profits from the prying eyes of the IRS. What it does mean to you is that you will probably see the *worst* profit picture. And that's good. It gives you a built-in hedge. It's far safer to gamble on understated rather than on overstated profits.

How much profit should you see? It really doesn't matter— providing the business is presently solvent and there's enough profitability to pay down long-term loans. Beyond that it's the owner's headache. You're only interested in a stabilized solvency.

The unprofitable business is another matter. This won't be the big white lie. If you see it, it's there. Quantify it. To what extent will the losses eat into solvency? What is the profit trend? What are the reasons for the loss? When will the loss become a profit? How?

Step 5.   Net Profit to Net Worth.   This calculation doesn't mean much in evaluating the small firm, but it is important with the larger company, particularly, if it's a subsidiary of a still larger firm.

Follow this calculation:

$$\text{Return on Investment} = \frac{\text{Net Profit}}{\text{Net Worth}}$$

Return on investment, you might think is only for the stockholders to think about. Think again. Many parent companies won't hesitate to close a small subsidiary showing too small a return on investment. And when it happens the creditors may easily lose out.

Later in this book I advise you to obtain a parent-company guaranty when extending credit to a subsidiary. In large measure that resolves the problem of checking out the subsidiary and instead you begin to test the financial strength of the parent.

Suppose, however, you can't obtain that guarantee. Now you're back to weighing the profitability, not only to ensure solvency but also corporate goals.

For example, the owners of a four-restaurant chain (each incorporated separately) with locations scattered around Long Island, found one of its restaurants producing only a meager $10,000 profit on a $100,000 investment. With a minimum return on investment goal of 30%, they decided to sell out, at a loss producing only 60% for creditors.

Still another reason for checking R.O.I. (return-on-investment) is to measure the efficiency and management effectiveness. Profits as a percentage of sales are never as accurate an indicator as return-on-investment.

To measure the growth potential of the business look to return-on-investment. If you find a customer showing a return well in excess of industry standards, you have a winning horse to ride. With steady performance it will have plenty of investors knocking on their door.

Put the profit picture in a framework. Correctly evaluated it should answer three important questions:

What are the profit *goals* of the business?

What are the profit *prospects* of the business?

What are the profit *uses* in the business?

Try to find out if the business is intended as a long-term operation or if it is a "cash cow" which can only generate income today without long-term prospects. Knowledge of the industry is one clue, the objectives of the owners, the other. Know the *goals*.

Be realistic in assessing *prospects*. Don't turn down the new business because of losses. Assess the future. Don't shy away due to an occasional bad year. It can happen to any business. Find out the reasons. Be a detective.

Check the retained earnings of the business. Profits, in itself, doesn't mean a thing if the owners are taking more money out of the business than it earns. Look for owners who keep plowing profits back into the business. Not only will you have a stronger customer but one owned by people who show their own confidence in it. What better reference can you have than owners who intelligently use profits.

How Liquid Is the Business?

Liquidity means the ability to generate cash to pay debts. And it's a vital financial indicator for creditors.

I suggest you look at it in two time frames: (1) The *immediate* liquidity and (2) the *long-term* liquidity. And to do it you only need two indicators:

Step 6. Sales to Working Capital.   Whenever I analyze a balance sheet, my eyes immediately gravitate to the number opposite the cash entry. I want to see the working capital available to the business. But is it enough? To find the answer, profile it against total sales:

$$\text{Working Capital Ratio} = \frac{\text{Cash on Hand}}{\text{Total Sales}}$$

You can't look only to the present balance sheet. Determine what the "normal" or average cash-on-hand position is. Check two or three year's statements. It may be the business is cyclical and always ends its fiscal year in a cash-poor position, while it operates with a healthy cash position during other months.

How do you find out. See if the owner can provide you interim or quarterly statements. Many businesses, even small businesses (thanks to computerized accounting), have quarterly or even monthly statements. If not, find out when calling for a bank reference. Be candid. Ask what the average balance is for the account. The banker will probably tell you "low," "medium," or

"high," or that it maintains a three-, four-, or five-digit balance.
Banks are like burlesque dancers. They never show you quite
the whole story. But you'll have an idea of the cash routinely
sitting in your customer's checkbook.

If you see the business with a chronically low or overdrafted
cash position, you're up against a character robbing Peter to pay
Paul. And even then Paul may not be getting paid. But go further.
Some owners operate with little cash and little debt. As quickly
as the money comes in it goes out, particularly if it's a COD-type
account.

Do the same even for the business with large cash reserves. It
may have even larger payables. The accounts payable aging (Step
1) will tell you. Place the two in perspective to see whether the
customer is holding on to excessive cash reserves while letting
creditors dance for their money.

The situation to beware of is the one with little or no cash and
excess payables. This is a definite credit risk. And don't be fooled
by the same business with good solvency ratios. The business
may have a high inventory or even receivables creating an overall
solvency, but the goods on the shelf can't help you if the customer
doesn't know how to convert it into bill-paying cash.

Step 7. Project Long-Term Cash Flow. This important indicator
doesn't have a simple ratio. What it does take is a long-term cash-
flow analysis to see whether the business can pay its long-term
loans.

Why is it important? Consider that 70% of all business failures
are not due to lack of profits, but inability to retire long-term
debts as they mature. Every main street is dotted with reasonably
profitable and temporarily solvent businesses that are heading
towards a brick wall. The owner doesn't see it coming, and suppliers are too busy worrying about today to consider tomorrow.
Even the accountants are daydreaming.

A good friend of mine is in that position. As an owner of a
furniture store, he's obligated to pay down loans at the rate of
$36,000 a year from a business generating profits of only $15,000.
The $21,000 cash-flow deficiency will eventually erode the solvency
of the business, and chances are the business can't be refinanced
on terms consistent with its cash flow. My friend realizes it but

doesn't care. In a year or two he'll be through engineering school. In the meantime he covers the cash flow by building accounts payable. Some creditors are in for a rude awakening.

Don't be caught off guard, particularly if you plan on becoming a major or long-term supplier. Roughly calculate what it takes a year to pay down loans. Check the profitability and cash flow. Can the business safely pay the loans from profits instead of by draining assets or building payables?

PUT IT ALL TOGETHER

Bring the numbers together so you can evaluate them in context to each other and industry averages, and spot the important trend lines. Exhibit 2, Financial Information Analysis, can help you.

Don't expect a customer to achieve high marks in every category. Some indicators will be on the plus side, others on the negative. Ultimately, your credit decision will be based on a balancing act, weighing indicators against one another.

Here's a reasonably accurate way to rank them in importance:

1. Profit trend.
2. Management experience and depth.
3. Ratio of current asssets to current liabilities.
4. Collateral.
5. Ratio of debt to net worth.
6. Ratio of profits to net worth.
7. Ability to amortize long-term debts.
8. Changes in liquidity and equity/debt position.
9. Growth rate in sales.
10. Age of firm.
11. Growth rate in assets.
12. Credit rating reports.
13. Accounts payable aging.
14. Working capital to sales ratio.
15. Size of the firm.

Ratio	First Year	Industry Average			2nd Year	Industry Average			Final Year	Industry Average	
		D & B	RMA	Other		D & B	RMA	Other		D & B	RMA
Accounts Payable Aging											
Current Assets / Current Liabilities											
Total Debt / Net Worth											
Net Profit / Net Sales											
Net Profit / Net Worth											
Cash on Hand / Total Sales											

Exhibit 2. Financial Information Analysis.

In a sense, processing and evaluating credit information successfully requires all of the attention—and some of the methods—of a major intelligence operation. Your customers want you to see them in the best possible light. Your objective is to see them exactly as they are. That's when credit decisions become intelligent.

4

CREATING FASTER COLLECTIONS

Legend tells of a coat manufacturer who owed a textile supplier $3,000 on a long overdue bill. Undaunted, the manufacturer placed a second $2,500 order. The supplier wrote back, "We can't ship until your first order is paid." Three days later the reply arrived, "We can't wait that long."

Every creditor has his stories. So do customers. But stories don't count. Only payments do. And those faster payments are needed to:

1. Improve your own cash position.
2. Reduce bad debts.
3. Cut down collection costs.
4. Enhance customer relations.

Those are the four objectives of every collection program. And each of those objectives can be realized if you are prepared to bring a new twist to the collection process.

WHY CUSTOMERS PLAY WITH YOUR MONEY

Before you can successfully approach the collection process you need know who the late payers are and why each requires its own matching collection strategy.

Here are the general types of customers who will slow down your payments.

1. *The Undercapitalized Customer.* This is by far the most common problem. From my own experiences, it's clear that 60 to 70% of all chronically slow payers consistently operate on a cash-short position. These same customers tend to be the least loyal because lenient or new credit terms are their primary consideration in selecting suppliers. One supplier offers thirty-day credit and when the customer exhausts the credit limit it looks for a new supplier. When these customers can't find alternate credit-granting suppliers, they end up on COD terms and pressure to work a pay-down on the overdue balance.

Collection problems with this type customer are almost always the result of a poor credit-clearance policy. Their financial statements and poor references signal the problem, but this is either not detected or it is ignored to create sales even at the expense of collectibility.

2. *The "Alternate Loan" Customer.* This is a term I coined for businesses that prefer to run overdue with suppliers' money rather than finance through bank loans. In a sense the firm is undercapitalized because they choose to remain undercapitalized. If you look closely at many of your customers' financials, you'll find many who can and should borrow on a long-term basis to clean up current suppliers. There are several reasons why they don't. Part of it is inertia. Seeking long-term financing takes effort. Small business owners, particularly, are the least likely to effectively go after the necessary long-term funds. Economics is another reason. Back in the peak interest periods of 1981–82 it was *cheaper* to use supplier financing. Most overdues accrued interest at 18% while banks were charging non-rated accounts 21 to 24%. And, of course, supplier service charges could always be modified or waived when it comes time to negotiate payment. A third reason is knowledge. Too many small business owners don't realize the significance of their financial condition, or that current debt is abnormally high. It's business as usual. Finally, there's the question of personal liability. I have had many businesspeople tell me they won't go for bank financing because they don't want to

pledge personal guarantees or assets. They want risk-free financing. Suppliers provide that risk-free financing.

The difference between the "alternate loan" customer and the undercapitalized firm is not the net effect, for the "alternate loan" firm has the borrowing power. It's your job to make them use that borrowing power.

3. *The Seasonal Delinquent.* Businesses with cyclical or seasonal sales, coupled with insufficient capital, are predictable delinquents during slack seasons. In some cases these firms can straighten out the cash-flow ups and downs by a properly structured long-term loan or bank lines of credit. Others don't have the borrowing power and must rely on supplier patience to tide them over during the slow season.

Substantial balances going into the down season always point to poor credit planning and monitoring. Admittedly, it is difficult to monitor because of the short selling season and the high purchases. Programming payments to match the buying demands very close account supervision.

The difficulty in collecting from this type account, once sales are down, is the lack of cash availability. The options are few. You can either push for payment during this period of financial weakness or extend terms until the next selling season. The choice centers on the balance amount and the possibility of payment.

4. *The Negligent Customer.* For every supplier who operates without an organized collection program, there are two customers equally disorganized when it comes to bill paying. It's not a matter of money, but slipshod paying procedures.

I see it often. You too can walk into a customer's business and see bills scattered around or thrown into a box or drawer. The only time this customer pays is when it's programmed to pay on a regular basis, such as invoice-to-invoice or week-to-week; or when the supplier puts enough pressure on the customer to dig out the bill.

This customer is an enigma. You never know whether he's undercapitalized or only slipshod because he's as inclined to ignore follow-up and dunning notices as is the insolvent firm. Only a scan at the financial statements or a bank inquiry can uncover the answer. Payments, when finally made, are also a clue. While the poorly funded firm can only handle an installment arrangement on a large bill, the negligent customer usually pays in full—once he gets around to it.

5. *The Casualty Customer.*   This customer is easiest to handle because you know the reason for slow or nonpayment and can project a payment date. Strikes, fires, and even a temporary traffic detour can put any firm—and your payments—in suspended animation. A retailer in my neighborhood draws its traffic from a nearby public transit station. When the station temporarily closed for repairs, sales plummeted by 75%. The suppliers will wait, and they should wait. And if a creditor can't show leniency at such time toward an otherwise good account it doesn't deserve future business. Don't destroy your own goodwill in such a situation. This is not a payment problem, only a payment interruption.

6. *The "Small Balance" Customer.*   Many customers will deliberately put a hold on small payables until it can add to the account. A wholesaler states that its collections are *slowest* on outstanding bills in the under-$100 category. The retail customers may wait 60 to 90 days to reorder and then punctually pay the entire balance. The "insignificant" bill is bypassed due to clerical costs in processing checks. Few customers worry about the impact on credit, knowing the small claim will seldom be turned over for collections. Some suppliers refuse to dun on a small balance for fear it will alienate the customer. It's a foolish policy for two reasons. Leniency on the small bill can be interpreted as leniency on the larger bill. And those small payments can collectively be significant to your own cash flow. Either you have a credit policy or you don't.

7. *The Confused Customer.*   Many credit books suggest this is a very common reason for slow pay. I disagree. It's rare for a customer *not* to know the due date on a bill. Invoices are usually sufficiently clear. Where the problem is most likely to occur is with special deals, dated merchandise, or opening stock orders and "turnover" orders.

When "confused customers" are the rule, instead of the rare exception, it is typically the result of inadequate invoice information, or salespeople who suggest alternate payment terms. The latter is the more common, and oftentimes you can see a pattern emerge within a given sales territory.

The confused customer is also the least troublesome. The follow-up notices usually bring in the check. The danger is not in losing the payment but in losing a customer who expected extended payment terms. When it happens, accept the responsibility for the misunderstanding.

Slow payers must be distinguished from nonpayers who may be the game-playing deadbeats we discuss in Chapter 5, or the seriously insolvent accounts discussed in Chapter 9. The slow payers *can* pay and *will* pay. It's a question of *when* and how you can make it happen faster.

INCENTIVES TO MOTIVATE CHECK WRITING

Consider all these slow-pay customers. Each has limited dollars and unlimited creditors. You are one of those creditors standing in a long line with many hands extended for payment. Now, Mr. or Ms. Creditor, why should your customer put his few scarce dollars in your hands instead of some other creditor's clutching fist?

I have asked that question of myself before. And I looked for the answer. But I had plenty of help; over 4000 debtor clients and their 500,000 creditors with their own hands extended. It wasn't difficult to see a powerful formula emerge. The successful creditors knew how to *motivate* their customers to pay. They waved a more tempting carrot and wielded a sterner stick.

Stand out from the crowd. Learn the fine art of motivating your customers to pay. You'll need more than your "throw-away" letters and tired phone calls. That's only communication. And it's convention. Your competitive creditors are up to the same thing. What you will need are the strong, enticing *positive* motivators so your customer *wants* to pay. Add to it the "no-nonsense" *negative* motivators so he *has* to pay. With the right combination of motivators, finely tuned and properly applied you'll have your check. Even a donkey will move off his duff with the right carrot and stick.

Product Demand Pulls Payments

Holding back on orders until overdues are paid is always a supplier favorite. You can get away with it if you're a single-source supplier of a high-demand item. But few suppliers are that single source, and fewer products have the demand to motivate check writing.

Even when you have a needed product, it doesn't get the old bills paid if the customer can buy COD and still ignore the old bills, or worse—switch to another supplier.

What you need is a program to *increase* product demand and "tie" it into a strict policy of dangling it as your carrot to collect overdues. Watch how some other firms do it.

A book publisher knows how to keep its bookstore customers current. Before it releases a "blockbluster" novel, it sends its accounts a promotional package on the book, complete with book review clipppings, ads, and all the other hooplah to show just what a "blockbuster" it will be. Attached is a letter—"Accounts must be current to order the book." The publisher admits that stores 90–120 days overdue manage to find the money. "And then we only ship COD if we think the customer will fall behind again," its credit manager adds. *Create product demand* and use it to collect money as well as to generate sales.

Arrow offered shirts regularly sold at $10.50 at a special $5.00price to all current (non-overdue) accounts. If you own a clothing store and deal with a California distributor, you'll see promotional ads like this twice a year. Few customers can afford to pass up the deals. The checkbooks open. Dangle that carrot, even if it's a *"special deal"* carrot.

A Boston drug wholesaler does it with a service policy. It started a high-powered cooperative advertising program for participating drugstore accounts. The one requirement for joining the advertising program is to stay current on all purchases. "Without the ad program, many of our customers would be 90 to 120 days in arrears," says its president. "And we didn't have the clout to make them pay 'catch-up.' There are plenty of other wholesalers around selling the same merchandise, so the customer was in the driver's seat. That's no longer the case. Now they need us because we have the ad program that can increase store sales by 20 to 40%. We're back in the driver's seat and that means fast checks." And your own *special service* or program.

Any sales-oriented program can work. Whenever your company has more to offer, make your high-powered program work twice as hard for you. Bring sales and credit together. Have the program land payments as well as sales. Being needed means being paid.

Make Your Cash Discounts Really Work

Cash discounts have only one purpose—to encourage fast pay. The trick is to break away from convention and double or triple its firepower.

In most industries a 2%–10-day policy is standard. Everybody plays follow the leader. Let's assume it's your policy, because it's also your competitor's or the industry standard. Right there you should see how your own cash discount loses incentive. Your customer has fifty suppliers, each offering their own 2% cash discount, but if it's undercapitalized it can't discount all its bills. Picking and choosing, your cash discount offers no greater incentive than your competitors. So why should he pay you? Balance the economics of a greater discount against the costs of slow receivables. Experiment, be different, innovate. You need the best formula. Consider the possibilities.

1. *Play with the Discount Size.* There's no magic in the words "2%." Look for the right number. One supplier, selling to large rated firms found out it was needlessly giving the money away. A fortunate supplier, 80% of its customers paid within 7 to 10 days. It dropped the discount and most of its accounts still pay within a week of statement date. In most cases, however, competition won't allow it. If profit margins are sufficient or your own cash flow tight, then gradually move up to higher discounts. A wholesaler acknowledges that when he doubled the cash discount from 2 to 4%, over half his customers paid within the

discount period compared to 20% before. It's arithmetic. Does the faster cash flow justify the extra 2%? Watch the numbers.

Financially troubled firms should always go for the higher discount if it brings in the cash. Cash flow is more important in these cases than added profits. The money market is another factor. When interest rates were 18 to 24%, a 2% cash discount wasn't much different than bank financing. Now with interest rates down, the 2% again has some meaning.

Discounts of 5 to 10% should be considered if you have a high markup (40% or more) and sell to marginal accounts. A printer experienced excellent results with a 7% discount. When he sold on 2% terms, nobody paid on time and 60 to 90-day receivables were the norm. Now it receives immediate payment from 70 to 80% of its customers. The extra 5% discount motivates the customers. It costs an extra $5,000 a year in cash discounts, but that's better than having $30,000 to $40,000 in overdue bills on the books.

2. *Shorten the Time Period.*   Ten-day-discount terms don't make sense with a higher-than-standard cash discount. Cut it to five days. If a customer can pay in 10 days, it can pay just as easily in five. Conversely, if it won't pay in five, you won't see the check in 10 days. For example, a plumbing supply firm switched from 2%–10-day terms to 5%–5-day terms. By offering an extra 3% discount it had the right to expect even faster payments. And it got them.

3. *How About a Year-End Discount?*   Cash discounts can be used even beyond the typical discount period. One of the most successful formulas was developed by an appliance manufacturer selling through retail outlets. It continued to offer the standard 2%–10-day terms but added a wrinkle. Customers who paid all their bills within 30 days during the prior year would receive an extra 2% cash rebate. It produced excellent results. The wholesaler correctly reasoned that many of its customers couldn't pay within the discount period, sending their bills into the 60- to 90-day column. Service charges on overdues weren't the entire answer either. Its customers made sure they didn't go beyond 30 days in any one month, because it would mean losing the 2% for the entire year. *That's* motivation.

4. *Sell the Discount.*   Constantly push your customers to take advantage of the discount. If you want fast money, you have to sell it.

There are several ways to do it. First, make the discount stand out so your customer sees it. The small print on the corner of the invoice isn't enough. Stamp across the face of the statement the available cash discount—the due date—and the discount in dollar terms. Make your customers see it as money he can keep in his pocket. Have it read:

PAY THIS STATEMENT WITHIN 10 DAYS AND DEDUCT

YOUR CASH DISCOUNT OF

$

AS YOUR SAVINGS!

Your billing clerk only has to calculate the discount and write in the amount.

Use constant reminders. Several firms send out postcards three days before the end of the discount period with the same type reminder.

Telephone reminders are used by a tobacco supplier. Its order clerks phone the customer stores on a daily basis for orders, so it has the order-takers remind the customer of the cash discount date.

You have to do more than have a convincing cash discount. You have to sell it.

Make Service Charges Costly

Service charges (interest on overdue bills) are motivators. It's a negative motivator, forcing the customer to pay to avoid costly carrying charges.

Many suppliers don't use it that way. They look at interest as what it costs them to borrow to finance the overdue account. It's the wrong perspective. The service charge should be a big stick to avoid delinquency. You want a service charge to prompt the customer to write checks to you.

Most industries use a 1½% per month (18%) charge. When bank interest was 20 to 22%, the supplier charge of 18% was a bargain. In 1983 prime rates are down to 10 to 11%. The supplier charges of 18% still mean little to the small or marginal account who can't borrow at much less than 16 to 17%.

It doesn't matter what your industry standards are. I think the only service charge that makes sense is 24% a year (2% a month). Customers rarely consider the service charge when selecting a supplier. Competition means nothing in this area.

Many creditors found that the 24% rate does produce results. Customers who would be chronic delinquents under an 18% rate now give them priority, while letting other creditors with a lower service charge wait. That's your objective.

A high interest rate also gives you some negotiating room. For example, a customer may be 90 to 120 days in arrears and show signs of turning into a "non-pay." Why not offer to cut the accrued interest back to 18% or even 15% as a compromise for full payment? The savings mean something to your customer, but what are you really losing?

Consider cash discounts and service charges together. A high cash discount to induce fast payment, and a high service charge if they don't pay within terms, is a double punch. Your customers now have two reasons to give you priority.

DESIGN THE BEST COLLECTION SYSTEM

Your collection system is based on your collection policy. You may need to vary your policy if you sell to different groups of customers, but every policy is based on:

1. *Maturity Date for Accounts.* This is the date when you have the right to demand payment. Your terms of sale should clearly state this date (usually 30 days is standard).

2. *Starting Date for Collection Action.* The number of days beyond the maturity date, that you begin to pursue follow-ups or dunning notices.

3. *Cut-Off Date for Additional Credit.* This is the number of days after the maturity date that you "freeze" the customer's account, refusing additional credit until the balance is paid. The cut-off date may come at any time the account goes beyond approved credit limits.

4. *The Phases in the Collection Cycle and the Time Duration for Each.* Typically firms will divide the collection cycle into three distinct phases:

The polite reminder stage.

The formal appeal stage.

The firm demand stage.

The policy will determine how form letters, telephone follow-ups, and other collection devices will be used in each step of the cycle.

5. *The "Bitter End" Date.* This is the number of days beyond the collection cycle that the account will either be turned over for collection or marked "no further action" because the amount is too small to justify turnover.

Within this framework, your system must satisfy two additional criteria. I must:

1. *Ensure Sound Control.* No matter what size or type company you have, your system must provide prompt notice of required action. This includes current information on the status of each account, and posting of collections to preclude collections after the account is paid.

There are hundreds of systems available, from a simple card file to complex computer systems. The objective is always the same: you must be able to stay on top of each account and move it along from one stage to the next in the collection cycle *automatically* and without delay.

2. *Ensure the Right Action.* Control is mechanical. The right action is based on strategy—decision making during the collection period with the objectives of not only obtaining payment but retaining customers as well.

Your collection program will be based on the same system and basic policy. Now let's go through the various steps to turn it into a winning system.

ACCELERATE YOUR SYSTEM TO SPEED COLLECTIONS

The collection system is "time"-oriented. Every step has a defined time period and collections can only be accelerated if the time period within each stage is shortened. Tighten up every phase of the process with these pointers:

1. *Use a Shorter Maturity Date.*   You may operate with a 30-day maturity. Can you cut it to a 15-day maturity? Competition will help you answer it, but don't be blinded by industry standards. Many firms have switched to 15-day billing/maturity cycles in the face of competitors offering 30-day terms. Theoretically, this one simple step can cut your receivables in half.

2. *Render Bills on Delivery.*   If you sell goods to a customer in infrequent intervals, then send the bill as soon as possible *after* the goods are delivered. Why wait to the beginning of the following month? One firm has its delivery service drop the bill off with the goods. You can't be much faster. The firm reports that 20% of the customers decide to pay on the spot, handing the delivery driver a check.

This is a form of cycle billing. In most cases cycle billing is staggered with so many bills going out each day based on the alphabetical order of customer names. Its advantage is a spread-out workload and greater control in monitoring receivables. A better cycle-billing approach is to base it on delivery date. You have the same advantages plus faster payments.

3. *Don't Delay Collection Action.*   Many firms wait 30 days beyond the maturity date to start collection activity. It's too lenient a policy. No action within the 30 days beyond the maturity date grants the customer an effective sixty-day maturity. Start your collection activity five days after the maturity date. The five days covers checks timely paid but in the mail. Make it your objective to let the customer know he's late as soon as he's late. Don't delay the message for another month.

4. *Accelerate the Collection Stages.* You may use a series of three dunning notices, for example, each spaced a month apart. Now, Mr. or Ms. Creditor, that's all plain foolishness. You already know the first letter (or phone call) should go out five days after the due date, but don't procrastinate with your second and third follow-ups. Space the second and third letter 15 days apart and no longer.

This is the most serious mistake in conventional collections. A 90-day collection cycle gives your customer too much time. You have to create a sense of urgency. You want to *get paid.* A lenient, slow-paced approach doesn't get that message across.

Consider it another way. If your customer doesn't pay, or work out a payment schedule, within 45 days after the due date, this same customer isn't inclined to pay within 90 days. If you have to reach the "bitter-end" date, have it come sooner when you can take decisive, timely action rather than later when it may be too late to collect.

A lumber supply can show you just how effective these accelerated collection steps can be. Under its old policy it billed customers the following month for current-month purchases and extended 30-day terms. The dunning cycle started 30 days after the due date, with no less than five "follow-up" letters spaced a month apart. Receivables constantly totaled about $260,000, average aging was 48 days, and bad debts were 5% of sales.

All that changed. It now bills the day following delivery with 15-day terms. Five days after maturity a reminder goes out. If that doesn't produce the check within 10 days, a second letter is mailed. They wait 15 more days and follow up with a phone call. If that doesn't settle the problem, a final notice before suit is immediately mailed. Their customers can't play with their money. Not for long. Receivables are down to $130,000, aging is cut to 21 days, and even losses have been reduced to 3%.

WHEN TO SHUT THE CREDIT SPIGOT

During this entire "hope and wait" period comes the question— When do you cut off further credit? Don't forget, that's part of your policy. And it's a critical part for two reasons: (1) You can't afford to risk further losses and (2) turning off the credit can in itself prompt payment. Remember, product need is a powerful payment motivator.

Shutting down credit must be based on both the allowed credit line and a cut-off date in terms of delinquency. Whichever comes first signals the termination of further credit. But you need *both* barometers. One alone is no protection.

Many suppliers will open an account and extend 30 days' credit without a credit limit. A customer can buy an awful lot of product in 30 days. I see it happening every day. A marginal clothing store client was recently granted 15-day terms from a new jobber. The owner had a picnic. Within the 15 days the store scored $36,000 in purchases. It was crazy. The defunct business could never handle the payments. The picnic continued, the 15 days extended to 28 days, and the store owner was still buying like a demon possessed. The final tally was $49,000 before the store was finally shut off 36 days after the buying spree started. The jobber will never be paid down and is screaming at the customer. In reality this jobber should be kicking the credit manager in the pants. That's the person who was asleep at the switch.

A smart credit manager would have set limits and controlled it. At best, the store was deserving of a modest $5,000 credit line. When $5,000 was reached the store should have been put on hold even if it was the initial order. If the account hadn't reached its credit line, the goods should have been put on hold if the company's check didn't arrive within five days of the due date.

The decision of granting additional credit is always troublesome with the overdue customer who is well below its credit limit. For example, a customer with a $10,000 line may be overdue by 15 or even 30 days, while owing only $3,000. Do you continue to ship? If not, when—and how—do you cut the customer off?

There is not one right formula for this decision. It requires an analysis of the customer, prior payment habits, and competitive pressures. A rule-of-thumb is to extend shipments for one more billing date (another 30 days, if you offer 30-day terms), provided credit limits are not exceeded.

Customer retention is an important factor here. Nothing can alienate an account more than curtailing credit without prior notice. Warn the customer, at least ten days prior to the shut-off date. The customer should have the last clear chance to pay before it loses future credit. But follow this word of caution: Watch the account's buying within the 10-day period. Many customers intending not to pay will "load up" once forewarned. If the buying seems excessive, immediately shut down credit or stall for time (out-of-stock, back-ordered) until you can see whether the check is on its way.

MAXIMIZE COLLECTION COMMUNICATION

The emphasis is on the word *communication*. And that means more than letter writing. You need a mix, including telephone calls and personal visits. Each method has its own purpose, and its own strengths and weaknesses. Moreover, each must be handled in its own special way to obtain the best results.

Beware of "over-kill." It's a common error to communicate *too* much. A customer doesn't need eight reminders to be reminded, or 12 phone calls to tell him you want your check. Overcommunication is counterproductive to collections. It's the old "cry wolf" syndrome. Why shouldn't a customer expect a ninth letter after the eighth?

I recommend a four-step communication mix:

1. A letter reminder.
2. A request for payment (mailgram).
3. A phone call or personal visit.
4. A final demand.

Each step has its own purpose. The most important is the phone call or personal visit. It can accomplish more than the letters, as you'll soon see. Remember timing. Accomplish the four steps within a 45 to 60-day cycle.

COLLECT WITH ACTION-GETTING LETTERS

Too many collection books dwell on the wording, style, or format of collection letters. Most of the various letters recommended for use try to play to customer psychology by appealing to their pride, fear, or sense of justice. There's nothing wrong with these approaches, but the successful letter goes further. It can be an extremely useful tool to:

1. Establish the validity of the debt, if the claim is later contested.
2. Retain customer goodwill.
3. Prompt a specific response.

The style is secondary, provided it's straightforward, polite, and concise.

These additional points should also be followed:

1. Make each letter self-descriptive of the obligation. Include the debtor's name, date of letter, invoice or transaction reference, together with amount due. This is vital for legal reasons as well as identification. If you must go to court you can reconcile the correspondence to the subject matter of the litigation.

2. Avoid form letters. Personalized letters are much more effective. This is particularly true on the "request for payment" and demand letters. In these cases target the letter to a specific individual, if possible. Many firms now specialize in sending out personalized collection letters for other companies—the cost is about half what it costs to send out individually processed letters, and it's not much more expensive than form letters.

3. Mix the format, using different-color envelopes for each letter.

4. Use certified mail for the demand letter. You want proof of delivery and it creates urgency on your customer's part.

5. If you have a promotional program or strong sales incentive to offer your customer, then send it along at the same time—but in a separate envelope.

What Reminds Best?

Hitting the right note in your first reminder notice results in early payment with a majority of your customers. Most customers need only be reminded before they pay. For many, payment would be on its way, even without a reminder.

There's a growing trend among commercial credit managers to use rubber-stamped invoices as reminders up to the "Final Notice" letter. A better policy is to use both the rubber-stamped invoice as one reminder and a separate reminder notice mailed simultaneously.

One of the most effective reminder letters reads:

This statement is overdue. Please give payment your immediate attention.

At the same time, you can send out a more formal reminder. Some firms use humor-oriented reminders. It's a matter of style, but shouldn't be used either from or to a large or prestigious firm. Make your correspondence fit the dignity and character of the firm.

Use your reminder to remind—not threaten. At this point in the collection stage, you should assume the customer will pay and goodwill retention is paramount. Courtesy is the only policy, coupled with a straightforward request for payment.

One of the most effective reminder letters reads:

Gentlemen:

You're one of our busiest customers, and undoubtedly that's why you overlooked payment on your overdue statement.

Won't you please mail us a check today in the enclosed self-addressed envelope?

Very truly,

Amount past due: $ _____ .

The supplier who used that form reports it worked well, but he has since added another touch to the letter. Although the letter is signed by the credit department, the salesperson assigned to the account scribbles a friendly note on the bottom, saying, for example: "Charlie—How about sending the check?" The salespeople give it a personal touch because they know how to talk to the customer. With the request, the sales rep may expand it to a quick question about a business problem, regards to the wife, or even reference to a side bet they had on the outcome of a ball game. What it does is take the "cutting edge" off the reminder and let the customer know that the salesperson is aware of the overdue. It's a terrific strategy. Customers don't lose face with an unknown clerk in the credit department, but the sales representative may be as close as a personal friend. This company reports the side comments by the salespeople increased results by 25%. Test the results with your firm.

Telegrams Demand Attention

If the reminder doesn't produce the check, then switch to a telegram or mailgram. Few customers ignore this unexpected form of communication.

Western Union recently started a new service of providing collection telegrams with maximum efficiency and low cost. The custom-tailored telegraphs are designed by you and brings the cost of a full-length collection letter down to the cost of a minimum-word wire.

You can send the same message to a list of slow payers, on a routine time-check basis, simply by filling in the customer's name and address and the amount due. Only the amount is transmitted by wire, yet your customer receives a full telegram that looks like it has been written expressly for him, and carries the same urgency and importance associated with a telegram.

Another advantage of a telegram is that short, concise, and to-the-point messages don't offend. People expect telegrams to be abrupt.

Use the telegram as the second step in your collection cycle. Sent 15 to 21 days after the reminder, it brings your communication from the politeness stage to one of urgency.

THE LETTER THAT DEMANDS ATTENTION

Although telegrams are very effective at the request-for-payment stage, a letter offers one advantage. It allows your customer to propose a payment plan and is very useful in cementing your legal case if the claim goes to collection.

The request-for-payment letter should go beyond its reminder purpose, and yet you're not quite ready for serious threats just now. It's the point of no return in customer retention and requires tact not force. The very best letter that I have seen in this category was stated this way:

Gentlemen:

Despite our prior reminders, your overdue balance in the amount of $, has not been paid.

Frankly, we do not know whether the delay is due to some dissatisfaction with our firm, or due to a temporary financial or other condition preventing full payment.

In either case, we want to hear from you. If the problem is with us, then take a few moments and tell us about your dissatisfaction on the reverse side of the letter.

However, if you have not paid due to financial circumstances, then we certainly want to cooperate in considering an extended payment date if you will tell us when payment will be mailed. If that is the problem, please take a moment to complete and return the extended payment request.

We expect to hear from you within 10 days.

Very truly,

The balance due can be paid in full by _____ .

_____
Customer

This letter has several strong points. First, it invites a customer response, and gives the *customer* a chance to propose a payment plan. That's the failing of most collection letters. The customer is boxed into a corner. It's either pay or else. With that ultimatum the chances are good the customer won't pay. Few customers take the initiative to write a creditor, explain a financial problem, and say when they *can* pay. You have to take the initiative.

If a customer does propose an unreasonable payment plan, you're not bound to accept it. But you know now what your customer can do. He's cooperating. He's talking to you. Negotiate mutually agreeable payments if you must, but the letter served its purpose—it broke the stalemate of silence.

MAKING PERSONAL CONTACT COUNT

Letters and telegrams can only take you so far. There's nothing easier for a customer to ignore, and perhaps no collection policy more costly than one based on letter writing alone. And it's costly because it doesn't give you the chance to see if the customer or your bill is salvageable.

It's all part of psychology. A customer falls behind and receives a first reminder. He's still financially strapped so he ignores it while receiving the sterner follow-up letters. After the third or fourth letter, and certainly by the time the lawyer letter arrives the supplier and customer are now antagonists. And to break the cycle, it may only take a phone call asking what the problem is and when you can expect payment.

So after your first two letters, put the letter writing on hold. It's time for some direct communication. There's nothing complicated about it, you're only talking about money.

1.   Talk to the person who can write the checks. If you can't get through, leave your number and the name of your firm. Don't expect a call back. You'll be the one to chase with a few more phone calls. But don't try more than three times. Switch to your final demand letter.

2.   When you get your customer on the phone, don't intimidate. Keep it cordial.

3.   Suggest the customer may have overlooked the bill. Let him save face.

4.   Have him acknowledge the debt by asking whether he received the goods. If there is a problem (nonreceipt, defective goods, etc.) have him issue a full written report.

5. Now you want a commitment to send the check. If it's full payment, you want a specific date. Don't be put off by stalls— "I'll send it as soon as I can," or other vague, meaningless promises. Pin the customer down to specifics. If it's installment payments that are agreed on, cement the entire deal. On a $2,000 bill, an agreement to send $250 the following week doesn't solve the problem of the remaining $1,750.

6. Confirm it in writing. As soon as the agreement is reached, send the customer a confirmatory letter stating the agreed payment date.

Use telephone collections for bills over a certain amount. Long-distance calls are usually not cost justified for collections under $200 to $300. However, if you do use extensive telephone collections, check into a lower cost WATS line or one of the new interconnect telephone services. Your labor costs are also a factor. Use capable but lower-cost personnel for the smaller accounts. In fact, some employees do an appreciably better job with telephone collections than do the boss, because customers are less intimidated and the employee may have a superior telephone style. Every organization has a personality who can charm the check from a customer.

Large accounts are another matter. This requires a personal meeting. The only use for the telephone here is to set up that meeting. I have seen large creditors who were owed $30,000 to $40,000, and a few who were owed as much as $200,000 never once requesting a face-to-face meeting to work out a payment plan. You may decide $5,000 or even less justifies the direct-meeting approach. Whatever your dividing line, if the money is important to you, don't overlook the need for the personal visit.

If the customer refuses to meet, you have no choice but to go to the enforcement stage. Usually they'll agree, however, if you keep the conversation cordial and show you're willing to listen and be reasonable.

Arrange the meeting at your customer's plant. It's less intimidating than at your office and gives you the opportunity to look around and size up the company's financial condition. And it's easy for a customer to throw up his hands and walk out of your office. It's harder for the debtor to throw you out of his office.

PROMISSORY NOTE

(Long Form)

FOR VALUE RECEIVED, the undersigned hereby jointly and severally promises to pay to the order of
the sum of
($) Dollars, together with interest thereon at the rate of   % per annum on the unpaid balance. Said sum shall be paid in the manner following:

All payments shall be first applied to interest and the balance to principal.

This note may be prepaid, at any time, in whole or in part, without penalty.

This note, shall at the option of any holder hereof be immediately due and payable upon the occurrence of any of the following:

1.   Failure to make any payment due hereunder within   days of its due date.

2.   Breach of any condition of any security interest, mortgage, pledge agreement, or guarantee granted as collateral security for this note.

3.   Breach of any condition of any security agreement or mortgage, if any, having a priority over any security agreement or mortgage on collateral granted in whole or in part as collateral security for this note.

4.   Upon the death, dissolution, or liquidation of any of the undersigned, or any endorser, guarantor, or surety hereto.

5.   Upon the filing by any of the undersigned of an assignment for the benefit of creditors, bankruptcy, or for relief under any provisions of the Bankruptcy Code; or by suffering an involuntary petition in bankruptcy or receivership not vacated within thirty days.

That in the event this note shall be in default, and placed with an attorney for collection, then the undersigned agrees to pay all reasonable attorneys' fees and costs of collection. Payments not made within five days of its due date shall be subject to a late charge of   % of said payment. All payments hereunder shall be made to such address as may from time to time be designated by any holder hereof.

The undersigned and all other parties to this note, whether as endorsers, guarantors, or sureties agree to remain fully bound hereunder until this note shall be fully paid and waive demand, presentment, and protest and all notices thereto and further agree to remain bound, notwithstanding any extension, modification, waiver, or other indulgence by any holder or upon the discharge or release of any obligor hereunder or to this note, or upon the exchange, substitution, or release of any collateral granted as security for this note. No modification or indulgence by any holder hereof shall be binding unless in writing; and any indulgence on any one occasion shall not be an indulgence for any other of future occasion. Any modification or change of terms hereunder granted by any holder hereof, shall be valid and binding upon each of the undersigned, notwithstanding the acknowledgment of only any one of the undersigned, and each of the undersigned does hereby irrevocably grant to each of the others a power of attorney to enter into any such modification on their behalf. The rights of any holder hereof shall be cumulative and not necessarily successive. This note shall take effect as a sealed instrument and shall be construed, governed and enforced in accordance with the laws of

_____

Company

CEMENTING A PAYMENT PLAN

Usually, this direct confrontation over a large debt will result in an extension or agreement to pay the debts back over time in installments. Your company's needs balanced against the customer's ability to pay provide the framework for the plan. However, you should bargain for these additional terms:

1. Structure payments to be made weekly, instead of monthly or quarterly. Smaller payments are easier to handle and you'll have less chance for default.

2. Request collateral security. In Chapter 6, you'll see how collateral can work for you.

3.   Personal guarantees are another bargaining point. If the principals won't guarantee the full amount, make the owners at least share the risk of delayed payments.

4.   Look for return goods if it can be incorporated back into inventory. In-hand inventory is oftentimes better than a payment that may never come. Negotiate further. Try to discount a 25 to 35% handling charge from the value of the returns. Credits on the return goods should be applied to the last-due, not first-due payments.

5.   Assess interest equal to your normal service charge.

6.   Go for as much cash up front as possible. If the customer has seasonal sales, profile the payments to the cash flow.

7.   Have the customer understand that future shipments will be on COD or cash-on-advance terms only.

8.   Try to make it a condition of the deal that the customer continue to buy from you. Quantify the amount and define the terms. Upon default in buying you should have the right to call the entire balance payable. Of course, an intervening bankruptcy or insolvency should also make the entire balance payable, as will any missed payment.

9.   If your customer is entitled to future trade discounts from future buying, reserve the right to apply the discounts to the last-due installments. If the customer balks, then try to compromise with half applied to the next-due installments and the other half to the final payments.

10.   Impose financial restrictions. Require financial statements to be periodically submitted. Define the criteria for determining future solvency. Also impose restrictions on the owner's salary.

The final agreement can take one of two forms, a promissory note or a formal extension agreement. The promissory note (on pages 84–85) has the advantage in that it can be more easily "factored" or turned into cash. The extension agreement is useful in that it can incorporate peripheral points. Both serve to acknowledge the validity of the debt and the terms of payment. In some cases a creditor will combine both a note and an extension agreement. Involve your attorney. You need airtight agreements.

AGREEMENT TO EXTEND DEBT PAYMENT

FOR VALUE RECEIVED, the undersigned
        (Creditor) and   (Company)
hereby acknowledge and agree that:

1.   The Company presently owes the Creditor the sum of $,
said sum being presently due and payable.

2.   In further consideration of the Creditor's forebearance, the Company agrees to pay said debt on extended terms in the manner following:

3.   In the event the Company fails to make any payments punctually on the agreed extended terms, the Creditor shall have full rights to proceed for the collection of the entire balance then remaining.

4.   This agreement shall be binding upon and inure to the benefit of the parties, their successors, assigns and personal representatives.
      Signed under seal this   day of   , 19

_____
Creditor

_____
Company

HOW BANKS CAN COLLECT FOR YOU

If your in-house collection efforts fail up to this point, your banker can be of help.

Many creditors try as a last-ditch collection effort the use of *sight drafts*. A sight draft is drawn up by a creditor, ordering the debtor's bank to pay the draft upon presentment to the debtor's bank. Now a sight draft won't be honored by the bank without the debtor's signature, so it certainly doesn't ensure payment. Its effectiveness as a collection tool is that the debtor's bank has the obligation to seek the debtor's signature so it can honor payment. This, of course, creates an awkward situation for your customer because customers seldom want their bank to know they are being dunned. That's only one purpose. When the debtor's bank presents it to the debtor, the banker should inform the bank why the sight draft will not be honored. The reason the debtor gives his bank can be a valuable legal tool, particularly if the debtor doesn't state a bona fide reason. Then again, there's always a chance the debtor will sign the sight draft, and then it has the validity of a regular check.

TEST YOUR COLLECTION EFFECTIVENESS

1. Is your average collection period below or above competitors in your area?

2. Do you limit credit based on both amount and overdue period?

3. Are your cash discounts and service charges above or below industry averages?

4. Is your billing and collection cycle tightened to the shortest possible time?

5. Do you use incentives to motivate payment?

6. Do your collection letters produce better or worse results than experienced by others in your industry?

7. Do you use a mix of collection methods, or rely on one method of communication alone?

8. How does your bad-debt loss compare to industry averages?

9. Does your collection system tell you the status of every account and trigger the next step in the collection process?

10. What steps in this chapter can improve your collection strategy?

= 5 =

GAMESMANSHIP: PLAYING TO WIN

Buckle up your army boots and grab your helmet. You're going into combat. If the check still hasn't arrived in the morning mail, it's time to leave diplomacy behind and fix bayonets. Why not? The deadbeats in the far trenches are planning to stick it to you.

This chapter is your combat manual. You'll meet the enemy with all their dirty, dangerous, and deceptive ways. And you'll learn how to fight them on *your* terms and on *your* ground.

But to fight, and fight effectively, you should first take a cram course in:

DEADBEAT PSYCHOLOGY

Deadbeats, wherever and whenever you find them, always think the same way. One way or another, they don't want to pay you. Your first big step in winning is to remember and react to just that message.

Robert Ringer eloquently stated it in his best-selling book *Winning Through Intimidation*. It was a best seller because he had the courage to write finally what everyone else only would think about. What was Ringer's message? A simple hypothesis. Deadbeats come in one of three categories:

1. Deadbeats who want to keep your money *and tell* you.

2. Deadbeats who want to keep your money but *don't tell* you.

3. Deadbeats who want to keep your money but *don't realize* it.

The first character is the easiest to deal with. At least you know where you stand. The second scoundrel is more dangerous because he knows what he's up to while you don't—at least not yet. The most sinister of the lot is the third type. He won't even admit to himself that he's out to stiff you. You may even know what he's up to before he does.

Since these game players have the same evil objective—keeping your money—you might think they all resort to the same devices. Not so. That's what makes the battle such a challenge. You never know what they'll pull on you until they pull it. But they do have plenty of stunts at their disposal. Some, the master deadbeats, know them all and use as many as necessary. And for others one stunt may be enough.

So the war between creditor and debtor is a pitched psychological battle from beginning to end. Let's go through their tactics one by one and turn their ploys to your own advantage.

THE "CONTESTED BALANCE" CON

This character never seems to owe what you say he owes. But, of course, he only wakes up to that fact once the day of reckoning is upon him and you go hunting for his check. Take a few Valium. He can do a worse job on your bookkeeping department than the IRS.

Recognize him? You should. You met him many times before. However, if you haven't been introduced, perhaps you should meet Sam T. He's terrific at making you prove what he says he doesn't owe.

For starters, Sam wants all his invoices for two or three years. How else can he reconcile the statement? And how else can he stall you for at least a month while you pull and copy them. Now Sam has his invoices. "Stop pressing," he shouts. It takes Sam at least three months to match up the invoices. After all, Sam is a busy man.

Four months drift by and Sam announces the invoices match the statement. That's if you're lucky. But for Sam it's only the start of the second round. Now he only wants to see if his payments have been credited. You wouldn't think it would be much of a job considering he paid you so few checks. Don't forget, though, Sam can't be rushed. He's the deliberate type. A month later Sam tells you he can't find his canceled checks. Copies are on order from the bank. Now everybody knows that banks are even slower than Sam. The stall works for two or maybe three months. Sam's scorecard now has him ahead in the game by about seven months. Still Sam doesn't agree with you. He's now checking out the credits and returns.

Nine months later, Sam should be ready to capitulate. But the Sams of the world don't capitulate. What they do instead is either:

1. Tell you all their records were stolen from the back seat of their cars, so they have to start all over again.
2. Go bankrupt.
3. Switch to yet another ploy.

What he *won't* do is pay you. That's the one guarantee you have.

Action to take: The only way to combat Sam is to follow this three-point strategy:

1. Put some teeth in your statement. Make your customers contest statement accuracy within 45 days or lose their rights to contest it thereafter. Why should you have to go back two or three years to reconcile what your customer has seen each month. Call your printer. Have this language added to the statement:

Any disputes or errors on this statement must be reported in writing within 45 days of receipt. No customer adjustments will be allowed thereafter.

Notice two key words. You want *written* notice. Also, make adjustments one-sided. Errors that work against you don't have a time limit. Only the customer is bound by the 45 days. The 45 days take care of end of month/beginning of month entries. This powerful clause can take the wind out of Sam's sails.

2.   Impose time limits. Even good, solid accounts may question your statement. But don't fall for the stall. Tell the customer when you expect an answer, make him give your statement top priority. Try a marathon. One good method is to have your credit manager offer to sit down for a full day if necessary to straighten out the account—Sam won't go for it, but your honest customers will.

3.   Watch your own bookkeeping. They say the customer's always right. It's sometimes true when it comes to billing. I have one large manufacturer client whose billings are so fouled up that I almost assume the customer *is* right. Strangely, the errors always seem to be in the manufacturer's favor. Don't play games. If the errors are deliberate, word gets around. Excessive legitimate errors mean it's time to shake up your billing department. Let Sam catch you in even one insignificant error and he'll never stop looking for more.

THE "MISSING GOODS" MASTER

Meet Sam's first cousin Walter. You can always tell them apart. Walter is considerably more clever than Sam, because he adds so many more tricks to the stall, confuse, and obfuscate game.

Listen to Walter. He never *received* the goods. If he did they were *defective*.

Walter can even say it with a straight face. I have watched several of them in action. The best performer was a Walter who owned a large health and beauty aid store, supposedly owing a wholesaler over $55,000 gradually mushroomed over three years. Around the conference table sat the wholesaler's credit manager and attorney, while I joined Walter on the other side.

The yellow legal pads flashed while the wholesaler's people expected a quick payment plan. Walter, another methodical type, was in no hurry. Reaching for three pregnant storage cartons loaded with invoices he started his spiel. "On invoice 2037, I'm billed for three 89-cent Prell shampoos. I only received two." Skipping down to the six $3.00 handbrushes, "Two brushes came with broken cellophane wrappers. . . ."

An hour later Walter was on his third invoice and only had 1074 more to go. The credit manager was sleeping, his attorney sat there working on another case, while I worked my calculator to tell me if Walter might be finished before I retire. Walter was enjoying it. I can hear him now . . . "And on line 14 a package of 49-cent hair pins had three bent pins."

As you'd expect, we had an offer. The wholesaler would accept $30,000 to wind up the charade. Not Walter. He was sadistic. The drums continued to beat . . . "And on line 23 it says 'beige' pantyhose. My notes say I received taupe."

Walter never did pay. Walters seldom do. And when they do it's usually a pittance. And Mr. or Ms. Creditor, it's always your own fault. You just didn't know there was a Walter sharpening his bayonet.

Action to take: Put on your armored vest.

1.   Call your printer back. This time you want some protective language added to your invoices.

All claims under this invoice must be made in writing within 30 days. This includes but is not limited to claims of non-delivered goods, defective or damaged goods, nonconforming goods, unordered goods, or any other claim under Article 2 of the Uniform Commercial Code.

2.   Don't waiver on your policy. If the customer doesn't make claim within 30 days, that's his problem. You have the language to protect you.

3.   Have the customer sign for receipt of goods. This takes care of the problem of a customer claiming nonreceipt of the goods — or the invoice.

4.   On large orders, or "one-shot" orders, have the customer inspect and acknowledge upon delivery. For example, why ship $15,000 worth of fabric only to have your customer come up with his stories two weeks later?

5.   If you haven't protected yourself, then go for a reasonable settlement and lick your wounds. Otherwise you'll wait three years to get to court and the judge will still throw you and your "Walter" out into the lobby to reach a settlement. Do you think the judge wants to grow old listening to Walter?

THE "LOAN-IS-ON-ITS WAY" LORE

How many of your customers are negotiating bank or SBA loans so they can pay you and your equally naive creditor colleagues?

Sarah may be one of them. She's both energetic and convincing. Call her on your overdue bill and she'll tell you how she has fifteen loan applications pending and next week she may even try the SBA. By next month, of course, she sadly announces she has been turned down by each and every bank. But wait, now the good news. The SBA is seriously considering a $50,000 loan, and as soon as the fat check arrives you'll be the first paid. The SBA is always a good story. And it can remain a good story for at least a year.

The beauty of the phony loan story is that it trades on hope while defying detection. And creditors always want to hope and believe.

Action to take: Call her bluff.

1.   You want copies of her loan applications. If you think the only way you can get paid is to pray for a bank loan, then at least make sure there really is an attempt to obtain the loan. You don't need stories. You need proof. If Sarah refuses, you can bet it's a phony story. If she shows you the application, you can at least assess the chances.

2.   Push for progress. It's a must if you are Sarah's only pressure point. If you sit back, she'll sit back. Demand constant progress reports.

3.   Move in for collateral security, a guarantee, and acknowledgment of the debt, or a promissory note. Don't let Sarah stall you with her stories for months and then try another escape ploy.

4.   Verify that you will be paid. Sarah may get her $50,000, but that doesn't mean you will be paid. If you're a large creditor, try to coordinate it so the bank cuts two checks—one for Sarah and one for you.

5.   Finance for her. Sound ridiculous? It's not to a large hard goods manufacturer owed $16,000 from a small retailer. After six months of listening to loan stories, the manufacturer arranged financing for the retailer. The manufacturer guaranteed a $16,000 loan to the bank, secured by the assets of the business. The manufacturer has its money, and with little risk on its guarantee considering the collateral behind the bank's mortgage. The retailer is not too thrilled because the company has to pay the bank. Sometimes you have to call their bluff.

THE "BIG BAD CUSTOMER" BLUFF

If Sam has Walter for a cousin, Sarah has Sally for a sister.

Sally's story is that there's a big bad customer who owes her a large chunk of money but is overdue in paying it. And as with Sarah's loan, Sally intends to pay you if and when the money comes in. Hear the words "if" and "when."

Sally's strategy is clear. She's "passing the buck," in the figurative sense, but never does it literally. Usually the "buck" isn't even there to pass. It's almost always just another deadbeat story. And when the receivable is on the way there will be fifty creditors in line ahead of you. Still, it works. Creditors continue to hope, pray, and believe.

Don't fall for the line. If your customer is solvent, then its collection problems aren't your problems. You can't worry about *your* receivables *and* your customer's receivables. One headache is enough.

Then again you may be facing a rather hopeless situation. Sometimes that illusive receivable is your only hope.

Action to take: The overall strategy is to double your chances of collecting. Here's how:

1.   Verify that the receivable exists. Since your customer is asking you to rely on it, you have every right to check it out.

2.   Here's the critical step. Try to take an assignment of the receivable. If your receivable approximates the amount of your customer's receivable, it makes plenty of sense. After all, your customer has been promising to turn the proceeds over to you, so why not have it turned over now? It's the old reverse bluff. But can a Sally dare refuse?

ASSIGNMENT OF DEBT

For good and valuable consideration, the undersigned hereby assigns and transfers to   [your firm], all right, title, and interest in and to a certain debt and obligation due and owing the undersigned from: , in the amount of $. This assignment is with full recourse.

Date:

_____
Customer

Use a side letter agreement to adjust. For example, if you're owed $12,000, but the assigned debt is $14,000, acknowledge the $2,000 difference will be immediately repaid your customer.

3.   Notify your customer's account of the assignment. That puts them on notice to pay you.

4.   If the account doesn't pay within 30 days, it's time to press *both* your customer and its debtor for payment. Read the assignment carefully. It's with full recourse. It doesn't let your customer off the hook. The transaction only gives you the added right to turn Sally's long-awaited receivable into your payment.

THE "INTIMIDATION" ARTIST

This chap is most unpleasant. Whereas other deadbeats only jerk you around for a few years with their phony stories. This one puts you on the defensive by taking a strong offensive.

Think how ludicrous it all is. The Intimidator has owed you money for so long your receivable ledger has turned a pale yellow. And now the intimidator raises his or her vocal cords a few notches and lets you have it.

You can always tell when you're up against intimidators. First, they never start the intimidation routine while your merchandise is flowing through their doors. That's when they love you. You probably won't even see the true spots while you're sending out your benign collection letters. Pieces of paper seldom disturb this character. But it's when you begin to seriously put the pressure on that the intimidator goes to work.

Intimidators come in two subspecies—the "big mouth" and the "letter writer." Some are hybrids sharing the characteristics of both.

Big mouths enjoy showering you with verbal abuse. They'll give you 205 reasons why they don't intend to pay, 310 reasons why you owe them money, and 406 things they'll do to you if you even have the audacity to call again. With the ringing in your ears and the churning in your stomach the bully can safely assume you have been scared away for good.

The letter writers are even more insidious. Their trick is to pepper the file with a barrage of self-serving and self-righteous letters telling you about your dastardly deeds and in the last paragraph the revenge ultimatum. And don't expect just one letter. The intimidators who think one letter is good believe ten follow-up letters are even better. And to show just how serious they are, the letters arrive by certified mail. After all, they mean business, which is the fine art of giving you the business.

The bully always looks for allies. Expect copies to be forwarded to the Attorney General, the Chamber of Commerce, the Better Business Bureau, and anyone else they can think of. Why not? Hasn't the bully been victimized?

Settlements rarely work with intimidators. To give an inch is to give a mile. If you're lucky they'll let you apologize and tear up your bill.

The intimidator always has an equally intimidating attorney on their side. The best ones continue the game by suing you before you have a chance to sue. It's all part of maintaining the offensive.

***Action to take: Faced with a bully you have very few options.
Fast action is the key.***

1.   The very first time the customer becomes abusive, ask for
the name of the company's attorney. You don't want to talk to
the lawyer, you want it to be an attorney-to-attorney situation.
That's all. Keep the conversation short and simple.

2.   With the letter writer, take an additional step. With the
very first letter you receive, write the customer back just one
letter, telling them why he is off base and that further letters will
be ignored. Never, never tell them that you intend to sue or when.
Don't let them jump the gun on you.

3.   Act fast in bringing suit. This is a critical step. You want
to be the plaintiff, not a mere defendant with a counterclaim.
Psychologically and in the mind of the court, when the customer
sues first it looks like he does have a legitimate claim. You have
to take the offensive.

I have pulled that stunt. I once represented a bully who owed
an exporter about $80,000. The exporter would call and my bully
would go into a tirade. He was almost believing it himself. Then
the exporter's attorney made a fatal mistake. He warned us that
he was preparing a lawsuit. We beat him to the draw by filing
first against the importer, claiming $300,000 in trumped-up dam-
ages. All the importer could do is sue back for the original $80,000.
But beside its name on the lawsuit was the ominous word "defendant." Do you think courts are quick to give defendants an
attachment against a plaintiff?

THE "PAYMENT IN FULL" PLOY

Occasionally you run into bullies with charity in their hearts.
One owes you $10,000, but through sheer benevolence mails you
a check for $2,500 marked "in full payment." Accompanying the
check is a long letter with exhaustive reasons for knocking $7,500
off the bill. If the reasons are due to the company's insolvent
condition, then I refer you to Chapter 9.

Most "payment in full" artists use other reasons, and they always try to intimidate you into accepting the check rather than risk the hassle of chasing for the full amount. This deadbeat is no dummy. He knows that creditors hate to part with money in their hands, particularly if there are some convincing reasons to keep it and swallow the balance. The bird in the hand is better than the two, three, or four in the bush. Besides, it may cost you almost as much in legal fees and collection costs to go after those flighty birds.

Action to take: Drop your rule book. This is a delicate situation and requires a case-by-case evaluation. But from years of experience in dealing with the "payment in full" manipulator, I suggest you use these pointers as a guide.

1. It's time for some more teeth in your paperwork. This deadbeat's chief weapon is the belief you will accept rather than run up costly legal bills to come chasing. The trick then is to make *the deadbeat* pay your legal and collection costs. To do it you need some additional language plugged into your contracts or statements. Try this terminology:

In the event this statement is not paid on the due date, then the customer agrees to pay all reasonable collection costs and attorneys' fees necessary to collect.

Look familiar? Of course. You'll always find it in promissory notes but almost never in open-account transactions. And in most states this powerful clause is binding. Check it out with your lawyer. It's time the "payment in full" artist and all your other deadbeats realize they may have to pay your attorney as well as their own. It brings faster and larger checks.

2. If you aren't prepared to accept the check, don't cash it. And don't try to cross out the "payment in full" notation. You have no right to alter the check. Either accept it or send it back.

3. Now the big question is, should you accept? Not without some negotiations. If a customer offers you 40% to settle, that's only the beginning figure. A phone call or two may increase it to 60 to 70%. It's only when you have your *best* offer that you can make decisions.

THE SELL-OUT CAPER

The sell-out caper has several themes. The most common is the deadbeat who sells the business for whatever can be gotten, pockets the proceeds, and goes into hiding.

It happens. In one recent case, such a scoundrel sold a food store for $20,000 which owed creditors over $60,000, while the foolish buyer forked over the money in return for a bill of sale stating the assets were sold "free and clear of all creditor claims."

To combat the situation you have to know a little law. The Bulk Sales Act, enacted in every state, is your ammunition. It provides that a seller of a business must notify creditors at least ten days prior to any sale. If the creditors are not notified they have six months to go after the goods transferred to the buyer. The notice requirements are also exacting. If payment in full is anticipated, the notice must state it. If partial payment is expected, then that too must be spelled out with considerable detail.

But a shrewd seller can get around even these creditor safeguards. For example, the seller may give a buyer a false list of creditors. The business may have $80,000 in creditors, and a selling price of perhaps $60,000. So the deadbeat seller gives the buyer a false affidavit listing only $40,000 in creditors and pockets the other $20,000 at the closing. Now the creditors are left chasing the gullible buyer. And that's always a hassle.

Other variations on the theme? Let's assume you receive notice of the intended sale, specifying that creditors should be paid in full. It's not payment and may not turn into payment. For example, the buyer may discover some last-minute creditors, or closing adjustments bring the price down. Only after the closing does everyone realize there's only enough money to pay 80% on creditors' claims. So just when you thought you were all set, in comes the "Dear Creditor" letter.

Action to take: No sale goes through unless you have complete assurance you will see your full payment. Here's how to do it.

1.   If you never received notice under the Bulk Sales, only to later discover the business was sold, then run—don't walk—to

your counsel. Stop the dunning notices. You need a fast attachment against the transferred assets and you have to do it within six months.

2.   If you receive notice of the intended sale, and that you will be paid in full, you still need follow-up. Before the sale, demand written acknowledgment from the buyer's and seller's attorney that (1) the debt is due and fully owing (you don't want a contest after the sale), (2) the attorney will escrow the proceeds until you are fully paid, and (3) payment will be made within 10 to 15 days of the sale. This last point is important. Even attorneys can sit on your money for months.

3.   Notices specifying that partial payment is anticipated require action within the 10-day period preceding the sale. Let's assume the notice says the business is being sold for $40,000, but since the debts are $80,000 creditors will receive about 50 cents on the dollar. That's your red flag. The business may be worth $100,000 and the buyer is the seller's brother-in-law. Enjoin the sale in court until you're satisfied you can't do better. Even then you should try to hold up the sale. Being a pain in the neck can pay big dividends. How do you know the buyer (or seller) won't find the few extra dollars to let the sale go through?

THE "VANISHING ACT VANDAL"

Some deadbeats you can't even find. Like Gary Cooper in the movie *High Noon* they mount up their steeds and ride off into the sunset.

A few use Cadillacs or Mercedes. Why not leave town in style, they figure. They have plenty of money after years of looting the business. And all they ever leave behind is a few worthless assets and a mountain of debt.

The enemy you can't find is the enemy you can't beat. Of all the scoundrels in this chapter, none is quite as frustrating as the "vanishing act vandal." First, the vandal was hiding behind a corporation to run up the bills. Unlike a consumer debt, the bills aren't even the vandal's. Go chase an empty corporation. Further, you never know quite who to chase or where.

Forget your money. Except for the few pennies you may reap from the business rubble, you probably will never see another dime. So don't play sheriff and go chasing off into the sunset. Your only objective should be revenge.

Action to take: Revenge requires a posse. If you want to make the vandal's life miserable, then group action is the only way to do it economically. After all, even revenge has a price.

1.   Round up the posse. You want as many creditors on your side as possible to share the costs and, of course, share in the joy.

2.   Now hire a "no-nonsense" lawyer. Let counsel know you don't expect recovery—only revenge. Ten creditors, each throwing in $100, can start a war chest of $1,000. It's enough to create serious aggravation. What your lawyer will do is sue the deadbeat personally claiming every type of fraud and embezzlement. It may be true, it may not be. Who knows? What you do know is the deadbeat has a bad choice to make. He can either come out of hiding and defend (which can cost him plenty of money), or he can ignore it and be officially declared the loser with a default judgment against him.

I remember one of my old clients, Tom, a deadbeat of the first magnitude. After living high off the proverbial hog by milking his business for two years, he saddled up and drifted south for the winter together with the other birds. There he was, sipping his piña colada by the pool when the sheriff handed him a $160,000 personal lawsuit from the suppliers. Rather than pay a $6,000 retainer to defend, he filed personal bankruptcy.

Sometimes getting even is better than getting paid.

THE "SAD SACK" STORY

It's enough to make a grown person cry. "My spouse deserted me," "my oldest kid has leprosy," "my in-laws moved in with us." Horror stories. Hopefully you'll fall for the line, and through sheer humanitarian compassion you'll stay off the "Sad Sack's" back so this deadbeat can continue to ignore you for a while.

Now when the stories are truly sad and very real you may have to give your customer some breathing room. Even creditors need a heart.

But how do you know what story is for real, and what's just another phony sympathy-evoking fable. You don't. You have to check out the facts. Then you'll discover the fiction.

Action to take: Operate on the premise that this deadbeat type only tells stories but rarely remembers them, and even less often covers his tracks.

1.   Test their memory. Today your customer tells you their *child* developed leprosy, so it's impossible to get to your bill. Fair enough. The customer's preoccupied. Call up next week and ask how the customer's *spouse* is doing. The deadbeat will tell you. The "Sad Sack" never remembers.

2.   Play detective. It only takes a phone call, a get well card to the hospital, or a thoughtful inquiry to an employee.

3.   When you uncover the big lie, let your customer know it. Then move in fast.

4.   Watch for the multiple-story artist. Even leprosy lasts only so long. Once the "Sad Sack" sees how successful the story is this deadbeat will be inventing a few more.

THE "COMPUTER CONVULSION" CLOWN

Time out for a little light humor. Now and then you'll come across a deadbeat who enjoys sabotaging your computer. Consumer deadbeats do it all the time. But even business deadbeats can find it a form of relaxation.

For Molly P. and Joshua Q. it's an avocation. Whenever they come across a computer-coded billing card they randomly punch a few more holes and send it back—without a check, of course. They find it interesting to test the results. Here's a sample scorecard for last year.

One company mailed them a $490 refund check.

Another victimized firm sent them 26 catalogues on the same day.

A third supplier rebilled them $1,643,900 when the company only owed $164.39. It didn't bother them. Playing the "Contested Balance" Con they patiently waited three months for a corrected bill.

Three firms never rebilled. The con artists were too much for the computer.

How should you handle Molly and Joshua if they throw your computer into convulsions? There's only one solution. Unplug your damn computer. Computers never win.

THE "FALSE IDENTITY" FAKER

These scoundrels pull the old "shell" game. Now you see it, now you don't. They somehow manage to get you to clear credit for big, healthy Company X only to find out $95,000 later that you have been shipping and billing Company Y, which turns out to be a mail-drop storefront or a $50 a month office in the low-rent district.

How do they do it? Ken B. can give you a quick lesson on the "false identity" caper. Ken managed to bamboozle $285,000 worth of creditors so his teaching credentials are impeccable. Here's how he pulled the gig. First he applied for credit for his Company X, a large, prosperous discount store. With glowing credit credentials, suppliers always give it the green light.

Now lurking and working in most shipping departments are $175-a-week clerks who don't appreciate the legal significance of a phone call politely requesting billing instead be in the name of Company Y. So when the bills come due about all you can do is chase Company Y and its $50 desk and rented telephone.

Third-party billings to phony, weak, or "throw-away" companies are more common than you may think. Ken didn't invent the game, although he boasts he slightly perfected it. "It's easy as pie," says Ken. "Once credit is established and the goods start flowing, get to know the people who handle billing. A phone call to let them know that they should ship and bill to another name or even address doesn't arouse their curiosity. Half their customers have divisions, trade names, affiliates, and other names. And why should the different address create suspicion. Between centralized warehousing and drop-shipping it's as common as grasshoppers in Kansas."

Ken, once he has his hands on his goods, immediately reships to his supermarket. Don't despair. You may get paid if Ken decides you're a worthwhile supplier. But if not, he leaves you chasing his phantom company.

Sure, you can file all sorts of fraudulent transfers and other nasty legal actions to right the wrong. You know it and Ken knows it. But it's costly and complex, and hardly worth it for a small bill. So Ken deals from his position of poverty and power, while you continue to wonder where the defunct Company Y came from.

Maybe you should protect yourself from Ken before he gets to you.

Action to take: It requires a strong before and after policy.

1.   Strengthen your billing controls. If you clear credit for a company under a particular name, insist billing and shipping be under that name. Don't allow your billing or shipping department to switch to another trade or company name or any other address until it's checked out.

2.   If a customer requests billing or shipping to another-named firm, either obtain a guarantee from the original firm which has cleared credit or have your customer agree to a "joint billing" where you have recourse against either firm.

3.   Don't hesitate to go after a final recipient of the goods, when there is an intercompany transfer. The phantom firm should either have payment or a receivable representing the value of the reshipped goods. If it doesn't, you have a very good fraudulent-transfer case. Your attorney can guide you through the complexities, but the remedy is there. This is one deadbeat that's easy to beat.

THE "RUBBER CHECK" ARTIST

This deadbeat isn't your long-standing customer who now and then sends you a bad check on a rendered statement. Bookkeeping oversights happen, and usually these checks clear on redeposit.

The rubber check artist is something else again, with more "rubber" floating around town than Goodyear Tire. And it always happens on a COD purchase.

In a few moments I'll show you the conventional ways to handle this chronic paperhanger. But I learned a long time ago that not all remedies are taught in law books. Sometimes it's better to take a lesson from Fillmore, a first-class jungle fighter.

Old Fillmore follows this counterstrategy. Let's follow how he handled his most recent rubber passer. The story unfolds as Fillmore receives a $1,200 order for stereo speakers from a nearby stereo shop. Since it was a new and nonrated company, Fillmore shipped on COD terms. Two weeks later the rubber check bounced back marked "account closed." A less spirited character may have run to court. Not Fillmore. He waited a week and phoned the stereo shop owner. "I know how bad things are. You can catch up on the bad check later. In the meantime how about some more business?" Mr. Rubber was amazed. There was Fillmore holding $1,200 in worthless paper and he wanted *more* business. Of course he did, but now Fillmore logically wanted *cash* on delivery. The stereo shop owner agreed, placing an order for $1,600 in new components. Fillmore delivered and quickly picked up the $1,600 cash. An hour later the stereo shop owner opened the box loaded with coal and Fillmore's $400 rebate check. As Fillmore would say, "The only way to win is to fight fire with fire. You can't go by the rule book."

Fillmore's clever ruse does work. Many of my clients now use it and report at least a 50% success rate. The only time they strike out is when the customer won't reorder on cash terms, or when they're smart enough to inspect the goods before they part with the money. But what can you lose by trying?

Perhaps this tit-for-tat approach doesn't quite fit into your style.

Action to take: Back to convention.

1.   Always use your criminal remedies first. A bounced check on a COD order is larceny by check in just about every state. And you'll collect faster with the authority of the criminal courts behind you. Besides, why pay an attorney to do what a young prosecutor will do for free.

2.   Never accept a partial payment on a bad COD check. In most states, acceptance of a partial payment (or commencement of a civil suit to collect) is a waiver of your criminal remedies. The only time you should accept a partial payment is when you obtain adequate collateral to ensure payment of the balance.

3.   Put your banker to work. If the check is returned "insufficient funds" or "uncollected funds," you stand a reasonable chance of getting paid if you place it with your bank for "collection." Your bank will phone your customer's bank each day for 10 days to inquire if adequate funds are on account to honor the check. If the funds are there, the money will be set aside to cover your check. In contrast, the redeposited check can only be cleared if the funds are on account on the day it's presented. This simple, low-cost technique of placing the check for "collection" improves your chances tenfold.

4.   People who bounce checks are deadbeats. But people who "stop payment" on checks are shrewd businesspeople. Since it's better to be considered a shrewd businessperson than a deadbeat, many of your customers will discover the goods were "defective" or find some other fabricated story to stop payment and make it a long, drawn-out civil matter. A check is only a promise to pay. If you want payment, make it *cash* on delivery.

Hear those words? Get cash. That's the only way you'll really win the game when you play against any confirmed deadbeat. But, unfortunately, you never know they're in the ring with you until they deliver the knock-out punch.

6

TURNING ASSETS
INTO COLLATERAL

To build a $20,000 credit line with Phoenix Hospital Beds, a customer needs only a profitable cash flow, sterling credit history, proven management with impeccable character—and $20,000 in solid collateral. "Collateral is the real key," muses Ken Benjoya, Phoenix credit manager, "without it we don't bother checking further."

Phoenix seldom loses in the collection arena. A case in point: When Brighton Surgical Supply folded, its other creditors mopped their brow, walking away without a dime on their $145,000 in claims. Benjoya showed up at the auction and waving his security agreement granting Phoenix first claim on assets, scooped $26,000 from the auction proceeds to clear the bill. The remaining few dollars were absorbed in bankruptcy expenses. Once again Phoenix made out while other less demanding and less imaginative creditors lost out. And all that separated Phoenix from the losers were a few pieces of paper.

THERE'S NOTHING QUITE LIKE COLLATERAL

Nothing takes the place of collateral in the credit and collection arsenal. All other criteria are frills and only take on meaning when collateral isn't available and you have no other basis to go on.

Pour over a customer's financial statements, cash flows, and P & L statements all day long. It only tells you if the company is healthy today. What guarantees does it give you for collecting tomorrow when the bills become due?

Credit history? As with all history it only shows what *was*, not necessarily what *will be*. At a given point in time every business can show a good track record. At some other point in time 80% of these companies will sputter or stop bill paying. Who can really predict the timing?

Character and management competence? A band of angels can't pay if the money isn't in the checkbook.

That brings us back to collateral. It has a power all its own. It turns the probability of payment into certainty of payment because it's based on preparation for the worst instead of merely hoping for the best.

Banks understand it. Masters of asset-based lending, collateral is the cornerstone of small-business borrowing. Whether it be business assets, personal assets, or both, banks demand adequate recourse when promises become prayers. It may be a "hard-nosed" attitude, but banks have learned collateral means strength while lack of collateral puts them in the weakest position to collect.

It's this very same collateral-hungry philosophy that gives banks an overwhelming chance of collecting while unsecured trade creditors have scant chance of seeing their money when a customer decides it can't—or won't—pay. The objective is to start thinking and acting the way the banks do.

EXPLODING FIVE MYTHS

Dig out your accounts receivables files. How many are backed by collateral security? Probably very few, if any. Selling on open account you're guided by faith, hope, and eventually charity.

It can change. You can benefit from the power and practicality of collateral once you shake loose the five myths most business people fall victim to:

1. Customers *won't* grant collateral.
2. Collateral *isn't* available.

3. Collateral goes *contrary* to convention.

4. Collateral is *too complicated.*

5. Collateral *isn't needed.*

And they are all costly fallacies.

1. *Customers Will Grant Security.*   Sure they will. And they will hand you collateral with far less resistance than you think. But there are two essential ingredients to make it happen. First, you have to make it policy to ask for it. I've yet to see the customer who ran to a supplier with a security agreement or personal guarantee. It's your job to go after it. And you have to sell it from the customer's perspective, showing him why it's in his best interests to sign. It's a two-step process few creditors accomplish.

Not long ago our firm liquidated a bakery, which went bust owing 50 creditors over $150,000. Free and clear of mortgages and encumbrances, the auction gave creditors about a dime on the dollar. Did any of these creditors even *ask* for a mortgage? "Not one," according to my client.

You're not going to ask General Motors for a mortgage for you to ship $500. But General Motors probably doesn't appear on your receivable roster. Learn to ask for and to sell collateralized credit. In this chapter I'll show you how.

2. *Collateral Is Available.*   You'll come across customers mortgaged to the hilt, and you may have to dig deeper to find collateral to protect your debt. So dig. Chances are other secured creditors overlooked valuable collateral you can latch on to.

That's one challenge of collateral. There are so many clever ways to achieve it, it's difficult *not* to find a way to put yourself ahead of less imaginative creditors.

Take a page from a shoe manufacturer who used one of those clever ways. A mid-sized shoe retailer hunted credit from competing manufacturers who consistently turned it down, citing its heavy secured debt and poor credit history. This shrewd manufacturer spotted the same problems but found a solution. It segregated a small portion of the store and stocked it with its brand shoes on a consignment basis. The store did eventually fail; however, the manufacturer didn't lose a dime as it carted away its unsold inventory. The bright side was this manufacturer sold $190,000 worth of shoes through this store before it collapsed.

Glance through your files. How many of your customers don't have collateral to pledge?

3.   *Collateral Can Be Conventional.*   You'll continue to stand out from the crowd as you go after collateral. You know your competitors aren't even thinking about collateral until it's too late. That doesn't make you noncompetitive. Just the opposite. You'll be even more competitive because collateral will allow you to do more for your customers than your competitors can selling on an open account (nonsecured) basis.

Consider it your good fortune that collateral does go contrary to convention. It offers you a clear field to be the imaginative supplier. Jackson Paper Products found that out. Before it became collateral-conscious, Jackson sold all its customers on open account. Now it aggressively pushes for collateral for large orders from nonrated accounts. Sixty percent of its receivables are now secured and bad debts are down from 6% to less than 1%. You can benefit the same way once you make collateral your rule.

4.   *Collateral Is Not Too Complicated.*   Many businesspeople shun secured transactions for the same reason I hide from computers. They don't understand how it works. Don't let collateralized credit intimidate you. No law degree is required. But lack of knowledge is precisely why so many creditors don't chase collateral.

At a seminar with twenty credit managers, I asked, "How many routinely go after security?" A candid bunch, two managers replied in the affirmative and the other eighteen honestly admitted they don't really understand it or how to go about it. They found it easier to gamble and ship on open credit.

What will it take to put a strong collateral package together? A few hours of your attorney's time to prepare documents you can use with almost any account and just a few minutes of your time to learn how to use them.

It's not complicated. In fact, you'll find all the ready-to-use forms you need in my own book, *The Basic Book of Business Agreements* (Enterprise Publishing).

5. *Collateral Is Needed.*   Whether you're extending $1,000 or $100,000 you need collateral and you need it with just about every customer.

Remember Brighton Surgical Supply's crowd of clammering creditors and their lost $145,000. They didn't think they needed collateral either. Brighton Surgical looked like a sure bet. Ken Benjoya knew better. The only sure bet you have is when adequate collateral backs up your debt. But why peek over Ken Benjoya's shoulder. Pull your recent loss files and ask the most important question of all, "If you had collateral would those receivables be in your loss column?"

USING COLLATERAL CREATIVELY

Collateral offers protection. That much is common knowledge even if seldom practiced. But it's more. It can be the best way to increase sales and retain customers. So collateral, used creatively, offers a three-pronged approach to increased profits. Here's how.

Collateral Can Land Customers

Without collateral you're limited as to who will receive credit and how much you'll extend. And all your competitors are navigating by the same yardsticks. Switch to a collateral-oriented approach and you have a totally different yardstick and a surprisingly large number of potential customers who can measure up. Let me introduce you to two enterprising suppliers who prove the point.

Commonwealth Beverage, a liquor distributor, actively goes after accounts based on collateral. One of my clients, Cameo Liquors, was a beneficiary of this approach. With a weak financial statement, spotty credit history, and rollercoaster profits, other suppliers remained credit-shy. Along came Commonwealth Beverage who looked over Cameo's operation and figured the business was worth about $50,000. Since the only existing mortgage against the business was $10,000 owed a bank, Commonwealth felt comfortable with the $40,000 collateral cushion. It offered Cameo a $15,000 credit line to be repaid over two years, provided Cameo stayed current on future orders.

It was a sensible deal. Cameo obtained the credit needed to boost inventory, sales, and profits, on a plan matching its cash flow. Commonwealth also viewed it logically from a "best case," "worst case" angle. If Cameo succeeded, Commonwealth would be locked into a high-volume and profitable customer. If Cameo went under, Commonwealth would easily recoup its $15,000 from the liquidation. Fortunately the "best case" is winning out. Cameo is alive and well, buying over $200,000 a year from Commonwealth. Commonwealth played the game right. They knew what they could gain and they saw how little they could lose. And the odds are always good when you go after accounts—and their collateral.

Atlantic Periodicals is an even more dramatic story. Atlantic struggled for years as a small distributor of paperbacks and magazines to drugstores, variety stores, and other typically weak and marginal Mom and Pop operators. Atlantic's competitors used a short credit leash, seldom extending more than one week's credit. How could Atlantic use one-upmanship over its well-heeled competitors? It scouted out prospective customers offering four weeks' credit provided it was backed by collateral.

"It was a terrific strategy," comments Harry Corsetti, Atlantic's Vice-President. "Our sales reps would hit a competitor's account and ask what they rang up a week in magazine sales. The customers would say $2,000 to $3,000 a week, and our people would then throw out our four-week terms. The customers could see how it would ease up their own cash flow, when they learned we'd continue to roll over the month's credit if they paid interest and future orders on time. But its success was in its simplicity. We were essentially making an $8,000 to $12,000 loan and buying a $100,000-a-year customer in return."

From a financial viewpoint, Atlantic's strategy was more than simple. Before their collateral-hungry sales campaign, Atlantic had 200 marginal accounts generating annual sales of $2 million. Now they have 450 accounts producing $5 million in sales. But it was the increased strength of their receivables that allowed this thinly capitalized firm to expand. Atlantic's bank will lend against their receivables because the receivables are no longer questionable. Either the customers are well-rated or Atlantic holds a good mortgage on their business. So the bank lends to Atlantic and Atlantic lends to land new customers. "We're nothing more than a conduit to pass the money through, winning increased sales and profits in the process—and far fewer credit losses," confesses Harry Corsetti.

Consider your own situation. How many additional, risk-free customers could you land if you offered more credit than your competitors?

Collateral Helps Retain Customers

If collateral can help you win customers, it's even more effective in keeping them loyal and profitable to you. Credit is the carrot to land the account, but their pledged collateral becomes the stick to retain them. And a mighty big stick it is.

Without collateral you're at the customers' mercy. They run up a $10,000 bill with you and then jump to Company X, leaving you without a customer and without their money. It's a fool's game, and the creditor is the fool.

Commonwealth Beverage admits it's not in the finance business. They're in business to sell liquor. So Commonwealth tied Cameo to an agreement, obligating Cameo to buy at least 75% of its wholesale liquor from Commonwealth. If Cameo defaults and decides to flirt with another supplier, Commonwealth can demand immediate payment on their secured $15,000 balance—or foreclose if the check doesn't arrive.

If it's a form of legalized bondage, it must be a bondage based on mutual benefit. And it is a fair deal for Cameo because Commonwealth sells at a competitive price, granting Cameo all the trade discounts and concessions available from other suppliers.

Atlantic Periodicals is no different. When the customer stops ordering, the outstanding debt is immediately due. How can Atlantic lose? They either have the customer or they have their money.

Commonwealth Beverage and Atlantic Periodicals are hardly the only two companies to discover the power of a hefty mortgage to bind customers. Its economic potential has attracted other shrewd suppliers to the same "load them up and lock them up" routine. It is indeed profitable.

Cameo Liquors shows just how profitable it can be. Shelling out $200,000 in purchases a year to Commonwealth, it adds about $20,000 a year to Commonwealth's profits. It's not a bad return on a $15,000 secured investment. Beyond that, Commonwealth even makes a few dollars on the interest spread, charging Cameo 21% interest, while Commonwealth borrows at the prime rate, now about 16%. "We're at the point where our competitors are becoming wise to our credit policy. Someday a smart competitor will come along, offer Cameo a $20,000 credit line to pay us off and add a few dollars in working capital and maybe even throw in an extra one or two percent discount to steal Cameo away. But until they do we can virtually retire our salespeople and let the mortgage take their place," admits Commonwealth's credit manager.

It can be an equally profitable strategy for you. But watch these pointers:

1. *Don't* let the credit line exceed the value of the collateral. Maintain that careful balance. It's easy to become too sales-oriented and forget collateral is also designed to protect.

2. *Don't* extend a large initial credit without agreement on how it will be paid down. Your objective is not to load an account up with $15,000 to $20,000 in new credit and expect them to pay it off the following month. If the customer had that cash-flow capability they wouldn't need you or your credit terms. Plan a repayment consistent with the customer's projected cash flow. In most cases, one to three years of installment payments are needed.

3. *Don't* penalize your customer. The company may owe you money and you may hold its mortgage, but it's entitled to the same discounts, benefits, service, and concessions other customers obtain buying in comparable volume. Violate this rule and you'll be up to your neck in Robinson-Patman price-discrimination violations.

4.   *Do* demand a profitable interest rate. For example, if your opening credit line is $20,000, have it evidenced by a note bearing interest *above* what you charge customers on open account. If your open account interest rate is 18%, you may be able to negotiate a 20 to 21% rate. And it's not discriminatory because you can charge a higher rate on a note than on open account (invoiced) obligations.

5.   *Do* spell out the buying obligations. You can't compel the customer to buy, but you can demand full payment if it doesn't. The best approach is to set a minimum monthly (or quarterly) purchases' quota. Excess purchases in one period may be credited to the quota for subsequent periods. Project buying capabilities carefully. Don't set requirements that can't reasonably be achieved.

6.   *Do* require the customer to remain current on all payments. If an installment payment or payment on current purchases goes beyond the due date, retain the right to declare the entire balance payable. Don't forget you're not just another creditor. You hold a mortgage.

MATCHING THE CREDIT TO THE COLLATERAL

The credit limit extended to the customer should not exceed the pledged collateral value upon liquidation of the business. This in turn requires a two-step process:

1.   Calculate the estimated liquidation value of the pledged assets.
2.   Subtract existing mortgages, liens, and encumbrances against the assets.

The net difference between estimated liquidation proceeds, and the amount necessary to pay prior mortgage holders represents the value of the collateral—to the extent you are relying on the collateral for credit purposes. Follow each step in closer detail.

1.   *What Is the Collateral Worth at Auction?*   If you were to accept real estate, a motor vehicle, or even a specific piece of

equipment as the only collateral, defining the value of the collateral is not difficult as these items have a reasonably fixed and ascertainable resale worth. Major suppliers, however, rely on a *blanket mortgage* (security agreement) consisting of a mix of collateral. Inventory, fixtures, equipment, and accounts receivable are common inclusions. The value of the whole, then, is represented by the sum of its parts.

Even within a specific category of collateral—such as inventory—the variables are considerable. Inventory in the retail liquor industry may liquidate out at 70% of wholesale cost. On the low side, clothing stores and customers in the soft goods line may see their inventory auctioned at five or ten cents on the dollar. Within a given industry, the variables are equally hard at work. The inventory mix and condition are factors. So, too, are the location of the business, market demand for that type inventory, and even the time of year when the liquidation takes place.

Fixtures and equipment go through the same wild fluctuations as does inventory, and for the same reasons. Not long ago we liquidated a printing plant with new equipment recently purchased for $60,000. At auction the same equipment brought only $4,500. Why? There was a rash of printing plant auctions in the preceding few months and the market was "soft."

The lesson to be learned is that you need an experienced eye to size up the situation and tell you what the assets will bring at liquidation. And experienced commercial auctioneers have the best eye. For $200 to $300 you can hire an auctioneer to walk through your customer's business and come up with a reasonably accurate liquidation value for the tangible assets. If you are thoroughly familiar with your customer's industry and attended a few auctions yourself, you may have already developed your own experienced eye.

Accounts receivable and other pledged intangible assets must also be appraised. A customer may be willing to pledge $50,000 in receivables, but what will you see on those receivables if the business goes under? You have to consider the collectibility of the receivables, not an easy task, particularly if the receivables represent consumer debt or marginal accounts. For this reason you may only place a $25,000 liquidation value on receivables with a face value of $50,000. In many cases you'll do well to collect even 20 to 30% of the receivables due a business under foreclosure or liquidation.

Considering Murphy's Law that all that can go wrong will go wrong, stay on the conservative side. Build a cushion or safety factor into the numbers. If you think assets will bring $60,000, mark it down to $40,000 to $45,000. Don't forget, there will be liquidation expenses, not to mention assets that may be depleted and certainly used and abused between the dates of appraisal and liquidation.

2. *Deduct Prior Liens.* In most cases you'll be offered collateral that is already pledged to prior mortgage holders. Their claims must be satisfied before yours is paid as they hold the superior position. These prior encumbrances may be mortgages (security agreements), tax liens, or attachments.

Don't take the customer's word on prior encumbrances. Some lie, others forget. You or your attorney can check out the existence of these encumbrances by checking public filings. Initially you should have your attorney show you how to go about it.

Assuming you do find prior encumbrances on file, your next two steps are to see if they cover the collateral being pledged to you and, if so, the amount due. Reading the collateral clause in their mortgage (or financing statement) will answer the first question. Amounts due require direct creditor verification.

One mortgage to watch out for is the "open-ended" mortgage. X Company, for example, may hold a mortgage against the same assets to be pledged to you. So you call X Company and they tell you the customer only owes $10,000. Read the mortgage carefully. X Company's mortgage may say it covers "any and all obligations now or hereinafter existing." Next week the customer may run up an additional $15,000 in credit with X Company giving them a claim of $25,000 ahead of you. This is a common problem with supplier mortgages. They usually are "open-ended" as to amount— and yours should be also. However, you can't predict the equity in the collateral at the time of liquidation with this type mortgage superior to yours. The solution is to have X Company and the customer agree that X Company's mortgage will not exceed $10,000. This may impair the customer's future credit with X Company, but it's vital to protect you. Another common error in computing prior encumbrances is to ignore interest, penalties, or attorneys' fees accrued. I recall a case of a sadder but now wiser dress manufacturer who loaded up a Chicago discount clothing store with $100,000 in merchandise on favorable credit terms. Why not? The retailer had plenty of assets, reasoned the manufacturer, and the only encumbrance ahead of the manufacturer's mortgage was a $30,000 tax lien. Believing the assets would sell for well over $130,000 the manufacturer could hardly lose—or so it thought. A year later the retailer collapsed and the assets were grabbed up for $148,000. But the Internal Revenue Service didn't settle for $30,000. With accrued interest, penalties, and all the other nasty assessments, compounding each year for six years, the tax bill was up to $78,000. It was an expensive $48,000 mistake.

Even with a solid fix on liquidation values, and an equally solid verification of prior encumbrances, the collateral value is only a theoretical number. That's what your customer's collateral is worth to you *today*. What will it be worth two months or two years from now if your customer goes down the drain? You know the answer. Your collateral will be long gone unless you have a mortgage with teeth in it.

FIVE IRONCLAD TERMS FOR YOUR MORTGAGE

Plugging power into your mortgage requires effective clauses and terms to:

1. *Increase* the scope and value of the collateral.
2. *Maintain* the collateral value.
3. *Monitor* the collateral.

In short, you want to grab as much collateral as possible, enhance its liquidation value, and make certain the collateral value doesn't decrease.

A simple security agreement may take the following form:

SECURITY AGREEMENT

Date:

BE IT ACKNOWLEDGED that:

_____

Name

_____

Address

_____

(Debtor) grants to   , and its successors and assigns (Secured Party) a security interest in the following property (collateral) as herein described:

This security interest is granted to secure payment and performance on the following obligations owed Secured Party from Debtor: [Describe obligation]

Debtor hereby acknowledges to Secured Party, each of the following:

1. The collateral shall also include any after acquired property of a like nature and description and all appurtenances, proceeds or products thereto.
2. The collateral shall be kept at the Debtor's above address, and adequately insured at the request of Secured Party.
3. The Debtor owns the collateral and it is free from any other lien, encumbrance, and security interest and the Debtor has full authority to grant this security interest.
4. Debtor agrees to execute such financing statements as are reasonably required by Secured Party.
5. Upon default in payment or performance of any obligation for which this security interest is granted, or breach of any provision of this agreement, then in such instance secured party may declare all obligations immediately due and payable and shall have all remedies of a Secured Party under the Uniform Commercial Code.

Signed in duplicate:

_____

Debtor

_____

Secured Party

Now let's build some strength into it by seeing how these additional terms can work for you:

1. *Increase Collateral.*   You may have bargained for inventory, fixtures, equipment, and accounts receivable, but why stop there? With an all-inclusive collateral clause you have *every* possible asset. Consider the potential value of tax refunds, insurance proceeds, patents, trademarks, contract rights, and even claims against third parties. Have your mortgage spell out that the collateral includes *all* tangible and intangible assets of every nature and description. Don't limit yourself.

2. *Enhance Value.*   What are the assets worth at auction? Twenty thousand dollars? Thirty thousand? What would the assets be worth if you could sell it as a "going business"? Far more. The trick is to be able to sell it as a going business, and the only way to accomplish this is by obtaining an "assignment of lease" to go along with the mortgage. With the assignment of lease, you can take over the location and allow the buyer to assume the balance of the lease term. Those same assets that would bring $20,000 at auction may go for its actual wholesale or replacement cost if you can sell the business intact.

A drug wholesaler in our area usually demands an assignment of lease. It pays handsome dividends. In one case a retail pharmacy customer failed, owing it $40,000. The inventory and fixtures weren't likely to bring more than $20,000 at auction. But the drugstore didn't go to auction. The wholesaler, armed with the assignment of lease, simply sold it as a going business for $65,000, recouping its entire debt. The best part was that the wholesaler sold the business to another long-standing customer, assuring the wholesaler profitable future business. If location is an asset, have your attorney prepare an assignment of lease for you.

3. *Maintain Value.*   Let's assume your customer has an inventory worth $60,000 at cost. You need this figure to estimate liquidation—and collateral value. You decide the $60,000 will produce $20,000 at auction, so that's how you set your credit limit. A year later the debt is still $20,000 but the inventory shrank to $30,000. Now the collateral is worth $10,000 at liquidation and you're no longer protected. And it will happen.

Typically, a troubled business will deplete inventory before it fails. Don't allow it to happen. Insert a clause in your mortgage that your customer must maintain an inventory at least equal to $60,000 (or its present cost value). If the inventory begins to shrink, you can call an immediate default and foreclose. It's the only way to protect yourself against dwindling inventory—and dwindling collateral.

Take the same approach with receivables, if they are secured. You may be relying on your customer's representation that *today* it has $50,000 in good collectible receivables. Once his business falls on hard times the customer may decide to stop further charges and pocket incoming receivable payments, leaving you with negligible receivables on the books. Make it a condition of the mortgage that receivables remain at the $50,000 level.

4. *Monitor the Situation.*   Words on a piece of paper don't mean much. You have to play watchdog. Unless you carefully monitor and review your customer's financial position, the words will indeed be meaningless. Inventory levels can be monitored in many cases by your sales personnel who can spot signs of depletion. If in doubt, take a physical inventory. Do the same with receivables. Require the customer to periodically provide for you a receivable list so you *know* the collateral is there.

Enforcing the terms of the mortgage is the only way the mortgage retains the value you bargained for.

A distributor of musical records and tapes now agrees with this advice. On the strength of a Chicago-based retailer's financial statement it opened a $25,000 credit line, holding a mortgage on inventory as collateral. Since the inventory had a cost value of $90,000, the distributor was confident it couldn't liquidate for much less than $25,000 to $30,000. And they were right. The only problem was the inventory was no longer $90,000 when the retailer finally failed. Sensing disaster, the owners ran a "closeout" sale for several weeks before the doors finally closed, working the $90,000 inventory down to $20,000. The bare shelves produced less than $6,000 at auction.

5. *Prevent Change of Ownership.*   This may be the most important clause of all. No matter how tight your mortgage may be,

you're relying to some extent on your customer's reputation and honesty. A mortgage doesn't offer much protection against an outright crook who won't think twice about selling the inventory out the back door, or peddling showcases and cash registers listed as collateral. They'll rape, pillage, and plunder the collateral to the point where it's near worthless.

Your objective must be to prevent a takeover of your customer's business by such a character. Certainly, your customer cannot sell the mortgaged assets without your consent, but he can sell his shares of stock in the corporation without your approval. So in reality you may be extending credit today to Honest Harry only to find out his corporation was sold by Crooked Charlie. Plug in a clause stating that the entire debt is immediately due upon a sale of the shares of stock in the debtor's corporation. Then you know who you're dealing with.

6. *Create an "Open-Ended" Mortgage.* The mortgage should cover all obligations, now existing or hereinafter due. Don't limit it to a specific amount. You may agree to extend $10,000 in credit. If your mortgage defines the debt as $10,000 you won't be protected for any debts accrued in excess of that amount.

7. *Don't Overlook Attorneys' Fees.* You can pass the costs of collection on to the customer, if your mortgage calls for it. If your attorney has to sue to recover a debt due on "open account," you will have to pay the fees. If the mortgage provides for attorneys' fees, it's payable above and beyond what the customer owes you. And with attorneys' fees averaging 25% on collections, it's an important point.

Don't look for these clauses in stationery store mortgages. You won't find it. But go over these points with your attorney. You need a mortgage with teeth in it.

FOUR MORE WAYS TO SECURE YOURSELF

Many credit situations are in the nature of a single transaction. You don't need a *blanket* mortgage on your customer's assets to protect yourself. What you do need is the right to reclaim the specific item being sold on credit if the bill isn't paid. That leads us to a wide range of effective possibilities.

Protection with a "Purchase Money Mortgage"

Assume you are selling a specific piece of equipment on credit terms. A used $2,000 copy machine is a good example. Of course you can sell it on open account and lose all claim to the copy machine if the customer doesn't pay. But that's not what this chapter is about. You want to be able to repossess the copy machine.

A security agreement (mortgage) secured by the copy machine alone will do the trick. But there may be a complication. What if the customer has a mortgage outstanding to another creditor who has all equipment as part of his collateral? Wouldn't that give the prior creditor first claim on your copy machine? Absolutely.

Enter the purchase money mortgage. You can obtain prior claim to your copy machine ahead of other secured creditors if you notify the prior secured creditors holding equipment as collateral. Notice must be in writing and delivered within ten days of the sale. (See page 126 for a sample notice.)

The purchase money mortgage only works if:

1.   The collateral remains definable. That's why it's widely used for fixtures and equipment. Conversely, it shouldn't be used for general merchandise, as merchandise becomes commingled and loses its identity as your property.

2.   You do the financing. A third party cannot secure itself under a purchase money mortgage. The collateral has to secure the price due the seller from the buyer.

Don't forget the fact you'll still need a mortgage on the equipment. But with a purchase money mortgage you can safely extend credit even if your customer is mortgaged to the hilt. And you can never lose. Either the customer pays or you have your equipment back.

Why Conditional Sales Beat Outright Sales

The conditional sale is still another possibility when selling a specific, definable item such as fixtures or equipment. Under a

---

**NOTICE TO PRIOR SECURED PARTY
OF PURCHASE MONEY SECURITY INTEREST**

Date:

To: (Prior Secured Parties)

    This is to notify you that the undersigned has or expects to acquire a purchase money security interest in and to the following described collateral: (Describe)

Said collateral shall be sold to:

_____
Name

_____
Address

_____ (Debtor).

    Insofar as you have an existing security interest on record as against the same type collateral, this notice shall inform you of our priority claim to the property being sold. The sale has or shall occur within ten days of receipt of this notice.

Very truly,

_____

CERTIFIED MAIL

---

conditional sale you retain title to the item until it's fully paid for. Upon final payment, title transfers to the buyer.

As with a purchase money mortgage, the customer's alternatives are few. Either he pays for the item or he loses it. To that extent the differences between a purchase money mortgage and conditional sale are more theoretical than practical. Some firms selling equipment prefer purchase money mortgages and others choose conditional sales.

CONDITIONAL SALE AGREEMENT

The undersigned Buyer agrees to purchase from

_____

_____

(Seller) the following goods: (Describe or attach)

Cash price	$ _____
Sales tax (if any)	$ _____
Finance charge	$ _____
Insurance (if any)	$ _____
Other charges (if any)	$ _____
Total purchase price	$ _____

Less:

Down payment $

Other credits $ Total credits $ _____

Amount financed $

Annual interest rate   %

    The amount financed is payable in   (weekly/monthly) installments of $ each, commencing one (week/month) from date hereof.

    Title to goods is retained by Seller until payment of full purchase price, subject to allocation of payments and release of security as required by law. The undersigned agrees to keep the goods safely, free from other liens and at the below address.

    The full balance shall become due on default; with undersigned paying all reasonable attorneys' fees and costs of collection. Upon default, Seller shall have the right to retake the goods, hold and dispose of them, and collect expenses, together with any deficiency due from me; but subject to the Buyer's right to redeem pursuant to law.

    THIS IS A CONDITIONAL SALE AGREEMENT.

Accepted:

_____   _____
                                   Buyer

Seller   Address

Your attorney can prepare a conditional sales agreement or for simpler transactions you can use forms availabe at commercial stationery stores. As with a mortgage, you should record your conditional sales agreement in the public offices required by state law.

Some firms call it a lease, with the buyer having the option to acquire the property at the end of the lease term by paying a nominal amount. It's the same as a conditional sale, and the requirements and advantages are identical.

Field Warehousing Can Make Sense

Field warehousing isn't a difficult concept. It's been used to collateralize agricultural products for years. But it can be equally useful with any type of merchandise.

Under a typical field warehousing arrangement, the seller has the inventory stored in a public warehouse near the buyer's place of business. The buyer is allowed to draw down on the inventory by paying the warehouse administrator a corresponding percentage of the purchase price with the warehouse administrator turning payment over to the seller.

Since the goods are segregated, it doesn't become subject to the claims of other creditors.

Field warehousing makes sense when the seller wants to ship the entire order in advance of payment, but retain title until paid for. Obviously, it makes little sense to use field warehousing if the customer will accept partial shipments on a COD basis.

There are many variations on the theme. For example, a large kitchen copperware distributor found an interesting wrinkle. It wanted to close out its copperware inventory and found a Dallas retailer willing to buy the entire $250,000 inventory. The distributor shipped the goods and had them stored in a nearby vacant store, and appointed the landlord his "warehouse person" to collect the money and release the inventory. Once a week the retailer would show up, deliver a certified check to the landlord, and be allowed to remove inventory of a corresponding value. The arrangement continued for six months until the entire shipment was released and paid for.

Look into field warehousing as a practical alternative when you're selling large quantities of goods in one shipment, and the customer can't satisfy you with a *blanket* mortgage.

Don't Overlook "Consignment" Sales

Consignment sales offer their own form of protection if you sell primarily to retailers.

CONSIGNMENT AGREEMENT

AGREEMENT made by and between
(Consignor) and   , (Undersigned).
The terms of consignment are:

1.   Undersigned acknowledges receipt of goods as described on annexed schedule. Said goods shall remain property of Consignor until sold.

2.   The Undersigned at its own cost and expense agrees to keep and display the articles only in its place of business, and agrees, on demand made before any sale, to return the same in good order and condition.

3.   The Undersigned agrees to use its best efforts to sell the goods for the Consignor's account on cash terms, and at such prices as shall from time to time be designated by Consignor.

4.   The Undersigned agrees, upon sale, to maintain proceeds due Consignor separate and apart from its own funds and deliver such proceeds, less commission, to Consignor together with an accounting within (   ) days of said sale.

5.   The Undersigned agrees to accept as full payment a commission equal to   % of the gross sales price exclusive of any sales tax.

6.   The Undersigned agrees to permit the Consignor to enter the premises at reasonable times to examine and inspect the articles.

7.   The Undersigned agrees to issue such financing statements for public filing as may reasonably be required by Consignor.

Signed under seal this   day of   , 19

_____

Under a consignment sale, you retain title to the merchandise until the retailer sells it. The retailer is obligated to place the funds in a separate account and periodically pay it over to you (less the commission or profit).

The popularity of consignment sales is not in its protection but in its mutual benefits in achieving product distribution. Many retailers will accept goods on a consignment basis realizing they can either sell or return the goods. Since the retailer isn't tying up capital, it will be more inclined to accept the product line on a "no-risk" basis.

The consignment approach can only be used if the merchandise is distinctive. In other words, it must not lose its identity if commingled with other nonconsigned merchandise.

If consignment sales can make sense from a marketing viewpoint, it looks even better from a credit viewpoint. Foxway Pewters

---

SALE ON CONSIGNMENT
ACKNOWLEDGMENT

Date:

To: (Customer)

This letter shall acknowledge that the goods described on the attached invoice or order are shipped on a consignment basis.

In the event you shall be unable to sell said goods, any unsold goods may be returned to us at your expense for full credit.

We reserve the right to reclaim any unsold goods at any time. You further agree to execute any financing statements as we may from time to time require to perfect our ownership claim to said goods.

Goods sold by you shall be paid on the terms stated in our invoice.

Very truly,

_____

Acknowledged:

_____
Customer

shows why. Foxway, a Providence, R.I. pewter figurine manufacturer, sold its pewter merchandise to only well-rated retailers to avoid credit risks. However, the pewter line could do even better in small marginal stores with a high traffic count. The only problem was Foxway didn't want to gamble on their credit in shipping the $900 standardized assortment displayed in its own $300 case. And not too many small retailers were anxious to lay out $1,200 to try out the line. "Consignment was the answer," says Foxway's credit manager. "We require a $100 advance against payments that may be due us, and put the displayed merchandise in on a consignment basis in any high-traffic convenience food, drug, or gift shop we can find. Our salespeople make the rounds every two weeks to collect on what was sold and replace sold inventory. We've had many retailers go out of business on us, but all we had to do was go in and take out our merchandise. If we had sold on open credit we would have been murdered, and have had much narrower distribution besides."

Do you sell a distinctive line of goods to retailers? If you do, check into consignment sales.

HOW TO WIN VALUABLE GUARANTEES

A guarantee is a form of collateral, for it allows you to go beyond the assets of the customer and look to the assets of the guarantor if the customer doesn't pay.

A letter of credit from a bank is nothing more than a bank-issued guarantee. And who can question its value? It's all the other guarantees you have to worry about. As with any other form of collateral, it requires an appraisal of value and a carefully prepared agreement to make it airtight.

What Is the Guarantee Worth?

Start with a credit check on the guarantor just as you would on the customer. What assets does the guarantor have? What's the person's or firm's financial condition?

When credit is extended to the small firm, the owner or principal stockholders are usually asked to sign a personal guarantee. Of course, a guarantee is only needed to obligate the owners when you're selling to a corporation, as the debts are automatically the owner's under a proprietorship or partnership form of organization. But the problem with a personal guarantee in such a situation is that the financial strength of the owner is seldom better than the financial condition of his or her corporation.

Even when a guarantor is solvent, it may be little assurance of solvency once trouble strikes the business. Consider the possibilities. During the time interval the owner may dispose of or lose his or her personal assets. It may be the demise of the business will in itself create personal insolvency. A law associate recently experienced that problem. His client, a large manufacturer, held a personal guarantee against a seemingly well-heeled owner of a toy distributorship. When the distributorship failed, other creditors popped up waving $2,600,000 in personal guarantees. What protection did the owner's $200,000 home or $50,000 personal savings really offer?

Unless the guarantor is exceptionally solvent—or the debt reasonably small—a guarantee only becomes valuable when it can be backed up by personal assets as collateral. If my law associate's manufacturer-client really wanted protection from the $30,000 guarantee, he might have asked for a mortgage on the owner's home to back up the guarantee. Now that's protection.

Even when an owner doesn't have personal assets to lose, a guarantee offers some *minimal* protection. Many owners, sensing business disaster, will try to pay down creditors holding personal guarantees, if only to walk away from the business "clean."

Subsidiary corporations offer other opportunities. Here you want a guaranty of the parent company *and* all its affiliates (sister subsidiaries). You'll also need a certified Board of Directors resolution with the guarantee to show it's authorized.

Don't hesitate to ask for corporate collateral to back up the guarantee. The subsidiary you sell to, Company X, may be heavily mortgaged or without assets to pledge. So you land the guarantee of its parent, Company Y. What can Company Y offer in collateral for its guarantee?

The reason collateral is so important when you have even a parent company (and/or sister subsidiary guarantee) is because the financial strength of any one subsidiary (or the parent) is no better than the strength of the remaining organization. Frequently, a corporation will file for Chapter 11 reorganization, consolidating its weak and strong affiliates and subsidiaries into one. The healthy subsidiary who guaranteed your debt now has its assets grabbed by creditors from its less solvent affiliates.

What the Guarantee Should Say

Unless you have a carefully drawn guarantee, the guarantor may be able to wiggle out of its obligations under a variety of guarantor defenses.

Use this checklist to avoid problems:

1.   The guarantee should be an absolute and unconditional promise to pay.

2.   The guarantee should cover all obligations due you from the customer. If a guarantor negotiates a limited guarantee (for example, not to exceed $10,000), limit the credit accordingly.

3.   The guarantor should agree to remain bound notwithstanding any extensions, waivers, settlements, or forebearances on the account.

4.   The guarantor should be primarily liable. Unless this is stated, you'll have to exhaust your remedies against the business *before* you can go after the guarantor.

5.   The guarantee should not be subject to counterclaim or setoff, and the guarantor waives all suretyship defenses.

These essential points, and a few others, can take the form of an iron-clad guarantee (see page 134).

SELLING THE COLLATERAL IDEA

You know what collateral can do for you—and you know how to use it. There's only one more hurdle to clear. You have to get

---

GUARANTEE

For good consideration, the undersigned (guarantor)
does hereby guaranty to (creditor)
, the full and punctual payment of all
monies now or hereinafter due creditor from (customer)

The obligations of the undersigned are absolute, unconditional, and not subject to set-off, counterclaim, or suretyship defenses generally. The undersigned agrees to remain bound notwithstanding any extensions, modifications in terms, compromises, settlements, forebearances, or the release of any other party obligor or guarantor, or the release, discharge, or substitution of any other collateral.

This guarantee shall extend to any and all monies due creditor from customer, whether now due or hereinafter due, including any and all interest charges or other allowable assessments and service charges.

The obligations of the undersigned shall be primary and not necessarily secondary and creditor need not seek recourse first against customer. If signed by two or more guarantors, liability shall be joint and several.

This guarantee is unlimited in amount or duration and shall be construed as a continuing guarantee.

Guarantor agrees to pay all reasonable attorney's fees and costs necessary to enforce the provisions of this guarantee. This guarantee shall be enforced in accordance with the laws of the state creditor conducts its business.

Signed under seal this   day of   ,
19

_____
Guarantor

---

it. And that takes sales expertise—the ability to sell the idea so that even your customer likes it.

Try these tips:

1. *Be Casual.* The mistake most suppliers make is to treat collateral as an extraordinary event. And that's how their customers see it. By far the best approach is one used by a New York food

wholesaler constantly looking for new accounts. Their sales personnel solicit new accounts with a suitcase loaded with the typical sales material. When the sales rep thinks the customer is hooked, he or she starts him signing a few routine applications and questionnaires. Next comes the guarantee. Finally comes the mortgage. "Don't make it a big deal," says the sales manager, "and don't have it come from the credit department. Customers expect nasty things from credit, but their off guard when handled by sales. Whatever you do, keep the lawyers out of it. Have the forms printed up in advance. Once it's all signed up, you can check the collateral value, prior mortgages, etc., and work up a credit limit."

2. *Sell the Benefits.* If the customer balks when you flash the guarantee or mortgage (always use both), you have some selling to do. Explain how the mortgage will allow for a larger credit line. Indicate the extended terms that may be available if the debt is secured. Show the customer how it will *help the business.* The customer already knows how it can help you. Don't talk in abstract terms or sweeping generalities. Talk in specific numbers. Let the customer know it may increase his credit line to $10,000 with the mortgage as oposed to $1,000 without it. Explain that you may be able to give twelve months to pay an opening "stock" order. Whatever the deal looks like, it has to offer more than what the customer can get from you—or someone else—without signing.

3. *Negotiate.* If the customer continues to balk at the idea of collateral, find out why. Some customers don't enjoy the thought that a creditor can step in and foreclose if payments run behind. Who can blame them? A mortgage is power. A sensible repayment plan can pacify the customer. References can also help. Let him talk to other customers who do business with you on a secured basis to verify you're not a tyrant who'll jump in and foreclose the minute a check is late. Your best argument is convincing customers they mean more to you alive than dead. You're there to sell merchandise. The mortgage is only there to collect if something goes very wrong.

Impact on credit is another resistance point. With some truth behind it, customers will say that your mortgage makes them a greater credit risk to other suppliers. Counter-argument? Tell the customer you'll act as a credit reference.

Problems with future borrowing is still another frequent customer hang-up. If the collateral is pledged to you, the customer can't use it for bank or SBA financing. Let the customer know you'll consider *subordinating* your mortgage to a bank or SBA loan if it makes sense. You can't agree to it in advance, but you will consider the proposal fairly if and when it should come up.

Stay flexible. A customer may agree to pledge inventory and fixtures but not receivables. One common reason is that they want receivables free to use for factoring or short-term borrowing. Take what you can get and set the credit on what you receive.

Customers usually will sign a mortgage with less hesitation than a personal guarantee. A guarantee represents a personal threat. Many businesspeople want to confine business debts to the business. If the customer refuses the guarantee, go on the strength of the mortgage alone. But first try some more negotiation. Perhaps the owner will sign the guarantee if you limit it to a specific amount.

The strategy is to avoid an "all or nothing" proposition. You generally *won't* get it all—and if you have any bargaining leverage you should get something more than nothing. Once you know what you will have you can translate it into a credit line.

4. *Selling "Yesterday's" Mortgage.* What's a "yesterday" mortgage? It's simply a mortgage you should have had yesterday when you sold on open account but expect today now that the account is overdue. And it's darned difficult to get because you don't have much bargaining power. The customer already has your merchandise, now you want the mortgage (or guarantee) to help you get paid. If the customer has any smarts, he or she will throw it in the "fat chance" file.

Don't give up. You should go after every delinquent account with a mortgage in hand and two possible motivators at the tip of your tongue.

1. *Extend Payment.* A customer may owe you $10,000 and is feeling some heat from your collection letters, or even more aggravation from your lawyer. What are your chances of collecting

as a nonsecured creditor if the customer fails, and how long will it take if the company does survive? Your proposition is inviting. Offer a lenient pay-down schedule in return for a mortgage. The pressure is off your customer and you have some protection.

Removing their blinders, a hobby supply firm used that tactic with one of my client hobby shops. The retailer owed the supplier $14,000 and legal action was threatened. But the supplier could see the situation. The hobby shop had more than $200,000 in liabilities but very few encumbrances. The supplier's attorney phoned and offered to freeze the $14,000 for one year, and accept $500 a month thereafter, if we gave a *blanket* mortgage on assets. It was a smart move. The hobby shop went under a few months later and the supplier was fully paid from the liquidation.

2. *Offer More Credit.* Back up a moment and read it again. That's just what I said. If a customer owes $10,000, why not suggest *another* $10,000 if the customer will secure the entire $20,000 with a mortgage. It's not good money after bad, but money to turn your bad debt good. And if the collateral is there to back it up, it's the best investment you can make.

I do it all the time and it makes sense. In a recent example, a drug wholesaler turned a $20,000 receivable over to me for collection. The pharmacy hadn't paid a dime in six months. It didn't take long to figure out the drugstore was on thin ice. But, interestingly, this same drugstore didn't owe a dime to any mortgage holder. The $80,000 inventory, new fixtures, and $30,000 in receivables were free and clear. I offered the druggist another $10,000 in credit *and* the right to pay down the entire $30,000 in monthly installments over three years in return for a mortgage. The drug wholesaler went slightly crazy over the deal but finally understood it's better to be a *secured* creditor for $30,000 than a *nonsecured* creditor for $20,000. Six months later the drugstore was sold to a large chain and, based on the price, general creditors received only thirty cents on the dollar. But we had our check for $30,000.

As Ken Benjoya said as he counted his $26,000 from the Brighton Surgical debacle, "Those mortgage papers really do have a certain power."

7

NEGOTIATING
YOUR BEST DEAL

Into every creditor's life, a little payment, like a little rain, must fall. And every now and then, it may be necessary to grit your teeth and accept that little payment as settlement of a much larger debt.

"Compromise settlements on outstanding accounts are no longer rare," reports Harry Febiger, owner of a Mid West tool and die firm. "Frequently we find we have to forfeit a large chunk of the receivable to collect any of it," he adds.

In that growing twilight zone between regular bill-paying accounts and those who offer no hope of payment due to liquidation or bankruptcy, the likelihood of a compromise settlement lurks. Contrary to popular belief, it's not always a matter of settling for less because the customer *can't* pay more but because he *won't* pay more. It's attitude as well as finances.

MEET THE COMPROMISE "WHEELER-DEALERS"

A mixed species, the "compromise wheeler-dealers" are in every type business and play the "let's compromise" game for an assortment of reasons. The objective is always the same—they want to pay less than they owe. And plenty of them get away with it.

The most dangerous breed is the character who has plenty of money to pay, and absolutely no reason not to pay, except for the important fact he doesn't need you or your product any longer. The inevitable chisel of the bill begins. Some debtors have it reduced to a science. A toy retailer rationalizes it this way, "Every year we drop ten to fifteen suppliers. Once we know we won't be doing business with them again we put a hold on their bill. Why pay them 100% of what's owed? We can never do worse than that. It's only a case of how much less we can knuckle and save."

In large measure, it's your own weakness as a creditor that encourages the nonjustified but costly compromise. Debtors trade on the fact that it will cost you 25 to 40% in commissions or fees, even if they do end up paying 100%. So the thought process becomes simplified. Instead of having you chase them for what can at best become 65 to 75 cents on the dollar, why not take the shortcut and discount the bill by that much now? And that's a generous customer.

Most aren't that generous. Plenty of solvent debtors will offer 25 to 50 cents on the dollar to call it a day. For some it's negotiating posture: start low and go up slowly. Others won't pay you a dime over 50% under any circumstances. Even if the case goes to litigation, they figure they'll come out ahead, including legal fees. It's not uncommon for a debtor to turn a $4,000 claim over to his attorney to defend, with the idea that legal fees of $600 to $800 and an ultimate settlement in the 40 to 50% range will still bring him out ahead by $1,200 to $1,800. And who can overlook the cash-flow benefits from delayed payment?

While this class of customers will arbitrarily try to compromise under some pretense for nonpayment, many customers honestly believe there's a valid reason for nonpayment or compromise. Arguments of late delivery or defective goods serve as two common examples.

The trouble is you can't easily tell whose faking a defense and who truly believes a valid defense exists. And it doesn't really matter, because few compromises are based on the legitimacy of any defense but on the practicality of the situation itself.

Listen to customers on the phone when you're dunning them for payment. You want your $1,000 but the customer's hard at work throwing out fifty reasons why they shouldn't pay a dime.

Finally the words come, "Look, I'll pay $500 to settle and call it quits." That's what it always boils down to: Do you take the $500 or fight?

Next in line with their partial-payment offers are the customers who can't pay the entire amount. They may be trying to cut just your bill or an across-the-board settlement with all creditors under a composition agreement. But whichever case it is, you'll have an easier time dealing with it because the only obstacle between you and your money is the hard reality of the numbers.

No matter how it happens, the reasons are seldom as dismal as the results. Rummaging through my own files shows just how dismal the results can be.

An anxious dairy supplier quickly settled for $12,000 on a $35,000 claim. What was remarkable about the case was the fact the delicatessen who threw out the offer had a $150,000 net worth and not a single defense to payment. Why was the dairy supplier in such a hurry to take a dive in the first round? The dairy firm owed the IRS back taxes and needed the money. Debtors can sense urgency on a creditor's part and use it as leverage for a quick but favorable settlement.

Here's a case where I was on the losing end. As assignees of a large construction firm under an assignment for the benefit of creditors it was our job to collect outstanding receivables. A large developer owed the construction firm over $80,000. We settled for $20,000. Why? The principals of the construction firm moved to Israel. Without their testimony we could never win in court. The debtor was smart. It assessed and parlayed our *weak legal position* into a $60,000 savings.

Then we come back to the debtors who can't pay. What's a pet shop worth at auction? Creditors owed $80,000 settled under a composition agreement for $10,000. Why gamble on the liquidation value of cocker spaniels and guppies? Shrewd debtors know how to use their *poverty for bargaining power*.

Debtors get away with it every day. Every year creditors with billions of dollars of receivables on their books agree to accept pennies on the dollar, counting the pennies as better than thin air. As one creditor aptly says, "What they owe is a statistic. What they can afford to pay or what you can actually squeeze out of them is reality. So we settle not on the basis of what 'ought to be,' but 'what is.' '' And that's where so many creditors go wrong. They never seem to know how to squeeze enough.

MEASURE YOUR BARGAINING POWER

Time for a quick pretest. Here's an actual letter received by an old friend and client George, who operates a lumber mill.

Dear Creditor:

  We owe you $96,000. However, our business is failing. The only way I can save it is to pay you $8,000 as full settlement. That's more than you will receive if the cornpany goes bankrupt.

  Please advise.

                                        Sincerely,

                                        XYZ Company

George had a quick solution. Twenty minutes after reading the letter, George suffered cardiac arrest and no longer worries about such earthly matters. But what about you? Let's assume you're a rugged individual with a strong heart. How would you handle it?

Enough time! Measure your bargaining power with a two-part approach:

1. What do *you* stand to lose?
2. What does your *customer* stand to lose?

Look familiar? Of course, Pick up any book on negotiation and you'll discover that's what the negotiation process is all about. Assess your alternatives and, with the same eagle's eye, calculate your opponent's position.

It's no different when negotiating a compromise settlement. But here's where it becomes interesting. You have plenty of creative alternatives. It should never be that black-and-white "take it or leave it" game.

What Can You Lose?

Your first step in the settlement process is to verify the economic reality of the situation. The world is full of "can't pay" debtors who throw out crazy settlement offers with the argument it's the best you can hope for. Sometimes it is. Usually it isn't. Few debtors really know what their business will liquidate for, or what you can expect to receive if it does liquidate. And even when they do they distort it for their own self-serving negotiating purposes.

XYZ Company played that crazy game. Believe it or not, several other creditors receiving the same "eight cents on the dollar" took it on blind trust and were prepared to accept. It takes more. You have to make sense from a jumble of numbers. Here's how to go about it:

Step 1.   Call in an expert appraiser or a well-recognized auctioneer to evaluate the assets and come up with a solid liquidation value.

Step 2.   Deduct the amount that would go to priority creditors. The following stand in line ahead of you:

  1. Auction fees and costs of liquidation.
  2. Debts owed secured creditors (creditor holding a mortgage).
  3. Legal fees, court costs, and expenses of administration. (Your attorney can give you a reasonable estimate.)
  4. Taxes due any taxing authority.
  5. Unpaid wages and funds due an employees' pension plan.
  6. Creditors who shipped within 10 days of bankruptcy.

Check the debtor's banks to obtain this information. If the debtor won't produce the books, hold out for full payment. Don't negotiate in the dark.

Step 3.   Subtract the priority claims (Step 2) from the total asset proceeds (Step 1). This shows the funds available to general creditors if the business does go under.

Step 4.   Once you estimate the funds available for general creditors, calculate the debt owed you against total general debt. If you did your homework and if the estimates are reasonably accurate, you have your bottom-line number.

Sound difficult? Let's run through XYZ Company's numbers and you'll see why we laughed at their offer.

The auctioneer gave us a written report showing the assets would liquidate for about $300,000. We hired an accountant to go over the priority claims and discovered only two—a small secured creditor owed $22,000 and back taxes of $8,000. With the priority claims of $30,000 subtracted from the $300,000, there would be about $270,000 left for general creditors. Since general creditors totaled about $500,000 they could look forward to about 50 cents on the dollar by throwing the customer into bankruptcy. Why should they settle for eight cents on the dollar?

Don't look for ironclad numbers. For example, the $300,000 liquidation value may be on the high side. It's only an estimate. There'll be some auction fees and incidental expenses. The bankruptcy court will eat up some of the money. So perhaps the $270,000 for general creditors would shrink to even $200,000. That's still 40 cents on the dollar.

I won't soon forget the day the creditors ganged up on Sam K., president of XYZ Company. Calling him into a meeting he sat there bluffing the creditors with his ragtime eight-cent settlement offer. The creditors had a few aces up their own sleeves. The chairman for the creditors' committee started the ball rolling announcing the *hard* facts. The documentation to support the 40- to 50-cent dividend was thrown on the table. Sam squirmed. The best was yet to come. "But we won't take the 40 to 50%. We have a buyer who'll take over XYZ Company and pay $500,000. That will just about give us 80 cents on the dollar!" Now Sam was more than squirming. A few weeks later we had our deal. A total payment of 90% to general creditors. Fifty percent would be paid within one month (funded by a bank loan) and the balance over three years.

Not all creditors took it as a victory. First there was one naive creditor who believes everything he reads, and scurried down to pick up a $2,400 check in exchange for a release on his $30,000 debt. And, of course, there was George. It's too bad he couldn't play out the entire nine innings.

What Is It Really Worth to Your Customer?

Numbers can be convincing, but you won't accept what the numbers show. Not if you're sharp. The debtor will show up with more than a calculator. He or she will bring along the desire to remain in business. And that carries a settlement price tag above the hard numbers. It's the human side of the settlement equation. And with creditors glancing over their left shoulder at liquidation values, the debtor glancing over their right shoulder at the possibilities of losing the business if agreement can't be reached, it all comes down to bluffing ability.

Joe T. knew how to bluff. The owner of a troubled supermarket, he conned creditors holding $200,000 in claims out of $180,000. Armed with the facts the business would upon liquidation yield the general creditors a token two cents on the dollar, he walked into the meeting of creditors and after the usual preliminaries threw his proposal on the table. "Folks," he said, "if the business liquidates, you'll end up with next to nothing. If you settle for ten cents on the dollar, I'll have your check next week." Figuring he'd pay a lot more to save his business the creditors began to test Joe. Out went the feelers to find out just how far Joe would go to stay alive.

Cecil, the credit manager of a baking firm owed $28,000, was a master negotiator. Cecil turned to Joe and quietly said, "Joe, you don't want to lose your market. We'll never accept 10%. Perhaps we'd let you stay in business if you paid us 10% now and 10% a year for the next nine years, with reasonable interest added, of course." There it was. A creditor staring at 2% haggling for a full 100%.

But Joe was a great poker player. Like a fox, he put down his cigar, extracted a prescription vial from his vest pocket and popped a few saccharin tablets which the creditors assumed was life-sustaining medication. Slowly Joe drawled, "The truth is I would rather quit the business and retire to Arizona. I'm not getting any younger and with my failing health and all. . . . The only reason I'm even here is out of respect for you people. I'd hate to see you get screwed if I walked away from the business."

The creditors fell for the line and, again thinking of their own self-interests, swallowed the 10-cent deal. A month after the $200,000 in claims disappeared, Joe sold the business and walked away with $175,000 in his pockets.

If Joe's story didn't convince you, Tom's might. His fabric chain owed creditors a whopping $300,000. Tom and his wife sat at one end of the conference table, ten angry creditors on the other. Tom started with his heart-wrenching tale of woe and a proposition—15% payment immediately and 10% for the next two years, for a total settlement of $35,000. The creditors knew the business was mortgaged to the hilt and they would receive nothing if it failed. That mattered little to the creditors. They were too busy watching Tom's wife. Whenever the creditors would hint at refusing the deal, his wife would start crying and muttering how much the business meant to her and Tom. It was like taking candy from a baby. The creditors ended up with a 100% payment, spread out over four years.

Tom should have hired Joe to do the negotiating. I could see Joe in action: He would have thrown the keys on the table and said, "Ladies and gentlemen, it's yours. I have a great new job lined up in California, but I'm willing to listen to any proposal you'd like to make." And do you know what the creditors would have said? "Give us a nickel or dime on the dollar. We'll take it." It's all a matter of style.

YOUR TEN-POINT NEGOTIATING CHECKLIST

While the numbers and the psychology draw the broad parameters for working out a compromise settlement, it's the finely tuned negotiating points that spell victory. As you do battle, keep this handy checklist at your fingertips. It includes virtually every negotiating point that's bound to arise and the counterpoints you can effectively use.

1. *How Much Will You Be Paid?*   Start with 100%. Let the customer work you down. Decrease the figure by 5 to 10% at a time, but drop slowly, looking for even greater offer increases from the customer. Rely on the numbers and your negotiating strategies to strike the highest possible settlement.

2. *Length of Payments?*   Most compromise settlements don't call for a lump-sum payment. And when they do, you probably made a negotiating mistake. For example, a debtor may offer an immediate 20% settlement. Assuming we're still talking about a "can't pay" character, try to go for more by extending payments. This same debtor may agree to 20% now, and possibly another 30 to 40% over time. Then again, maybe you'll get lucky and find the debtor willing to go for the entire 100%, given enough time.

In counseling debtors, I suggest they not go beyond two or three years. For how long can any businessperson mortgage their future before they are out of the woods? Many debtors don't see it that way. They *will* go for long-term payments, sometimes out of conscience and sometimes out of desperation.

3. *How Much Now and How Much Later?*   Once the total payback and agreed length of time is established, try to apportion payments in your favor. For example, attempt to take as much up front as possible with higher installments in the early periods with tapered installments later.

There are two obvious reasons for this advice. First, you want to recoup as much as possible for the sake of your own cash flow. The second reason is safety. A mere agreement to pay is far different than payment. You've seen debtors who cut fancy deals only to collapse six months later. You want as much money under your belt as possible should it happen.

But counterbalance this objective with reality. Don't push a debtor to pay dividends of $20,000 a year if the business can only afford $10,000. What have you gained? You may see the first few checks only to have the customer—and your future payments— go down the drain with an unrealistic schedule.

It's a common error. In about 90% of the cases I'm involved in the creditor demands a fast pay-down and the debtor foolishly agrees to it. Eventually they both lose out or are forced back to the drawing board. Do it right the first time. If serious money is involved, base payments on a prepared cash-flow projection.

4. *What About Interest?*   It's a negotiable point. If the pay-out is beyond 2 to 3 years it certainly is a reasonable one. Some debtors negotiate a settlement imputing the interest factor into the settlement. When you raise the question of interest, they'll

say, "Look, I proposed 50% over five years, and that includes the consideration of interest. If you want interest, I'm cutting the offer down to 35%."

A shrewd debtor will remind you that under a bankruptcy you may have to wait 2 to 3 years for your money, and the bankruptcy courts don't pay interest.

The question of interest typically dovetails with the compromise offer. Both you and the debtor have to look at the two in context with each other.

5. *Will You Obtain a Mortgage to Secure the Balance?* Don't ignore this vital protection. Without it your debt will be commingled with subsequently accrued debt, diluting the proceeds available to you should the debtor fail.

For example, a debtor may owe you $20,000 today, and you settle for $10,000 payable over two years. If the debtor later runs up another $50,000 in debt and fails, the new creditors will share equally with you in the proceeds. With a mortgage you stand first in line, after existing mortgage holders, but ahead of new creditors who are no longer of concern to you.

Another reason for the mortgage is to enhance the enforceability of your claim. Consider the ridiculous position of a creditor who reduces his claim for $20,000 to $10,000 only to have the debtor default. All the creditor can do is go chasing his $10,000 with a lawsuit. But if he has to resort to lawsuits he might as well have chased the original $20,000.

Since most composition settlements involve all creditors (or at least a large majority) each receiving the same pro-rata settlement, then one mortgage would cover all the participating creditors. The creditors appoint an individual (usually an attorney for one of the largest creditors) to act as trust mortgagee. The debtor mails one check to cover the dividends due all creditors and the trustee issues the respective dividends.

6. *What About Personal Guarantees?* It's only additional collateral, so why not ask for it?

If the debtor refuses, don't cancel the idea. You may be able to negotiate a limited guarantee for a portion of the balance. It's certainly better than nothing.

Another bargaining point is to ask for a pledge of the shares of stock as collateral for the guarantee. If the debtor defaults you can sell the stock ownership of the company. It gives you added control in selling the business as a going concern as an alternative to liquidation.

7. *Is the Settlement Conditional?*   Don't throw away dollars on promises alone. You should forfeit the balance of your original claim only when the payments are actually made.

For example, on a $20,000 debt reduced to $10,000, the agreement should read, "If the debtor fails to make any payment, the entire $20,000 (less payments made) shall be reinstated as the balance due, and the cancellation of $10,000 is expressly conditional upon the timely making of all payments."

This frequent oversight was a costly error for one creditor. Owed a whopping $80,000 he settled for $15,000, payable $5,000 up front and two annual payments of $5,000. The creditor was smart enough to take security for the $10,000 balance, but that's when his brains took a short vacation. He didn't make the cancellation of the remaining $65,000 conditional upon the payment of the $15,000. Several months later the debtor had substantially more assets, and a corresponding increase in new creditors and predictably went bust. All the creditor was entitled to was his $10,000 balance. Had the agreement provided for conditional cancellation he would have recovered his entire balance on the original $80,000.

8. *Will the Customer Be Committed to Future Buying?*   From an economic viewpoint, this may be more important than what you'll receive on the old balance.

Look at it this way. The customer is asking you to cancel part of your bill so he can stay in business. Now isn't it logical to say that you should also benefit from its longevity?

It's not difficult to visualize a customer begging you to cancel 60 to 70% on their debt and, with that accomplished, then switching to a competitive supplier.

In earlier chapters I emphasized the importance of weighing the future business of a customer in designing a credit and collection approach. Put it into play here.

One technique is to have the customer commit to a certain volume of purchases for a specified time period. It should certainly extend for as long as the payments. When you agree to a lump-sum settlement, you can still impose the same condition. Your remedy in the event of default is to have the balance of the original debt reinstated.

I recall one cantankerous seafood restaurant owner who was quick to remind his creditors about the value of his *past* and *future* business. Growling at his meat supplier who he owed $25,000 Nathan asked, "Walter, how much business have you done with me since I started the restaurant?" Walter didn't have the ready answer but Nathan did. "Over $1,200,000," Nathan snapped. "And how much more business will you do with me before I retire?" Nathan asked. Again Walter shrugged his shoulders. "About another $2,000,000," Nathan suggested. "So what's the big calamity if you knock $20,000 off your bill so I can get over some unexpected problems. What is $20,000 against $3,200,000 in sales?"

Around the table Nathan went, one creditor after the other succumbing to the logic of it all. Grateful for the past sales, and hopeful for the future, the creditors said good-bye to $240,000 in receivables due from good old Nathan. A week after the papers were signed, Nathan promptly dumped most of his benevolent suppliers for new ones.

Bargain for future business (COD or limited credit) but don't go on verbal promises. Lock it into the agreement.

9. *What About Return Goods?*   The debtor may be cash short but be able to return excess inventory as part of the settlement.

In a multi-creditor composition, the creditors must be based on equality. That presents one complication with return goods. Why should you accept $1,000 in merchandise for return, while other creditors are receiving their pro-rata payment in cash? If you discount the returns—a 50% credit on returns, for example—other creditors may challenge it as too favorable to you.

Nevertheless, explore the possibilities. You may be able to work out a return goods formula acceptable to yourself, the debtor, and other participating creditors.

10. *How About Shares of Stock in the Company?* Some creditors reason that if they can't make out as a creditor, why not become a partner?

It's not a common creditor demand, particularly when the debtor is a small or stagnant firm. However, it can make sense when the debtor is a "fast-growth" business.

In one classic case, creditors of an electronics firm dropped 75% of its claims in return for a 35% stock ownership in the business. They made out like bandits. The $280,000 in canceled debt is now worth nine million dollars in publicly traded stock.

There's plenty of precedent for it. Venture capital firms, for example, frequently invest in a startup by loaning 90% of the money and acquiring stock for the other 10%. The venture capital firms routinely have the right to convert the debt into additional shares. Isn't that exactly what you are asking for as a creditor who can't be satisfied with cash? There's more than one way to getting paid!

COMPROMISE SETTLEMENT STRATEGY

In a typical case the debtor will initiate the settlement proposal, by mailing each creditor a letter explaining his financial condition and outlining the terms of settlement. Accompanying the letter will be the compromise agreement to be signed and returned, if accepted.

Multi-creditor compositions, as a debtor's remedy, are usually used only by smaller firms. Experience shows that it is seldom successful for the larger firms. Handling many creditors, oftentimes with diversified interests and priority rights, is too cumbersome to handle through an out-of-court arrangement, necessitating Chapter 11 reorganization proceedings. Even for the small firm an attempted compromise settlement may be nothing more than a precursor to a Chapter 11. The debtor first tries the competition and if that fails it either uses Chapter 11 or liquidation as its fallback position.

Compositions can offer both the debtor and its creditors considerable advantage over a Chapter 11 reorganization. A debtor can be more generous in its offer because it saves considerable legal and court fees required for a Chapter 11. A second advantage is its flexibility. Free of bankruptcy code restraints, a compromise (composition agreement) can be more creative.

There are also disadvantages. Under a composition you may not have full access to the debtor's books or be able to effectively investigate its affairs. Preferences must also be considered. Under a Chapter 11 you can seek to recover preferential payments (or returns) made to other creditors within the prior three months. This avoidance power doesn't exist with a compromise.

All factors balanced, creditors usually would do somewhat better in working out a compromise settlement instead of forcing the debtor into Chapter 11. However, in practice it doesn't always work that way because creditors all too often fail to unify and coordinate efforts.

Follow this strategy when facing a debtor attempting a compromise settlement:

1. *Don't* accept the initial offer. A debtor will throw out a low settlement proposal and make it sound like a first and final offer. It rarely is.

2. *Do* organize the creditors collectively. This is the most important point of all. Debtors frequently win a favorable compromise because they divide and conquer. If each creditor approaches the problem on his own it prevents a coordinated negotiation. Make some phone calls. Bring a few of the largest creditors together as a bargaining committee. Let the smaller creditors know the committee is investigating and negotiating on behalf of all creditors and to wait for final recommendations. That's how creditors orchestrate under a Chapter 11. Why should it be different in a composition?

3. *Do* investigate. The creditors' committee should check out the finances, prior dealings, liquidation values, and everything else needed to make "thinking cap" decisions. You can't effectively negotiate without the facts.

4. *Do* use the ten-point negotiating checklist to strike the best deal.

5.   *Do* sell the compromise plan to other creditors once you're convinced you have the best possible arrangement worked out. This, too, is a critical point. A compromise settlement usually requires acceptance by 80 to 90% of all creditors to become effective. You have accomplished nothing to spend several meetings in negotiation only to have the proposal fail because some creditors are holding out. So it's not only the debtor's responsibility to sell. The assenting creditors (or the committee) should also be hard at work.

6.   *Do* agree to have the large creditors pool some funds to pay off small nonassenting creditors. Typically, a few creditors in the under $1,000 range won't agree to anything but 100%. They simply don't have enough at stake to care about the success of the composition. Usually a composition proposal provides that small creditors ($100 to $500 range) will be paid in full by the debtor. However, it doesn't require too many creditors owed beyond that amount to sabotage the plan. If creditors do pay nonassenting creditors to obtain the necessary assents, they should buy the claim and charge it back to the debtor.

7.   *Do* demand equality. It's the foundation of a multi-creditor composition. All creditors (above the $100 to $500 class) should be treated equally with the same percentile recovery and payout. The one area where equality is not needed is on future buying commitments. That's where each creditor is on his own to carve his own deal.

HANDLING "ONE-ON-ONE" SETTLEMENTS

You may be the only creditor asked to compromise your debt. Although multi-creditor compositions are more common as the only way for a "can't pay" customer to achieve financial stability, some debtors will only target one or at most a few of the major creditors alone. That puts you into a "one-on-one" arrangement.

Some creditors resist a unilateral compromise because they resent sacrificing part of their claim while lesser creditors are receiving 100% of theirs. But it's not necessarily a valid concern.

About a year ago we handled an interior design studio which was in trouble. It had 45 creditors, with the major creditor owed $26,000 and all the other creditors combined owed only $17,000. In fact, the next largest creditor was owed only $4,500. It didn't make any sense to try an across-the-board settlement with all creditors. The $17,000 owed 44 creditors wasn't the problem. It was the $26,000 owed one creditor.

The major creditor was upset at being singled out, but it was really in his own best interests. Had the debtor tried to compromise the other 44 claims, it's doubtful a compromise would have succeeded. The $26,000 creditor would have had the most to lose.

Don't worry about other creditors if you are the one largest creditor. If there are several others of near equal size, then you should insist they be asked to compromise collectively with you. It spreads the loss and should give you a proportionately higher recovery.

Back to the negotiating checklist. The one overwhelming advantage in being singled out for compromise is that you can be so creative, since you don't have to worry about equality of treatment with other creditors. For example, you may reduce a $30,000 claim to $10,000 but end up with a mortgage on the business ahead of the other creditors expecting full payment.

Frequently you'll find a troubled customer cutting deals first with its principal creditors thinking it will solve the problems. Six months or a year later the customer finds itself still up to its neck in trouble with the smaller, or newer creditors and then tries an across-the-board composition or Chapter 11. You don't want to be whacked a second time. Your best protection is the mortgage coupled with an agreement that the compromise is conditional upon the customer *not* filing bankruptcy or Chapter 11. If you play your hand right, today's compromise can turn into tomorrow's bonanza should the customer eventually fail.

TACKLING THE "WON'T PAY" CUSTOMER

Let's turn our guns on the scoundrel who has the money to pay but for any one of a 1001 fabricated reasons won't write out the check—unless it's at a substantial discount.

No two creditors seem able to agree on the right approach. I don't think there is any one sure-fire method. There are just too many variables to consider. But I can tell you what to watch out for:

1. *Watch.* "Won't pay" customers who are hiding under the cloak of "can't pay." There are loads of losers who'll cry poverty and pending disaster while sitting on a pile of money. Always ask for bona-fide financial proof.

2. *Watch.* Customers who are likely to hit you with an expensive counterclaim if you sue for full payment. Listen to their reasons for nonpayment and however "hocus pocus" it may be see if it's likely to cause you more money to defend.

3. *Watch.* Settlement offers of less than 65 to 75%. Anything below that amount should only be accepted if the customer offers a justifiable reason. If the amount in controversy is substantial, then allow your counsel to check out the merits of the defense and translate it into a minimum-settlement figure.

4. *Watch.* The precedent you'll be creating by allowing an unjustified, but nominal discount. Eight creditors out of ten will throw up their hands and snatch any offer over 75%. That's all they can hope to clear if the claim is turned over for collection. It can be deceptively costly. Word does get around. Customer X bluffs you out of 10 to 20% and before you know it customers Y and Z are trying it.

Negotiating your best deal is more than doing what seems practical with any one customer. You need a realistic yet tough attitude to set the groundwork for your next deal.

8

OBTAINING POWERFUL
HELP FROM OTHERS

There comes a time in the collection war when you realize the unopened letters, discarded telegrams, and unanswered phone calls won't produce the check. You're out of ammunition. It's time to turn the claim over to someone with more firepower—collection agencies and attorneys.

TIMING IS IMPORTANT

The one problem many creditors encounter is discovering the "right time" to turn the claim over for outside collection. Some creditors act prematurely, others wait too long. Each has its own dangers.

The hasty turnover is probably the more dangerous of the two extremes in the delicate question of timing. The central danger is that it breaks "diplomatic" relations between you and the customer. In reality, your customer no longer is your "customer" but becomes only a "debtor." Just as the appearance of a collection agency or attorney signals stronger action, it also communicates the end of a business relationship. Rehabilitation of the account as a retained and profitable customer is gone. Chances are that any possibilities of a creative—and mutually advantageous—workout of the debt are also gone. The adversarial approach may bring in the payment, but it seldom brings back the customer.

I frequently see it. A creditor will send out two or three routine collection letters and without further warning the customer is hit with a collection agency letter or a lawsuit. In a good number of these cases the customer would have paid with a different *direct* approach, and in almost all cases this very same customer still considered himself a *customer*, albeit a slow-paying or delinquent one.

Cost is another factor in the timing equation—and not an insignificant one. The moment you turn the account over the *best* you can expect to receive is 50 to 75% of the claim, as the difference will be eaten up by commissions or fees.

Conversely, delayed turnover has its own special risks. The principal one is that your customer may be in the terminal stages of insolvency when collections are all but hopeless. Delay in turnover is not necessarily a creditor's conscious attempt to retain or salvage a customer or to save the fee. In most cases it's due to lack of policy.

Robert Braunstein who manages a large Cape Cod law firm specializing in collections endorses the observation that creditors generally are not tuned in to the importance—or reality—of timing. "About 70% of our claims are premature. The claim may not be premature from the viewpoint of aging, as most claims are four to six months old. They're premature from the viewpoint of *attempt*. The creditor did not try hard enough to collect. They didn't need us to collect. They only needed a new approach to collections. Many of the others arrive too late. The creditors hold on to their claims for seven or eight months while the accounts disintegrate into bankruptcy. It's always a matter of timing," Braunstein cautions.

So when is the right time to hunt out a collection agency or attorney?

1. Dig out accounts more than 120 days in arrears. If the account is nonactive and doesn't respond to your collection effort, it's a candidate for turnover.

2. If an account is both inactive and in extreme financial difficulty, don't wait the 120 days. Faster action is required. Ship the claim out as soon as you detect a pending failure.

3. Move slowly on active accounts, or accounts that show promise of slow but eventual payment. Chances are the collection agency or attorney won't appreciably speed up the payments.

4. The true acid test is not the calendar but your prior *effort*. Have you tried every collection strategy at your disposal? Until you do, hold on to the file. Collection agencies and attorneys are not miracle workers. Why pay them to do what you can do for yourself?

PREPARING FOR COLLECTION

Preparation comes in two forms. First, you want to prepare your customer. Next, you must prepare the file.

Preparing the Customer

Preparing your customer is simply a last-ditch effort to let your customer know you will turn the claim over for collection. If your prior collection letters or phone calls conveyed the message, then the job is done. Don't bluff, and don't tell it to the customer for the second, third, or fifth time. Once is enough.

But one customer warning is essential. It throws the burden back to the customer. Many customers will ignore six or seven collection letters silent on lawsuits, but wake up once you threaten litigation.

If the claim is being forwarded to a collection agency, leave that point silent. Just say you will turn the case over for collection. Let the customer think he'll be hearing next from an attorney. It brings better results. On the other hand, if the claim *is* going to your attorney, that should be stated. Debtors know that lawyers have bigger teeth than collection agencies. It's a good idea to indicate on the letter that a copy is forwarded to your attorney.

Give the customer about a week to respond. And always let him know you'll listen to his proposal for payment.

Preparing the File

While you're waiting for the phone call (or check) that probably won't come, you'll have a whole week to put the file in order.

It may seem like an obvious housekeeping matter, but every collection agency and attorney will tell you the same thing. Unless the file carefully documents the claim, the debtor will have a picnic amidst the confusion. For example, a client will send us a file consisting of one invoice for $3,500. So we sue for $3,500. The debtor shows us a merchandise credit for $1,200 and another for $900 in authorized merchandise returns ready for pickup. We look like idiots, the creditor looks like an idiot, and of greater importance we have to start all over again.

Send a complete file. Include all invoices, credits, correspondence, and internal records. Provide the collection agency or attorney with a brief letter as to what the case is about and how you arrived at the balance owed. Of equal importance, disclose any possible disputes, counterclaims or reasons for nonpayment. Let the agency or attorney know what they can expect for a defense.

Also include a narrative about the debtor. You know the debtor and are familiar with his financial condition, size, and history. It's only a name and address to your agency or attorney. Why is it important? It helps define strategy and needed speed. If it's a small, weak account your attorney may try some fast pretrial attachment remedies that won't work against a large solvent firm. It's communication. Before the agency or attorney starts, it should know as much about the customer—and your claim—as you do.

COLLECTION AGENCY OR ATTORNEY?

It's a controversial issue. In reality it's not a question of which is better—for they each have their own purpose—but whether you should start with a collection agency only to end up with an attorney.

The primary problem with collection agencies is their lack of power to collect if the customer won't pay. Although agencies are craftier at collections than the typical businessperson, they are still limited to the letter writing and phone calls tried by the creditor. That casts collection agencies somewhere in the middle between the creditor and the attorney who has the power to collect through legal action.

Collection agencies are used far too often. In most cases involving commercial collections you'll do better to bypass the collection agency and go directly to an attorney. The reason is obvious. Your customer also knows the collection agency is limited to the same tired letter writing and phone calls you are. Why fight with one arm tied behind your back?

Most of my debtor clients actually sigh relief when a creditor turns the case over to a collection agency. They realize the collection agency can't throw lawsuits at them, and they also know the agency will hold on to the file for 90 to 120 days before turning it over to an attorney who will. It's like a vacation from serious concern about the bill.

One garment manufacturer explains the thought process. "We stiff a creditor so he turns it over to a big-name collection agency. Big deal. A month later the first dunning letter arrives. But we know the cycle. The computer has two more letters to spit out before the agency gives up. Sure enough, a month later the second letter shows up, and then the final notice arrives. What did the agency accomplish? All it did was stall the collection for three months before it went to a lawyer who has the teeth to collect."

As you would expect, collection agencies, who do serve as go-between for about 70% of all commercial accounts, will be less than thrilled with this public revelation of how debtors think in private. But that's just how many debtors do think.

Waving a fistful of payments, any collection agency can point to their successes. Sure collection agencies get paid. How do you think they stay in business? But whenever an agency is paid the customer usually would have paid the creditor had he been more patient or creative. And it would be difficult to find a debtor who would pay an agency and ignore an attorney worthy of the name.

Collection agencies, however, do have their place. Use them in these instances:

1. For consumer debts. Consumers are intimidated by collection agencies and agencies have an excellent record with consumer accounts considered too small and time-consuming for an attorney.

2. For small commercial debts. Claims less than $1,000 to $2,000 should go to an agency. Attorneys seldom give the small claim enough attention because they are not fee-justified. There

are exceptions. Some attorneys will be aggressive to satisfy a profitable client or to win bigger cases from a new client. Beyond that it's difficult for an attorney to make money chasing a small claim.

3.   When you have a claim that only needs mediation to settle, you'll probably do better with an agency. Collection agencies are excellent at mediating settlements, while an attorney with a litigious approach may be counterproductive to settlement.

4.   When you don't know a good collection lawyer, a collection agency can help. If they can't collect, they'll refer the case to a collection specialist and they generally find the best.

Creditors have many other reasons for using an agency. Some say that agencies are better systematized and methodical in their collection approach than attorneys. No doubt about it. Agencies are systematic. But if an attorney isn't, it only means you have selected the wrong attorney.

Ability to obtain information about a debtor is another common reason for going with an agency. It's particularly true with an agency specializing within an industry. I think it's a tossup as to who can learn more about a debtor. An agency has the ability to cross-index against other creditors, but an attorney has geographic proximity to the debtor and his own network of other collection lawyers.

Fees are another factor. Some agencies charge only a few dollars for each collection letter, resulting in lower fees than what an attorney would charge. But even here the savings can be deceptive when weighed against the wasted cost if the letters aren't productive, not to mention the needless losses from delayed collection results.

Finally we come to the major reason many creditors choose collection agencies. It's a matter of convention. Creditors go to agencies because agencies have sold themselves as "go-betweens" in the collection game, to the extent that 70% of all commercial claims go to agencies rather than attorneys.

Don't go by convention. If you have a large commercial claim, don't waste time. Go directly to an attorney. You need fast, aggressive action from someone who can bite as well as bark. And who has bigger teeth than lawyers?

FINDING THE BEST COLLECTION TEAM

Considerably more important than "what" you use is "who" you use. Collection agents and attorneys have their winners and losers just like any other business or professional group. The losers couldn't collect if the debtor strolled by with a wheelbarrow loaded with money. The winners somehow manage to squeeze the last ounce of blood from the proverbial stone. So how do you find the winners and bypass the losers?

Collection Agencies Who Collect

Generalizations are always dangerous—except when you talk about collection agencies. Then the rule *is* the rule. Here's how I rank collection agencies.

1.   Small local firms rate top marks. They are better than the large national firms because they are geographically close to the debtor, they are hungry, and they can be an awful pain in the neck. The small two- to five-man agency won't stop with letters. They'll be on the phone once or twice a week, and when that fails they'll haunt the debtor's business. I've met some sluggish small agencies, but they don't last long enough to count.

Inevitably, my clients pay the small local agencies because they are such a nuisance. But isn't that what a collection agency should be? One local agency in my area gives the word "nuisance" a new meaning. Whenever my clients come across them I recommend a quick settlement payment. It's therapeutic and far cheaper than buying pills and incurring medical bills for an ulcer.

2.   Agencies that specialize in your industry come next. They offer an advantage and a disadvantage. Since they are likely to handle accounts from within your industry they may have four or five pending claims against the same debtor. This can benefit you as it does pinpoint a customer in deep financial trouble. But this same factor creates the disadvantage. One agency specializing in the giftware lines may end up with two or three claims on a particular debtor. The debtor begins to play one creditor against the other, offering to pay X dollars a month to be apportioned and applied to the three claims. If the agency pushes for one

account, it cuts off cash available for another. It comes back to what I said in the first chapter. To collect you have to *beat* other creditors. And you can't very well beat other creditors when they're handled by the same agency.

3.   The large national firms suffer from size. Although systematic in following through, they primarily rely on letter correspondence rather than the more effective phone or direct contact. Distance is another weakness. Debtors don't attach the same significance to a collection agency located 1000 miles away as they do a local firm.

Dun and Bradstreet is one national firm who uses size to good advantage. Despite extensive use of letter correspondence, they do better than many other national firms because they do have the name. For example, many debtors pay Dun and Bradstreet, for fear the collection division will report the claim to the credit division. The mystique continues. I can even tell you about a furniture store owner who quickly anted up $2,100 for D & B. Why? He thought D & B was a federal agency!

The man or woman within the agency is also a factor in the selection process. This is particularly true with smaller firms who turn the file over to an employee who is encouraged to use his wits instead of a bound policy manual controlling the large agency. Success then may chiefly depend on which desk your claim lands.

Brand-new startup agencies are the most aggressive in hunting new business, and in their pursuit they tend to promise more than they can deliver. Prompt remittances of collected funds are another common problem with the startup firm, as it's not uncommon to find them using creditors' money to help cover their own cash-flow problems. However, the principal danger of the new agency is in their tactics. All too often they go beyond aggressiveness into the realm of illegality.

The two best ways to locate the best agency is to look for growth and references. Fast growth is a positive sign of performance and satisfied clients. And there is no substitute for references. Ask around. Start with the National Association of Credit Management. They maintain a file of agencies with good track records. Credit insurance companies can also lead you in the right direction.

CREATING YOUR OWN COLLECTION AGENCY

In the past, many creditors had the best of both worlds. They would simply set up their own "in-house" collection agency. It had the dual effect of saving fees while enjoying the psychological clout of the letter with a collection agency imprint. Coventry Collection, a division of American Express, was a more notorious example.

The Federal Trade Commission squelched this deceptive practice by regulation. The prohibition extends even to "in-house" attorneys who pass themselves off as independent counsel. Your firm, however, can use a collection agency imprint provided it clearly identifies its affiliation as part of the company.

One alternative is to set up an independent collection agency. Sound complicated? Not really. I know a clothing manufacturer who spent over $80,000 a year on collection firms. Tired of hefty commissions, the enterprising manufacturer set his wife up in the basement of their home and for $290 had the stationery printed up. Since the wife had no direct affiliation with her husband's manufacturing firm and occupied a separate location, it ostensibly was legal under the FTC guidelines. One other criteria is that it must be a *bona fide* collection agency. And it was. The spouse-operated basement collection agency does solicit outside accounts and can prove it's more than an alter ego of her husband's firm. The manufacturer is thrilled. He reports his wife has a 47% collection rate compared to his old agencies paltry 29% rate. And he's saving about $50,000 a year besides.

If this plan sounds too ambitious, you can legally use collection agency devices. For a nominal fee many trade organizations and law-letter publishers will provide form collection letters. All you do is fill in the blanks. Since these letters usually bear the collection agency's letterhead, the debtor lingers under the impression that the letters originated from the collection agency itself.

This scheme has been challenged in the courts, but so far the courts have endorsed its legitimacy on the grounds that (a) the service is provided by a *bona fide* collection agency; (b) the agency is paid for the service and consents to it, and (c) the account eventually will be turned over to the agency if the "in-house" attempt fails.

When are these various fee-saving techniques cost-justified? One retired credit executive recommends it as an alternative to the outside agency when annual commissions begin to exceed $20,000. You may not look at it that way, as saving fees may be a secondary consideration. You may be seeking a higher collection rate, with the belief you can do a better job than the outside firm—armed with a collection agency letterhead.

YOUR ATTORNEY: TIGER OR PUSSYCAT

Forget your Uncle Joe who prepared your will, and you can also ignore your high-priced corporate counsel who may only deal with corporate matters. What you do need is a *bona fide*, dyed-in-the-wool collection attorney.

Most businesspeople don't consider collections a legal specialty. They mistakenly figure any attorney can handle a simple "goods sold and delivered" contract action. They're dead wrong. I'll concede that just about any attorney can send out a collection letter, and virtually any attorney can draft a lawsuit (although I have seen some that apparently flunked that course in law school), but the reality is that it requires much fancier legal footwork to collect.

Consider the complexities of a collection case and you can see the required skill. For starters, the attorney needs the network to obtain *information* about the customer. Collection lawyers have their own network. They exchange notes on chronic delinquents much as you'll find in a credit association. Outsiders have trouble getting quick answers about a customer. They're not members of the same club.

Next comes *strategy*. A sharp collection lawyer can quickly digest the information and figure out the one best approach to the account. And it's more than a simple lawsuit. Maybe he'll try to negotiate collateral security instead, or a pretrial attachment. Facing a near bankrupt customer he may focus instead on return goods or even help with a creditor saving sale of the business. The collection attorney has to know everything you do about collection strategy and alternatives and more. He has to know the added legal techniques.

Protecting you in a *bankruptcy* situation is another trademark of the collection lawyer. Bankruptcy can be a mystery for many attorneys. Shy of experience in the bankruptcy courts they don't realize the remedies a creditor has. But a proven collection lawyer does.

Negotiating ability is the hallmark of a collection lawyer. He understands debtor psychology and how to deal with it. Not only does the attorney know how to negotiate, he equally knows what to negotiate for. A master at getting paid, he's a tough man to beat.

Above all, a collection attorney is *geared* for collection cases. It's not an intrusion on his regular work but the reason for his existence. Like his collection agency counterparts, the firm is of necessity streamlined, efficient, and systematic in its approach to collections.

Debtors pray for an inexperienced adversary. Just as a shrewd debtor can ignore a collection agency for two or three months, it's possible to put a novice lawyer on ice for several years. Once the typical lawsuit arrives, all a debtor need do is pump out an imaginative defense listing any one or more of 43 legitimate reasons for nonpayment. With a claim for a jury trial, *voilà*, the case won't be heard until 1990. Justice moves slowly. Time is always the debtor's best friend and the creditor's worst enemy. But meanwhile the case continues to collect dust and the creditor continues to collect nothing.

A clever collection lawyer can anticipate and neutralize these stall tactics. They have a grab bag of remedies from pretrial attachments to threatened bankruptcy to keep a debtor bobbing and weaving. Admittedly, even experienced attorneys may strike out, but I'll tell you this, if they can't collect it's indeed an uncollectible claim.

The problem, of course, is that it's extremely easy for me to tell a good collection lawyer from a poor one, just as a physician can distinguish surgical skill from malpractice. But you're a layperson. You don't know what a good lawyer does, so you can't tell who that good lawyer is.

The good news is that capable collection attorneys are easy to find if you stick to two surefire sources:

1.   *Check the Commercial Law League.*   This is the national association of collection attorneys. Unless collections are their specialty, the attorney won't belong. You can obtain a roster of members by writing them for their directory. Contact the Commercial Law League, 222 West Adams Street, Chicago, Illinois 60606. You can also find their membership directory at most law libraries.

2.   *Check with Collection Agencies.*   Collection agencies refer uncollected claims to forwarding attorneys in the state where the debtor is located. And since agencies want results, they consistently use only the best collection specialists. Dun and Bradstreet is an exceptionally good agency to follow. They are very selective in their choice of forwarding attorneys.

Cross-reference the lists. Try to find an attorney who is both a member of the Commercial Law League and who routinely handles collection referrals from the larger collection agencies. It's as foolproof a formula as there is for locating your tiger.

SIX WAYS TO REDUCE FEES

Before you can negotiate your best fee arrangement, you should understand that agency and attorney fees are not regulated. Many firms adhere to the recommended rates suggested by their national associations, such as the Commercial Law League, and others have their own fee schedule. In neither case is the fee carved in stone. If you can show the agency or law firm you may be a volume client, you're a candidate for lower rates.

The strategy in negotiating with agencies and attorneys follows the same guidelines:

1.   Most firms work on a contingent-fee basis. If they don't collect, they don't get paid a commission or fee. Agencies and attorneys usually are competitive with each other and follow very comparable fee schedules. Typically the fees will be on a sliding scale. For example 25% on the first $1,000 collected and 20% thereafter.

Unless you are a very large client, it's not wise to negotiate a change in the firm's rates. First, you will meet resistance, if only to avoid precedent for other clients. Even if a firm accepts a reduced fee it may be counterproductive to results. Some firms will "back burner" a low-fee case to concentrate on the more profitable. Try to negotiate other points.

2.   The best place to start is with an arrangement whereby an agency or attorney agrees to send out the first letter on a flat-fee or reduced-commission basis.

For example, an attorney may agree to send out the initial letter for a $10 charge. If the customer pays without further followup you've saved a substantial fee. Many collection agencies will do the same; however, they are less inclined since letters are their stock-in-trade.

One large Boston ambulance service saves about $10,000 a year with this approach. But they make it even more attractive for their attorney. The attorney provides the ambulance service with a stack of letterheads. The client's computer prints out the letter saving the attorney clerical costs. The attorney only has to sign and mail the letters in return for a $10 per letter charge. If the letter doesn't bring in the check within fifteen days, the attorney has a collection case at his customary 20% fee.

Incidentally, you can prepare letters for your attorney; however, it's unethical for anyone but the attorney to sign and mail.

3.   Don't overlook your company counsel. He may be willing to send out the initial letter on his own letterhead as part of his general retainer, or for only the clerical cost. It can even work for out-of-state debtors. An attorney in Ohio, for example, may send the letter to a distant account in California. Your Ohio attorney is not better than a collection agency because he can't sue in California. But debtors don't realize out-of-state attorneys must forward the case to local counsel. All they see is the word "attorney" on the letterhead. Talk to your corporate counsel about it.

4.   Will a commission be paid on return goods? There's not a set rule on this. Some agencies and attorneys expect full commission and others no commission. Now here's where I'll tell

you to be generous. Offer at least a one-half commission on returned goods (subject to your approval). Without this incentive, an agency or attorney may try to negotiate anything but return goods. And in many cases return goods may be your best solution.

5.   Watch fees on counterclaims. Frequently an attorney will accept a case on contingency and file suit. The debtor files a countersuit against you, alleging for example defective goods and $100,000 in damages. You are no longer only a plaintiff, but a defendant as well. Most firms will not defend you on a counterclaim as part of the contingent fee. They will expect their customary hourly rate on the defense of the counterclaim.

Anticipate the problem. Debtors dream up all kinds of fancy countersuits, but they nevertheless must be defended. Here's where an attorney should cut his hourly rate, and it should be negotiated in advance. A reasonable compromise is a fee reduction of 25%.

6.   Use the small claims courts—but without your lawyer. I don't know why creditors habitually have their attorneys handle small claims cases. It doesn't make sense. In most states you can sue in small claims courts for claims even as high as $1,500. You'll still need your credit manager or whoever is familiar with the facts to testify, so why bring your lawyer along? You'll be paying 20 to 30% to an attorney who is losing money to stand in a courtroom he doesn't belong in. Small claims judges usually favor the poor, hapless debtor outmatched by a lawyer. So why give him that advantage and pay for the privilege?

WORKING FOR THE BEST RESULTS

Teamwork is an essential ingredient in the collection process. Your job doesn't end once the claim is in the attorney's hands. The most successful collections, in fact, come about when the creditor continues to play an active and closely coordinated role with counsel. What can you do to help the case along?

1.   *Follow-up.* Demand periodic updates on the case. Collection agencies routinely provide clients with progress reports. It's not universally true with attorneys. Oftentimes you'll find

an attorney with a heavy caseload continually deferring action on yours. Sometimes you do have to push your own counsel to obtain the fastest action possible. It happens with even the best firms. Juggling several hundred cases, it's only human nature they'll give top priority to the cases where a client shows interest. However, that doesn't give you a license to nag. Every attorney can tell you stories about clients who phone every day and can't understand why the case is taking so long. Your attorney isn't a miracle worker. Have him explain the game plan when he takes the case and watch it to make sure it stays on track. Beyond that only hope that for you justice will move somewhat more swiftly.

2. *Communicate.* You have contacts in the business, so you can find out what's happening with the debtor. If you hear about a change in financial condition or probable bankruptcy on the horizon, let your attorney know. The information can be useful in changing strategy.

In defending one of our own clients against a $65,000 lawsuit for unpaid merchandise, the creditor attempted a pretrial attachment over my client's assets. The judge refused the attachment on our showing the client had a healthy financial statement and the ability to pay if a judgment entered against him. Nine months later my client found himself on a financial tightrope and with this same creditor back in court again looking for an attachment. And he got it, salvaging most of his $65,000 claim. The creditor's lawyer confessed his client phoned him and heard the business was in trouble. That phone call saved him $65,000. Don't keep your lawyer in the dark. Communicate.

3. *Offer Solutions.* You're not practicing law when you suggest possible approaches to the problem. Two heads are better than one. For example, you may be willing to accept return goods, or a long-term pay-out if it's secured. Chances are you'll come out ahead if you can devise a solution without running into court. But these are primarily business rather than legal solutions, and you may see some overlooked by even experienced attorneys.

With about 30% of our cases, that's exactly what happens. A creditor's attorney may phone and suggest a very practical alternative to litigation. In most instances the solution originated with the creditor rather than his attorney. So think hard about possible solutions, and encourage your counsel (or collection agency) to try it.

4. *Be Reasonable.* Keep an open mind to compromise settlements. Just as a customer may try to talk you into accepting partial payment in full settlement, or a long-term pay-out, your attorney and agency constantly receive the same message. If the debtor retains counsel, you'll be sure to receive a compromise offer, at best. After all, the debtor's lawyer has to justify his own fee.

An agency or attorney has the obligation to report all settlement offers to you, even the ridiculous ones. With the report should come a recommendation of acceptance, rejection, or counteroffer. But here's where it gets sticky. Your agency's or attorney's recommendation may *not* be in your best interests to accept. Sometimes the attorney's perception of a reasonable settlement is faulty, and oftentimes the creditor has his blinders on.

Attorneys and collection agents, being human, can also be lazy. For example, you may hand an attorney or agency a $4,000 collection case, and on the strength of a letter or lawsuit receive a settlement offer of $2,000 the attorney may be inclined to grab it on the basis that fast nickels are better than slow dimes. The one letter may earn him a $400 to $500 fee, while he may have to invest many hours only to double it and win your $4,000. The reality is that the attorney's economic interests don't always coincide with yours, although the professional interests certainly should.

There are only two solutions to this age-old problem. The first requirement is to make the attorney or agency back up the wisdom of his recommendation with facts, figures, and hard reasoning. Make him convince you it's your best deal. Next comes the comparison approach. As I stated earlier, you can't really tell what constitutes a good lawyer until you can make comparisons. Spread your work around. You'll quickly recognize the fighters from the phonies.

Now let's turn to you and your own perception problems. Every attorney and agency hears it from clients, "Give me, get me, and I gotta have"—and what the client "gotta have" is 100%

of his money overnight. Of course, the creditor found no magic wand to make the money appear when he was chasing the claim, but now that it's in the hands of an agency or attorney it should be different. And creditors do see it that way, arbitrarily declining even generous settlement offers.

Barry Levine, a Boston collection attorney, doesn't mince his words when he says, "A good collection agency or attorney should be able to do something for the creditor even if it's to convince him a paltry offer is the best settlement possible. Sometimes creditors forget that when they hire an agency or attorney they're also buying advice and objectivity. And it can be an excellent investment."

9

BANKRUPT ACCOUNTS: DIGGING MONEY FROM ASHES

The longest, saddest faces in the business world can always be found in the back rows of any bankruptcy court. That's where the creditors sit, moaning and groaning as the wheels of justice grind their receivables into bad debts, or a pathetic two cents on the dollar dividend. The only consolation to be found is another creditor who lost even more. Misery loves company.

There are plenty of smiles in the front rows. That's where the debtors—the bankrupts—congregate as they rid their firms of haunting creditors, endless collection letters, and the steady stream of sheriffs. One after the other, the names are called. The debtors stand and answer. Owners of small firms and large, each with his own story, and each with his long list of creditors who will no longer be creditors. But one thing unites them: They can't pay their bills.

WHAT'S BEHIND THE SUDDEN RISE IN BANKRUPTCIES?

Business bankruptcies are an everyday occurrence. For many of your customers it will be the terminal stage of a festering financial disease. They start out as slow payers, turn into nonpay accounts, and finally graduate into full-fledged bankruptcy.

The tremendous rise in bankruptcies over the past two years is an eye opener. As recent as 1980, about 200,000 firms went belly-up. In 1982 the number soared to close to 500,000. Nobody is quite sure of the final tally. Most firms that fail are never recorded as bankruptcies because they are instead liquidated under non-bankruptcy procedures, such as assignments for the benefit of creditors, tax seizures, or foreclosures. But the type liquidation is not important. What is important is that when a customer fails and liquidates, you can't expect more than a few cents on the dollar.

There are several reasons for the soaring bankruptcy rate. Look first to the causes. New business startups have grown from 265,000 in 1970 to over 550,000 in 1980. A recessionary economy coupled with inflationary interest rates took their toll. Lenient credit terms are also a culprit. The average liabilities of a failed firm in 1982 was over $400,000.

The new Bankruptcy Reform Act of 1979—now called the Bankruptcy Code—also helps explain it. The new code gives bankrupts considerably greater rights and opportunities for con- tinued survival than the prior law. Reciprocally, creditors have few rights, and less to say when a debt-riddled customer decides to leave them holding the bag empty of money.

The fastest-growing bankruptcy proceeding is the Chapter 11 reorganization. Rather than liquidate under a Chapter 7 Bankruptcy (Straight Bankruptcy) many firms, even small firms, use the new code as a way of survival. Our own firm handles 30 to 40 Chapter 11 cases a year. Some of these companies are no more than corner stores or shoestring operations. Ten years ago their owners would have abandoned the troubled business. Today they fight to stay alive, because they are smarter and better informed debtors. They see how large firms made it through Chapter 11 and they realize it can work equally well for them.

The bankruptcy stigma is also gone. In business circles, a Chapter 11 is almost fashionable, a status symbol, the American way of business. The theme is always the same. When the business ends up a financial mess, don't give up the business, but give up the creditors. And the bankruptcy court is always there to help them.

CLIMBING THE WALL OF FEAR

Creditors may be the victims in a bankruptcy situation; however, the reason is usually their own willingness to be victims. And they become victimized because they don't know the practical steps to take to protect themselves. A high wall of fear separates them from their powerful remedies and imaginative debt-saving alternatives. They become an immobilized pack as the debtor works its way through the process. The fatalistic attitude replaces an action-oriented plan.

That's the purpose of this chapter. It won't make a bankruptcy lawyer out of you and you don't need the technical nitty-gritty of what goes on in the bankruptcy court. Much of it is beyond your control and doesn't require creditor involvement.

Here's what this chapter *will* show you:

1. The best ways to protect yourself *before* a customer fails. And from a creditor standpoint this is the most important phase, because you do have the last clear chance to bail out your claim while it may still be salvageable.

2. How to maximize your recovery *during* a bankruptcy.

3. How to recoup your debt even *after* a customer fails and goes through bankruptcy.

KNOW THESE NINE EARLY WARNING SIGNALS

Business failure is seldom a surprise. Most firms go through a long period of financial turmoil before the final death throes. With even casual monitoring of a customer you can see the early-warning signals that separate the firm going through normal or cyclical problems from the one destined to go under.

Surprised creditors are always a mystery to me, particularly if they are geographically close and can see what's going on. A few months ago we filed a Chapter 11 for a large stereo shop. One of its major suppliers was alarmed. It was the last thing they expected. But why the surprise? The customer hadn't paid the supplier for several months, inventories were depleted, and the few old checks it did receive never cleared. You almost have to be blind to miss the bankruptcy candidate.

There are the exceptions. Johns-Manville, the giant asbestos manufacturer, was a picture of financial health before it unexpectedly filed Chapter 11. But Chapter 11 was the only way to rid itself of the thousands of asbestos-related consumer lawsuits. Braniff Airlines was another surprise. Its Chapter 11 was the only way to cut back operations to a profitable base. But these are among the few exceptions.

Remove your blinders. Scan your customer rosters and see which accounts may be in the front row of the bankruptcy court. Look for these nine telltale signs.

1. *Dwindling Inventories.* This one is hard to miss. A retail firm, for example, that typically operates with a $50,000 inventory may see its inventory depleted to $30,000 or even $15,000 before it goes under. An experienced eye can walk into a business and see the "dummied up" shelves, and "out-of-stock" situation. This should be your sales rep's responsibility to report. Inventory depletion doesn't happen overnight. The salesperson can see the trend.

2. *Frozen Payments.* The customer a step away from bankruptcy may stop all creditor payments. In some cases it's because it has no funds to pay back bills, channeling its limited cash flow to operating expenses and COD payments. Even when cash is available, the customer planning bankruptcy will hold on to the cash, knowing old bills will be eliminated under the bankruptcy. Any change in payment pattern is suspect. It's particularly true with the slow payer or one on an installment plan who sputters or stops. Check the payments you've received lately.

3. *Bounced Checks.* When rubber checks are routine or on COD purchases it shows a very acute and chronic cash-poor position. Usually a firm with continued operating strength can turn other assets into cash, but the seriously weakened firm doesn't have that capability. Inventories and receivables are also at their low point.

4. *Reduced Purchases.*   A customer who cuts buying by 25% or more, and for no other explainable reason, should be looked at as a troubled firm. The company goes into a "bankruptcy cycle." Without cash to buy inventory, it loses sales, and the reduced sales create even less cash to replace inventory. During the process the firm drains existing inventory for overhead. In some cases, sales and purchases can be down by 60 to 70%, as the firm becomes a skeleton of its former self. Check the buying volume.

5. *Employee Termination.*   Another telltale sign. When the firm becomes insolvent, the reduced sales bring about layoffs. Employees may leave due to insecurity about the firm's future. It's all part of forced retrenchment.

6. *Watch Unusually Heavy Buying.*   Just as the firm poor of cash and credit will cut down on buying, the insolvent firm with some credit lines open may do just the opposite. Many firms planning a bankruptcy will tap its few "open account" suppliers for as much inventory as it can and scout out as many additional credit-extending suppliers as possible. Even if the account is on COD with you, watch for the quick inventory buildup.

7. *Watch the Customer Base.*   Lost customers are still another clue. In a closely knit industry it's not difficult to learn about your customer losing its own key accounts. One warning, of course, is the drop in buying. However, lost customers can be an even earlier warning signal because it may start the firm on the road to bankruptcy.

8. *Read the Financials.*   The one problem with financial statements as a bankruptcy detector is the timing. Statements a year or two old won't help you. At best, stale financials can only forecast a long-term trend, and if you had that long-term forecast you wouldn't (or shouldn't) be a creditor when the bankruptcy comes about. Firms contemplating bankruptcy rarely give out new financials. That alone is an indicator. But if you detect any other signs, press for new statements. Test the response.

9. *Listen Carefully.*   You're not the only one dealing with the troubled firm. It has other creditors, banks, employees, and

customers. Word gets around as to who's in trouble. It's never a secret. But if you hear it, believe it. There's always some truth to the rumor.

ACT FAST TO PROTECT YOURSELF

Time for a quick pretest. Let's suppose you have a customer who owes you $20,000 on a long-overdue bill. You have gone through the collection ritual without favorable results. Now you're convinced the customer is heading toward bankruptcy. Now the question. What steps would you take to collect before it happens?

It's an interesting question. Most creditors come up with one answer: "I'll turn it over to my attorney and have him push like hell for whatever we could grab." And that's precisely the wrong answer. Here's why.

In the two or three months prior to a bankruptcy, the practical legal remedies are few and far between. The lawsuit will still be collecting dust when the bankruptcy is started. Even prejudgment attachments mean little, because they will be set aside under the bankruptcy. So while your lawyer is spinning his wheels and wasting your money on court filing fees, the customer is content to plan his bankruptcy. And it's all counterproductive because the only real hope you have is one of debtor cooperation.

In almost every case I have participated in where a creditor salvaged his claim against a near bankrupt firm, the success was based on the creditor and debtor cooperatively working together for their *mutual* interests. The key word is *mutual*. Don't expect the debtor to pay you unless you can offer something in return. He doesn't have to. Since your lawsuits no longer scare him, you have to think in constructive terms. Negotiate so you both end up winners.

What do you want from your customer? Payment. But that payment can take several forms, including return goods or collateral security to ensure future payment. Now what will your customer want in return? More inventory on credit terms is your best bargaining chip. Watch how these mutual objectives can be satisfied, once you know how to salvage the unsalvageable.

A wholesaler can show you how to obtain *security* for your debt. This firm was owed $17,000 from a large auto-parts store in obvious financial trouble. Checking out the store's financial statements, it discovered the store had $200,000 in general, unsecured creditors, but there were no creditors holding a mortgage. The wholesaler realized that under a bankruptcy, it wouldn't see more than twenty cents on the dollar, considering the other creditors sharing in the pie. But if it could obtain a mortgage on the assets, it would be safe, because the assets have an estimated liquidation value of about $50,000. So the wholesaler made a proposition. In return for a mortgage to secure both the $17,000 debt and future purchases, it would extend another $10,000 in credit. The auto-parts owner snapped at it because it offered a way to land needed inventory, and the mortgage to the wholesaler could even help him negotiate a lower settlement with other creditors once he was in Chapter 11. All he had to do was point out the wholesaler would be entitled to the first $27,000 on a liquidation, leaving the other creditors very little. The mortgage essentially shifted money that would be shared by all creditors to the wholesaler. Besides, the wholesaler agreed to let the customer pay-down the $27,000 over two years with nominal interest.

Few debtors will refuse collateral if you couple it with added credit. Your job is to show them how giving you a mortgage only takes money away from other creditors rather than themselves. The second step is to make certain the collateral is adequate to cover your total indebtedness.

An even more imaginative manufacturer used this approach when negotiating with a hardware store struggling with $120,000 in debt. The manufacturer, owed $21,000, agreed to accept a mortgage to secure the $21,000 and extend $20,000 additional credit. Since the assets were worth about $40,000 to $50,000 at auction, it was protected. Now in addition to the added $20,000 in credit, the manufacturer dangled another incentive. If the hardware store couldn't strike a favorable settlement with its other creditors, the manufacturer would do a "friendly" foreclosure on the assets, and sell it to a new corporation to be formed by the hardware store owner. It was attractive. The owner's new corporation wouldn't have to pay more than the $40,000 to $50,000 liquidation value, and since this would be payable to the man-ufacturer as the secured party, it agreed to finance it over three years. How could the debtor lose?

Return goods is another possibility. One of my drug wholesale clients constantly uses this approach. Let's say a troubled drugstore owes the wholesaler $5,000. If security is out of the question, the strategy turns to return goods. The proposition is simple. The wholesaler will accept for return $10,000 in excess or "dead" inventory and replace it with $5,000 in "live" inventory the drugstore needs. Since the $5,000 in live inventory has a greater operational value than $10,000 in dead stock, the customer always goes along with it. The wholesaler returns the $10,000 in dead stock to the manufacturers for full credit and is bailed out.

There's more than one way to skin a cat. Sometimes you'll need a combination approach. Perhaps you'll accept returns for part of the debt and a mortgage for the balance. In return you may offer some immediate credit and possibly some credit after the Chapter 11.

There are many ways a debtor and creditor can get together on a mutually beneficial deal. But stop the fighting, you need each other to make it work. Call him up, set up a meeting, and put the cards and your bargaining chips on the table. Let the other creditors wonder why they never got paid. You know how you did.

WATCH OUT FOR VOIDABLE PREFERENCES

Obtaining the upper hand over other creditors is not without its risks. Under the bankruptcy code, any preferential treatment to a general creditor can be set aside if it occurred within 90 days of the date of a bankruptcy or Chapter 11. A preference can be granting your security, allowing you to take return goods or even payment. However, for it to be a voidable preference, it must be in payment of an antecedent debt—one existing prior to the pref-erence. For example, if a customer grants you a mortgage to secure a prior existing debt, the morgage can be set aside. If a customer pays you $10,000 on a prior debt within 90 days of a bankruptcy, the $10,000 is recoverable.

However, if you receive a mortgage for simultaneous or future credit, the mortgage cannot be set aside, because you benefited the business by extending credit in reliance on the mortgage. Likewise, if you were paid $10,000 on a prior debt, but subsequently extended $10,000 in new credit, the $10,000 could not be recovered.

What does all this mean?

1.   The *worst* that can happen under any strategy I outlined is to lose what you bargained for. You *can't* lose more, but you may find yourself back where you started.

2.   Try to keep your customer out of the bankruptcy court for at least 90 days. If your preferential mortgage or payment occurred *more* than 90 days prior to a bankruptcy filing you are absolutely safe. In most cases a debtor can control the timing. Very few businesses are petitioned into bankruptcy by creditors. In most cases it's the debtor who filed bankruptcy or for a Chapter 11. Since he's a co-conspirator in the deal, make certain he watches the calendar.

3.   If the business is to be liquidated within 90 days of your payment, encourage him to use a nonbankruptcy remedy, such as an assignment for the benefit of creditors. The rule of preferences only applies to bankruptcy. An assignee or state court receiver cannot recover a preference.

Many creditors, sensing a bankruptcy is on the horizon, refuse to chase payment on the belief that even if successful, it's all futile because of the preference rule. It's faulty thinking. Chances are a creditor receiving a preferential payment will never have to repay it. In fact it rarely happens even though the law provides for it. The major reason is that bankruptcy trustees are too busy winding up an estate to start suing to recover preferential payments. A mortgage as a preference is likely to be set aside because the trustee must deal with it to liquidate the firm. Cash or return good payments are another matter. The trustee has to go looking for it. Few do. Unless it's a large amount of money, or you're up against a very diligent trustee, you probably won't have a problem. But as I said before, what do you have to lose?

SHOULD YOU THROW YOUR CUSTOMER INTO BANKRUPTCY?

Creditors are quick to threaten bankruptcy against noncooperative customers, although the threat is illegal under the Bankruptcy Code. But very few creditors actually carry through with their threat. The decision is never easy. But as with most decisions there are times to do it, and times you should refrain.

The safer rule is *not* to file bankruptcy against a customer. It has special dangers. First, the burden will be on you to prove the customer is insolvent (the most common ground for the petition) and your legal fees on a contested bankruptcy proceeding may exceed the value of your claim or what you could recover under the bankruptcy. And the debtor can make your life miserable. One possibility is a requirement that you post a cash bond to indemnify him for any losses as a result of your petition. Finally, if the court decides it was a "bad faith" filing, based on vindictiveness or revenge rather than a true belief of insolvency, you may end up paying the debtor's legal fees and substantial penalties and damages besides.

So it's risky business. Perhaps the largest risk is losing the customer. Of course, you no longer attach a value to his business because it's not buying and not paying. Understand what's happening. The customer is neither buying nor paying because it is planning its own bankruptcy or Chapter 11. If it is a Chapter 11, the debtor will resume buying and you want to be there for the future business.

When should you file a bankruptcy petition against a customer? In any of the following situations:

1. When the business is being looted and delay can only cause further dissipation of the assets. And this doesn't extend only to dishonest debtors. Even honest operators can work assets down to nothing so there's nothing left for creditors. In these instances, creditors usually don't work fast enough.

2. When the debtor gave another creditor a substantial preference over you and other creditors. For example, if you discover a small customer allowing another creditor to cart away $20,000 in inventory, while leaving behind only another $20,000 in inventory, then a bankruptcy within 90 days is the only way to recover the returned goods. But here it's justified. The recovery will double the size of the estate, and double your own recovery.

3. When you have a buyer for the business and the sale will give you more than what the debtor can possibly give you under a bankruptcy. For example, I recently represented several creditors of a large health and beauty aid store with debts of $150,000. The owner is killing the business and ignoring creditors. A buyer was found who would pay $150,000 for the business so we petitioned the store into Chapter 11, and applied to the court for permission to sell it for the $150,000 to bail out the creditors. The only way the owner will get to keep his business is to match the offer. Sometimes you have to grab the pleasant alternatives when they come your way. Incidentally, you'll notice we petitioned the customer into Chapter 11 rather than straight bankruptcy. That's an interesting feature of the new Bankruptcy Code. Creditors can now elect to file a Chapter 11 against a customer instead of a liquidating bankruptcy.

The new Bankruptcy Code offers you other interesting points. The most important is that it is no longer necessary to base a petition on a preference, which was the most common grounds under the old Bankruptcy Act. Now you can simply allege as grounds that the "debtor is insolvent, and is unable to pay its bills as they fall due." But even this definition is subjective. Never file against a customer unless it is handled by an attorney who can make sure you're on firm ground, and don't allow yourself to join with other creditors unless your counsel approves.

One remaining requirement to petition a customer into bankruptcy is obtaining the requisite number of creditors. If the business has twelve or more creditors, then three creditors owed an aggregate of $500 is required. Many creditors are stymied by this, since they can't find two other assenting creditors. You can allege less than twelve creditors and petition on your own. The debtor can contest it, claiming it has in excess of twelve creditors but it must give you the list. If you can then find two other creditors to join with you, the case proceeds.

Don't look at the bankruptcy court as your own personal collection agency. Many creditors mistakenly petition a debtor hoping the debtor will panic and pay them to withdraw the bankruptcy. You cannot accept payment as a condition for withdrawing the petition. Your petition is on behalf of all creditors.

THREE ALTERNATIVES THAT BEAT BANKRUPTCY

For liquidating a troubled customer, bankruptcy offers some disadvantages. The primary disadvantage is the length of time it takes to wind up a case so the trustee can pay you a dividend. A typical case may require two or three years. Since bankruptcy courts don't pay interest, the time delay erodes what little dividend you do receive. Expense is a second disadvantage. In a good many cases a trustee and his counsel can earn more than the creditors receive.

There are two liquidating alternatives that beat bankruptcy because they are faster and usually require less administrative expenses, leaving more for creditors.

An assignment for the benefit of creditors is the more common method of the two. Under this procedure, the debtor assigns and transfers all the assets over to an assignee. The assignee is usually an attorney representing one or more creditors, although most states allow any person to be the assignee. The assignee liquidates the assets, and after deducting its fee, pays the creditors the balance in order of priority.

The same can be accomplished by having a state court appoint a receiver. The receiver's duties and functions are the same as an assignee's, and the only practical difference between them is that the debtor appoints the assignee whereas the court appoints a receiver. The only other distinction is that the assignee operates without court supervision while the receiver is answerable to the appointing court.

From my experience, a case handled by an assignee or receiver can be settled within 4 to 5 months, compared to the 2 to 3 years under a bankruptcy.

There are situations where a bankruptcy does offer advantages over an assignment or receivership:

1. *When the Debtor Made a Substantial Preference.*   Don't forget, a preference is only recoverable under a bankruptcy.

2. *When the Owners Are Suspected of Concealment, Looting, or Other Debtor Fraud.*   A Trustee has considerably greater investigative and enforcement power than an assignee or receiver.

3. *When the Debtor's Lease Represents an Asset.*   Under a bankruptcy the trustee can assign the remainder of a lease to a buyer, even against the consent of the landlord. An assignee or receiver doesn't have that power. In the case where we are planning to sell the health and beauty aid store for $150,000, the buyer is really bargaining for a very favorable lease at an excellent location, as the other assets are not worth more than $70,000. Under a Chapter 11, or even a straight bankruptcy, a lease can be a valuable asset.

Other than in these three situations, you should try to talk the debtor into an assignment rather than a liquidating bankruptcy. Of course, an assignment is beneficial to the debtor also as it avoids the "red-tape" of a bankruptcy. Its popularity as a non-bankruptcy remedy can be seen in Massachusetts. About 70% of all small business liquidations are through an assignment.

Even when the debtor plans to remain in business, instead of liquidate, there are alternatives superior to a Chapter 11 reorganization. In Chapter 7, I discuss out-of-court compromise settlements. That's what a Chapter 11 reorganization is all about. But why go through the complexity and expense of a Chapter 11 if the creditors and debtor can strike a reasonable out-of-court settlement? Again, the advantages are in the economics and timing. A small firm can easily spend $10,000 to $15,000 in legal fees to go through a Chapter 11. That same expenditure can be added to the creditor settlement if the expense can be avoided. It's not always possible for a debtor to use an out-of-court settlement instead of a Chapter 11 for several reasons. One reason is that the debtor may need the protection of a Chapter 11 to stop a secured party foreclosure or a tax seizure. Even without problems from these classes of creditors, a debtor may have too many unsecured creditors or at least too many who won't cooperate in reaching an out-of-court settlement to avoid Chapter 11.

YOUR RIGHTS TO RECLAIM GOODS

There are two fast steps you should take against an insolvent account.

1. Stop all goods in transit.
2. Reclaim goods sold within ten days of the insolvency. It pays to know a little law in these two areas.

Many creditors have these rights available to them, but lose out because they didn't know these rights exist.

Stopping Goods in Transit

Upon learning or even hearing of insolvency or poor financial condition on the part of a customer, you should stop all goods in transit. Your rights to stop goods exist under the Uniform Commercial Code, enacted in all states.

It's not necessary for your customer to actually declare bankruptcy or file for Chapter 11 for you to stop goods. Any indicator of insolvency is sufficient. The safe rule to follow is that if you hear or learn anything to impair the customer's credit, then put a hold on the goods.

Your rights exist while the goods are in actual transit, unless the customer has a negotiable bill of lading. Usually the goods will be in transit with a common carrier. Follow this procedure:

1. Immediately phone the common carrier or warehouse holding the goods. Put them on immediate notice, before the goods reach the customer and you lose your valuable right.

2. Follow up with immediate written notice. No special form is needed, however, I have successfully used the following form:

NOTICE TO STOP TRANSIT

To: (Common Carrier)

Gentlemen:
   Pursuant to our telephone instructions, you are directed to stop transit of all goods shipped by us as consignors to:

> XYZ Company
> 100 Anywhere Street
> Anytown, U.S.A.   (Consignee)

   The goods are represented by freight documents numbered   , and generally consist of (describe)

   This shipment should be returned to us immediately. We guarantee the return freight costs. Please confirm.

> Very truly,

Send the letter certified mail, special delivery. A telegram may serve the same purpose.

3.   Notify the customer. Tell him why you stopped shipment. Now the burden is on the customer to convince you it is a good credit risk. In most cases, the debtor will already be in bankruptcy or liquidation so this point may be moot.

Reclaiming Delivered Goods

Here's an important point that even experienced credit people overlook. The Uniform Commercial Code provides that goods delivered within 10 days prior to an insolvency can either be reclaimed (if intact) or you can establish a priority claim for the payment and stand ahead of other general creditors.

It's not necessary for the account to go bankrupt or file Chapter 11 within the 10-day period. You have the same rights if the account makes an assignment or undergoes a receivership within this same time period. However, unlike stopping goods in transit, you can't merely allege an insolvent condition, but require the act of insolvency, such as filing a Chapter 11 petition.

Now I'll show you how to extend your protection from 10 days to three months. There's a provision in the Code which states that a creditor can reclaim the goods, or establish a priority claim for payment, if the insolvency occurs within *three* months of delivery. To obtain that extended protection the debtor must affirm its *solvent* condition at the time the goods are ordered. That little-used clause is not known by most attorneys but is there and it can work for you. It's easy to comply. Have your order forms contain the printed language:

> The customer acknowledges its solvency to the seller, with the understanding the seller relies on this representation to extend credit and ship the goods.

Make certain the order form or document bearing this vital language is signed by the customer.

Consider the importance of this clause. In the typical insolvency case, 25 to 30% of all debts are incurred within three months of the actual insolvency. Those are the odds you'll be in the same position. With those few words you'll have the advantage over other creditors on your claims.

Always try to reclaim the goods if intact. It's a better remedy than attempting to establish a priority claim for payment. The reason is obvious. Once you have the goods back, you can lose nothing. A priority claim for payment, on the other hand, gives you priority over general creditors, but there may still be secured creditors or expenses of administration ahead of you.

Send written notice of your intent to reclaim goods as soon as you discover the insolvency. Usually the goods will be reshipped if they are still available. However, if you meet resistance, retain an attorney. The procedures for establishing a priority claim can be complex. But try this form letter first.

NOTICE TO RECLAIM GOODS

To: XYZ Company (Customer)
     100 Anywhere Street
     Anytown, U.S.A.

Gentlemen:

On January 3, 1983, we delivered to you certain goods, as listed on the enclosed invoice(s), with a balance owed of $1,260.00.

Insofar as you have commenced insolvency proceedings within ten days of delivery (or three months, if applicable) you are hereby advised of our intention to reclaim said goods, or such goods as shall presently remain in your possession. Would you please communicate with the undersigned to confirm shipment.

In the event said goods are not available for return, we hereby notify you of our intent to file a priority claim for the balance represented on said invoices.

Very truly,

DEALING WITH THE CHAPTER 11 CUSTOMER

No insolvency proceeding is more complex or difficult for a creditor to understand than a Chapter 11 reorganization. Even attorneys unfamiliar with bankruptcy fail to understand its intricacies.

In concept, the process is to rehabilitate the debtor and give the company a fresh start free of excess debts or burdensome contracts and leases. Procedurally, the Chapter 11 is based on the debtor negotiating a plan of reorganization with creditors based on a settlement fair to both. Generally, only unsecured creditors are affected by a Chapter 11, although during the proceedings secured creditors and lien creditors cannot foreclose without court permission.

Chronologically, the typical case proceeds as follows:

1.   Either the debtor or its creditors file a petition under Chapter 11. If a prior Chapter 7 liquidating bankruptcy is pending, the case will be converted to a Chapter 11.

2.   The case is assigned to a bankruptcy judge.

3.   The debtor files its schedules, listing its assets and liabilities and other required information. This may be filed with the petition.

4.   A first meeting of creditors is called. During the meeting the court will appoint a creditors' committee (usually 7 to 10 of the largest creditors) to negotiate a plan of reorganization with the debtor.

5.   After negotiation with the committee, the debtor will file a proposed plan of reorganization and copies will be mailed to all creditors. At the same time the creditors' committee will notify these creditors of its recommendations on whether or not the plan should be accepted.

6.   For the plan to be confirmed, it requires an assenting vote by a simple majority of creditors, provided their claims represent at least 67% of the outstanding unsecured debt.

7.   If the plan has the requisite votes, the judge reviews it to make sure it's fair to all parties, and feasible for the debtor to perform.

8.   If the requisite votes are not obtained, the debtor may amend (change) its plan, with the hope of obtaining the requisite votes. After the debtor has been in Chapter 11 for four months, the creditors may file their own plan.

9.   Ultimately the court either approves a plan or decides a reorganization plan cannot be achieved, adjudicating the debtor into a Chapter 7 liquidating bankruptcy.

There are many intervening steps during the proceedings. For example, the court will decide whether a trustee is required to supervise the debtor. The committee will investigate the affairs of the debtor, preferences may be set aside, and the validity of claims will be contested.

And during this entire process, creditors do play a passive role, since they are represented by a committee and its counsel and accountants. Still, there are three distinct areas where you can, or must be actively involved as an individual creditor.

1. Deciding whether to ship goods on credit.
2. Filing a proof of claim.
3. Approving the plan.

Should You Extend Credit to a Chapter 11 Firm?

Debts incurred after filing the Chapter 11 have priority status. These debts are not subject to the compromise plan as are prior debts. Many creditors think this insures payment should the firm fail and be liquidated. It's not so. Upon liquidation, debts are paid in the following order:

1. Secured debts.
2. Expenses of administration.
3. Tax claims.
4. Wages due.
5. Priority claims.
6. General creditors.
7. Stockholders.

As you can see, four classes of creditors must be fully satisfied first. Whether there will be sufficient assets will depend on the amounts due these other classes, and the proceeds on liquidation. In Chapter 8, I show you how to calculate the probability of payment.

The best approach is to take the recommendation of the creditors' committee. They are fully aware of the numbers and resultant protection available to priority creditors extending new credit. Even then, limit credit to very small amounts, preferably week to week or order to order. Even if the money is available upon liquidation, you may have to wait 2 to 3 years to see it, so make it a small gamble.

Extending credit has two objectives from your viewpoint: (1) Credit may be necessary to keep the firm afloat, which may mean a greater dividend to you, and (2) credit is a customer-retention strategy. Firms in Chapter 11 tend to continue buying from suppliers who helped during a Chapter 11 and are quick to drop those that curtail credit. It's an important consideration if you think the customer will make it.

Filing a Proof of Claim

Creditors must file a proof of claim to vote on the plan, although it's not mandatory to receive dividends if the debtor listed the creditor on its schedules. In all cases, the creditor should file a claim to fully protect itself.

Generally, claims should be filed prior to a vote on the plan. Filing a proof of claim, but not assenting to the plan counts as a "No" vote.

Procedurally, it's not difficult to file a claim. Legal stationery stores have the form, or they are available at the Bankruptcy Court. Priority creditors, secured creditors, and landlords should have the claims prepared by attorneys because documenting their claim requires special care.

Accepting the Plan of Reorganization

The only policy to follow is to follow the recommendation of the creditors' committee. The reason for this advice is because they know the alternatives, the finances, and ultimately whether the plan is in the best interests of creditors.

In many cases, the committee will spend months investigating the debtor's affairs, and negotiating a plan of reorganization. If they have done their job, they have looked for buyers for the business, and every other way to increase recovery for the creditors.

As a practical matter it seldom does much good to go against the recommendation of a creditors' committee. The members of the committee, being the largest creditors, typically control the outcome of the case based on their aggregate debts.

If you should disagree with the committees' recommendations, then discuss it with the committees' counsel. You may see alternatives they haven't considered.

As one example, a committee recommended acceptance of a plan that would give creditors about a 20% dividend. A small supplier was upset. He knew a prospective buyer for the business who would pay a sufficient price to yield a 50 to 60% dividend. Sure, it was a valid alternative to the debtor's plan, but the committee didn't know about this buyer. Communicate.

FINDING MONEY IN THE BANKRUPT FIRM

Customers undergoing liquidation may represent the ninth inning in the ballgame, but you still have the final chance at bat. Your objective should be to have it put money in your pocket.

Consider these two possibilities:

1.   *Do You Have a Customer for the Business?*   Turn yourself into a bloodhound and hunt a buyer for the business. The goal isn't necessarily to boost the liquidation price and your dividend but to obtain an even greater direct benefit.

A greeting card manufacturer is very good at the game. When an account goes under they immediately get on the phone with every other account in the area. The manufacturer wants one of its existing customers to buy the business to retain sales to the firm. In one recent case, a gift and novelty firm failed owing the greeting card company $8,700. The buyer, a long-standing customer, purchased over $90,000 in greeting cards from this manufacturer last year. The *future* business was worth many times the prior loss.

A paper supply firm selling to printing shops adds a twist to it. It not only scouts out a buyer who will continue to buy from the firm, but tries to coax the buyer to assume the debt owed from the prior owner. "Why not?" asks a vice president of the paper firm. "If the deal is good enough and our bill isn't too high, it's still a sensible deal. And for us it's very sensible."

2. *What Are the Assets Worth to You?*   Assets at auction can go for a dime on the dollar. Sometimes the assets have considerably greater value to you as a creditor, and you can recoup your losses by buying low and reselling at your full price. Sometimes you can even make a profit.

A kitchenware distributor is always at a customer's auction. In its last round it picked up inventory for $16,000 with a wholesale value of $60,000. With a quick markdown the distributor resold it to other customers for $42,000. The $26,000 profit more than covered the $9,000 debt the defunct customer owed it. And don't forget, the distributor will still share in the auction proceeds.

The interesting point is that suppliers will fight for return goods before a bankruptcy—as they should—but ignore that same inventory when it comes up for auction. Attend a few customer liquidations. That's your inventory on the shelves.

BUSTING THE BUST-OUT ARTIST

Most debtors are reasonably honest. At most, they tend to stick a few stray dollars in their pockets to tide them over in case they have to go job hunting.

Bankruptcies also have their share of crooks, bandits, and bust-out artists. These are the people who need the whistle blown on them. Watch out for these tactics:

1.   Bankrupt firms that order inventory from anyone who will ship on credit terms, but show neither payments or an inventory to match the purchases. These are the "bust-out" artists who "backdoor" the inventory for whatever it can bring and then vanish.

2.   Owners of a multiple-store chain also need watching. When one store goes bankrupt they may be tempted to move inventory to the remaining stores. If the stores are separately incorporated, then demand strict accountability and be on the lookout for sudden increases in inventory in the other units.

3.   False financial statements are another con game. If the statements are materially false, you may have a mail-fraud case.

What can you do in these instances? Document the evidence you have and call the United States Attorney in your district. It probably won't put any money in your pocket, but it will help your reputation. Word will get around that you're a "no-nonsense" creditor, and it may save you from involvement in a few future bankruptcies.

10

LEGAL HASSLES
YOU MUST AVOID

Step carefully. Credit and collections are a legal minefield. Even a cautious creditor can chase a customer for $5,000 and instead end up owing the customer $50,000.

Sometimes you can end up owing even more. Willie Kurcon shared that not-so-unique distinction. Willie, the owner of a small paint factory, started his sad saga by shipping a $14,000 paint order to a paint and hardware distributor. When the check failed to show up, Willie became creative. His first step was to call twenty-three paint manufacturers to "blackball" the distributor. However, Willie was only warming up to the job ahead. In rapid succession Willie started to picket the distributor, flashing his famous "deadbeat" sign before interested on-lookers. The distributor stood firm. As a final gesture Willie decided to use some "self-help" and promptly helped himself to $6,000 worth of paint occupying the distributor's loading platform.

Now it was the distributor's turn to strike back. The distributor filed civil and criminal charges alleging libel, interference with contract rights, invasion of privacy, and theft. It took the court exactly two hours to render judgment against Willie and his firm for $240,000. But the worst was yet to come. Willie, unable to handle the $240,000 judgment, was forced to turn ownership of his plant over to the distributor who still hasn't paid the $14,000 bill. And why should it? The distributor is now its own creditor.

It was a bizarre case, but absolutely true. And you can find many minor-league versions of creditors being sued by debtors who catch them stepping out of bounds in their zeal to collect.

Michael Yerardi, a Boston attorney who represents several credit associations, reports, "Creditors are owed a few dollars so they mistakenly believe they have a license to do whatever they want to collect. What these creditors don't realize is that the books are loaded with laws to protect debtors and shackle creditors."

So true. There are at least eight federal laws throwing a protective cloak around debtors, buttressed by thousands of state laws and countless case decisions added to the debtor's arsenal. And who can stay on top of it all? No sooner do you become familiar with existing laws then new ones are passed, old ones repealed or reinterpreted.

If creditors seem unaware of the laws, debtors seldom are. They are learning faster and faster to use what they have learned. Nowadays, when you sue a debtor to collect, the first thing they ask is, "What can I use to get back at the creditor?" Estimates are that 20% of all creditor lawsuits are rebutted with debtor claims alleging creditor violations. An increasing number are successful. Ask Willie.

The scope of potential liability is another eye opener. Pitfalls exist in virtually every phase of creditor-debtor relations. It starts with the design of a credit policy and infiltrates every activity from credit references to collection practices. No area in the credit and collection process escaped the lawmakers, and fewer still elude the attention of a debtor anxious to fight back.

This chapter will guide you through the most common trouble spots. Learn a little law. It won't—and isn't supposed to—take the place of your attorney, but it may save you the trouble of calling him quite so often.

SIDE-STEP DECEPTIVE COLLECTION PRACTICES

The surest way to find yourself on the legal defensive is to engage in deceptive collection practices. It ranks first in the number of debtor claims.

The *Federal Trade Commission Act* protects against deceptive collection practices. Consumers enjoy even greater protection under the *Fair Debt Collection Practices Act*. Most actions are not based on federal laws but on state laws that make any "unfair" or "deceptive" trade practice a financial bonanza for debtors.

Massachusetts has a rather typical statute. A debtor who can successfully assert a deceptive or unfair collection practice is entitled to collect triple damages and attorneys' fees. The triple-damage possibilities provide the motivation to sue. A debtor's imagination furnishes the inspiration.

For example, who can really define a "deceptive" or "unfair" collection practice? When does a collection technique over-step the bounds of creative legality into the troublesome area of debtor deception? Only a judge or jury ultimately knows.

Debtors use that to good advantage. You may have a $6,000 claim against a customer. Once you sue, the customer begins to look for any collection activity that can even remotely be considered deceptive or unfair. Absent any other defense, the customer can still tie the case up in knots while it pushes its counterclaim. As a creditor you not only have a defenseless case suddenly defendable, but you continue to wonder whether your unusual or aggressive collection practice will be seen as deceptive or unfair by the court. And in the back of your mind is the fear of the triple-damage award. It's small wonder so many cases are settled for a fraction of what the claim is truly worth.

These laws can make even the most adventurous creditor extremely cautious and "gun-shy." Few are willing to experiment with unusual or novel approaches because the *imaginative* or *different* approach can be construed as deceptive or unfair, simply because it is different. It's a classic Catch-22 situation. If a creditor uses a hard-hitting collection strategy, the debtor yells "foul" and goes running into court. If he follows the crowd, he trades effectiveness for legal safety. Between the two lies a tightrope.

Unfortunately there is no precise list of *dos* and *don'ts* to guide you. Debtors will continue to interpret it liberally, while creditors construe it strictly. But follow these guidelines:

1. *Don't Disguise Yourself.* If you are not an attorney or collection agency, don't pass yourself off as one. In fact, any false

identity on a letterhead or phone call can be a deceptive practice. Even a failure to identify yourself can be deceptive. In one case the creditor phoned his customer on a daily basis but refused to disclose his name, although he did represent himself as calling for the creditor. The court held it to be deceptive and awarded nominal damages.

2. *Don't Use Phony Collection Gimmicks.* Beware of documents tailored to look like summonses or official court papers. Stationery-supply firms make a bundle selling them and debtors make a bundle collecting from creditors who use them. Some are quite convincing, complete with gold or red seal, gothic print, and the large letters "LEGAL NOTICE" or "NOTICE PRIOR TO SUIT." Even a lawyer has to look twice.

I have never seen such a phony device work. If a debtor foolishly believes it is a court document, he invariably turns it over to his lawyer, and if he doesn't, it ends up in the wastebasket. In either case it's both a waste of money and a deceptive practice. The courts have routinely held that a collection notice camouflaged as a court document is deceptive if a debtor could reasonably believe it to be a legal process.

3. *Don't Send Out Inflated Bills.* It was a clever but costly error for at least one creditor. For months the customer ignored a $900 statement. Frustrated, the creditor decided to mail a $1,500 bill to encourage a response. The customer responded with a lawsuit. The creditor defended claiming "clerical error," but the creditor's bookkeeper testifying it was deliberate turned it into an $1,800 victory for the customer.

4. *Don't Make False Threats.* Telling a customer you'll notify other creditors, his bank, employer, or any other disinterested party is always a deceptive collection practice because it borders on extortion. You should only state you'll turn the case over for collection. Beyond that you're in quicksand.

5. *Don't Violate Other Laws.* Even a nonintentional violation of the countless creditor–debtor laws can reciprocally be construed as a deceptive practice. Usury on interest charges is one example; discriminatory credit practices another. A deceptive act does not require intent to deceive. Mere deception on the part of the creditor is sufficient.

BEWARE EXCESS HARASSMENT

There comes a point when aggressive—perhaps diligent—collection efforts become harassment. It's an "unfair" collection practice and as actionable as a deceptive one.

Fortunately, the guidelines in this area are reasonably well defined. You have another safeguard because a harassment charge usually requires the debtor to warn against continuation. It's only when you ignore the warning or cease-and-desist request that a strong case comes about.

One axiom of commercial collections is that any amount of pressure is legal, provided the customer doesn't complain. But once you have the complaint, you have to know when to stop.

Visiting a customer's business to collect is a common situation. And you have every right to be there—until you are asked to leave. But leave you must. Remaining against the consent of the owner is both harassment and trespass.

One local collection agent enjoys pretending he's a toadstool. Invariably he'll show up and park himself in the debtor's waiting room or wherever the most comfortable chair is situated. In about 40% of the cases the debtor tires of watching him gather moss and pays to get rid of him, although in one case he proudly proclaims he waited four hours to collect $36. The remaining 60% immediately or eventually throw him out. But until they do, he's on solid legal ground sitting there.

Supposedly, a London collection agent devised a surefire way to make his presence known on the debtor's premises. Before starting out each morning on his appointed rounds, the enterprising agent doused himself with garlic juice. The stench, combined with his slovenly appearance, would shock both the sense of sight and smell. But there he would sit, reeking and waiting. Reports are he prospered with the highest collection rate in London town.

How you handle yourself in the debtor's business also counts. For example, loud demands for payment within earshot of customers or even employees can put you on the wrong side of a lawsuit. Libel is an added possibility.

Telephone calls offer their own form of harassment. It depends on "where," "when," and "how often." A business owner can refuse calls at home, a consumer at work. You can phone a business anytime during business hours, while a consumer debtor is limited to calls between 8:00 A.M. and 11:00 P.M.

Years ago Boston was plagued by a notorious collection lawyer who sadistically enjoyed phoning business owners at home in the middle of the night. The bleary-eyed debtors would always ask why he was calling at the bewitching hour only to hear the famous line, "I couldn't sleep thinking about the money you owe my client." The Bar Association put a stop to it.

How many times a day can you phone? Just once. More than that is harassment. But there's a wrinkle to it. You can phone as often as necessary until you reach a person with check-writing authority. That protects you on repeated phone calls to get through to the boss. It can still be harassment if you're told the boss is "out of town" or in extended conference. Repeat phone calls must be spaced to reasonably reach the boss and not simply to annoy the employees.

The disguised phone call isn't the answer either. Unable to get through as Creditor X you phone back as prospective Customer Y. It's a deceptive and harassing practice.

Can a customer command you not to phone at all? Some courts think so. In one case a debtor told the creditor not to phone, and the creditor persisted in making several more unanswered calls. The court suggested that an unwanted phone call can be as annoying as an unwanted visitor. Other courts disagree saying reasonable phone calls are no different than letters.

Speaking of letter writing, it may surprise you to learn that letters can be another form of harassment. The occasional letter certainly isn't. But one Miami wholesaler didn't send his defaulted retail account an occasional letter. Every day, five or six letters would arrive, each in an envelope with different markings. The court ruled it was harassment because it went far beyond what was reasonably required to communicate with the debtor.

A debtor has the right to shield himself from any further creditor contact by referring you to his attorney. Once the referral is made, all communication must be directed to counsel. You may, however, continue to send the debtor regular monthly statements. This rule is particularly enforced when a debtor is in bankruptcy proceedings.

Despite these lingering prohibitions, many creditors nevertheless find it profitable to be a "pain in the neck." Many debtors don't realize their power to stop it and those that do rarely wind up with more than a court-issued injunction or very nominal damages at best. But more times than not the creditor winds up with his money.

FOUR THREATS TO AVOID

Extortion—the science of extracting money through unlawful threats—seems to work for the Godfather in the famous movie by the same name. But you're not the Godfather. For you, it can be an extremely dangerous practice.

Since extortion is a crime, its penalties go far beyond the nickel-and-dime possibilities of deceptive or harassing credit practices. And unlike so many crimes, extortion doesn't necessarily require wrongful intent. Even a well-intentioned conversation can land you in the pokey.

Here are the four threats to avoid:

1. *Don't Threaten Criminal Prosecution.* It's a common form of extortion. If you suspect a debtor of criminal wrongdoing you can report it to the authorities. Mere reporting, in itself, is never extortion. It's only extortion when you tell a customer you will report it *unless* payment is made. Even then there are dangers. For example, if you commence criminal prosecution without sufficient reason to believe a debtor is engaged in a criminal act, the debtor can hold you liable for malicious prosecution. Always clear it first with your attorney.

It's easy to fall into the extortion trap. Take a lesson from a manufacturer owed $70,000 from a wholesale account. The wholesaler was suspected of concealing massive amounts of inventory while under bankruptcy. And the manufacturer armed with evidence of the concealment demanded "$50,000 to settle the bill, otherwise it would be turned over to the FBI and U.S. Attorney." When the wholesaler balked, the manufacturer followed through on his threat. The wholesaler ended up with a two-year sentence for bankruptcy fraud, but only two cells away resides the manufacturer serving a five-year rap for extortion.

One exception to the rule are bad checks. Some state laws require a creditor holding a bad check to expressly inform the maker of the check that criminal action will be commenced if the check is not paid. To be protected you must follow the language of the statute carefully.

The only threat you can levy against a debtor is that of civil litigation. The statement "The claim will be referred for legal proceedings" is acceptable. Even though it may include criminal action, it equally and more logically refers only to the permissible civil proceedings.

2. *Don't Threaten Bankruptcy.*   Few creditors realize it, but the Bankruptcy Code makes it illegal for a creditor to threaten bankruptcy. You can, of course, petition a debtor into bankruptcy if you meet the conditions; however, it can't be used as a club to coerce payment.

Under the new Bankruptcy Code a creditor can elect to petition a debtor into a Chapter 11 reorganization instead of a Chapter 7, liquidating bankruptcy. Legal minds are unsettled on whether it's a violation of the Bankruptcy Code to suggest a forced Chapter 11. Stay clear until it's resolved.

3. *Don't Threaten Disclosure.*   A threat that you will actively disseminate information on the bad debt is a subtle form of extortion—but, nevertheless, it's still extortion.

For example, threatened publication to other creditors is actionable. A creditor does have a qualified privilege to notify credit-rating bureaus and credit interchange associations; however, when the notification is based on malice or reprisal, the protection ceases. The best evidence of the malicious intent is the prior warning or threat itself.

This doesn't suggest that you must provide a good or even neutral credit report. What it does mean is that you can't threaten a customer with an unfavorable report. The threat alone is sufficient with any type extortion. You don't have to carry through with the threat to be liable. However, both the threat coupled with the act carries a greater risk because the customer would incur greater financial injury once other parties were notified.

4. *Don't Use Physical Threats.*   The danger is that even respectable creditors can become emotionally upset over the pros-

pects of losing a bundle of cash and resort to something more than polite conversation. Commonly, a creditor will start out with conversation but somehow end up with either physically threatening language or fists flying. Whether it be extortion or less exotic assault and battery, you don't need the headache.

Recalling one situation, a collection agency representative demanded $500 from the owner of a typewriter sales/service shop. One word led to another and next came the pushing and shoving. As you'd expect, each claimed the other started the fight. It was a sight to behold. Standing in the courtroom were the 6'2'', 240-pound collection agent. Beside this towering hulk stood the older 5'3'' owner, topping the scale at 140 pounds. Who do you think the judge believed?

It takes a special type to directly confront debtors. Frequently creditors will send a character with a marked resemblance to King Kong and an intellect to match and wonder why they're constantly being dragged into court.

Our own firm spends half its time trying to harness a vitriolic client, Noel, who only wants his own brand of justice. With him it's an "either/or" choice. Either the customer pays up or he threatens to tear out a few vital organs. Noel will get on the phone, pretend he's only a block away from the customer, and go into his threatening spiel. Customers don't know he's all bark and no bite. They hear the bark and have every right to expect the bite. Noel has been hit with at least two assault charges and convicted once of extortion. You can't convince Noel that words alone can spell trouble.

LIBEL: WATCHING WHAT YOU SAY

Some creditors don't care what they say about a debtor—or to whom. The words flow: "crook," "deadbeat," "swindler," "thief."

Tap my phone and you'll hear it. Irate creditors throw around the adjectives even when they talk to the debtor's own attorney. You can imagine what they say to other people.

Don't set yourself up for a libel suit. All the debtor need prove is that you made a *defamatory* statement and *communicated* it to a third person. And it can easily happen.

What is defamation? It defies a precise list of words, but any statement which tends to injure the reputation, business standing, or character of the debtor is sufficient. It's in the ears of the beholder.

Communication is more easily defined. All that's needed is for someone other than the debtor to hear (or read) the remark.

You can defame a business as well as an individual. To say that X Company is a deadbeat would give the company a claim. Go further and say Jones and his X Company are both deadbeats and you have two lawsuits to contend with.

How can you avoid libel problems?

1. *Avoid Name Calling.* The debtor may be a swindler or a phony, or make Attila the Hun look like Rebecca of Sunnybrook Farm. That doesn't give you the legal right to say it. I can use the words "deadbeat" and other adjectives in this book because I'm not referring to a specific person. But you may be. That's when the adjectives become expensive.

2. *Avoid Contrary Terms.* To say a customer is "less than honest" is to say he's dishonest. To suggest a debtor doesn't act legitimately is to imply he's acting illegitimately. Even a couched statement can be a defamatory one.

3. *Avoid Conclusions.* One creditor reported a customer "Had a very poor credit rating." It was a conclusion and one the creditor couldn't prove. It cost him $10,000. You may have certain facts about the debtor, but that doesn't justify sweeping generalities or costly conclusions.

Truth can be a defense to a libel case unless the statement was maliciously made. So what? The burden is on you to prove the truthfulness of the statement, and that's seldom easy. Besides, who needs legal fees and a week in a courtroom to try? Watch what you say.

Communication problems are easier to control. As long as you direct your comments to the debtor himself you're safe.

Correspondence is one trouble spot. Envelopes indicating it's a dunning notice are outlawed. So, too, are postcards. However, you can use postcards for regular billing or to state a *future* due date on a bill.

Questionable comments concerning an individual within a firm should be specifically addressed to the individual. A letter opened by a secretary containing a defamatory statement directed to the boss is still a third-party communication.

Some communications are privileged. This means they are protected from libel claims, provided they are not maliciously made. Within this category are:

1. Responses to credit inquiries by existing creditors or prospective suppliers seeking information. The privilege only applies however, if the statement is made in good faith and reasonable.

2. Reports to mercantile or credit agencies and reports from these services to subscribers with a direct interest in the business are privileged. Reports for general circulation are not privileged.

3. Disclosure of bankruptcy or other insolvency proceedings of a public nature are privileged. Even widespread disclosure is privileged, providing it's factual. Pick up the *Wall Street Journal* and you'll see mention of firms in bankruptcy. The privilege wouldn't exist if a company was cutting an out-of-court settlement with its creditors

The libel laws are complex. The only safe axiom to follow is either to say something positive—or say nothing. Admittedly, it's easy for me to write, and difficult for you to practice while you're chasing a scoundrel for $25,000.

EVEN A DEBTOR DESERVES PRIVACY

Invasion of privacy is a close cousin of libel. Whereas libel requires a derogatory statement, privacy violations encompass any unwarranted disclosure about a debtor.

The most common case is where a creditor furnishes information without debtor approval, as to a person with no apparent interest in the credit information.

You do have the right to disclose financial or credit information to:

Credit reporting services.

Credit interchange clubs.

Existing creditors.

Prospective suppliers.

The customer's bank or other lenders.

Even in these situations, the right to extend information is qualified. A customer, for example, has the right to prohibit disclosure to even these parties, although it does not prevent continued reporting to credit bureaus.

The type and scope of information is also qualified. It must be limited to what the recipient reasonably requires to make a credit decision and nothing further. Finally, the information must be actively solicited by the recipient.

Credit interchange clubs frequently violate this last point. A creditor will openly discuss a customer's credit history with all other members present. But most of these members have no direct interest because they are not present or contemplated suppliers to the firm. As bystanders the information falls on the wrong ears. It's surprising more debtors don't contest this practice.

Follow the safe course before providing information:

1. *Obtain Customer Approval.*   If in doubt about your right to issue information—don't. You can't be sued for refusal. Obtain customer approval. But protect yourself. Have the customer consent in writing, generally describing the information to be released.

2. *Don't Violate a Customer's Request.*   Honor a customer's request *not* to disclose information. You do have the right to tell a caller why you can't comply.

3. *Refuse Disinterested Parties.*   Most lawsuits center on disclosure to parties with an interest adverse to the debtor. A spouse, for example, frequently solicits information for use in a divorce case. Employees may want information for a variety of self-serving reasons, including verification of the firm's financial stability.

Labor unions have been known to call hoping to probe the financial strength. Disclosure can not only lose you a customer but win you a lawsuit.

CREDIT REFERENCES WITHOUT RISK

Credit references pose a dual threat. Issue a negative report unsupported by the facts and you can be liable to the customer based on diminished credit opportunity. On the other side of the coin, a false report to a prospective creditor encouraging credit and you can be liable for his resulting losses.

A large New England bank is facing that problem neatly wrapped in a $36,000 lawsuit. Here's how it happened. A cannery equipment supplier received an order for $36,000 in equipment from a local cannery. Phoning the cannery's bank for a credit reference, the supplier was told "The cannery is in excellent financial condition, and is current on all loans." Relying on the report, the supplier shipped only to have the cannery fail three weeks later.

The supplier could only conclude that either the bank didn't know what was happening with its cannery account, in which case "excellent financial condition" was a negligent statement, or the bank did know and was fraudulent. I don't envy the bank's attorney.

A credit reference is more than a casual favor. The recipient has a right to rely on the accuracy and objectivity of the report. That's the reason for the call. Issue anything less and you may end up paying your customer's bill.

Lawsuits by customers arising from an unjustified negative report are far less common. One reason is that a customer has difficulty proving monetary damages when credit is declined. Besides a negative report can be subsequently corrected to rehabilitate credit. The major consequence is usually the loss of a customer.

Button-up your credit-reporting policy:

1. *Assign Credit References to a Responsible Person.*   Credit reporting requires someone who knows precisely what to say, how to say it, and who to say it to. Frequently it's a $175/week

credit clerk talking to another credit clerk about a credit reference involving $100,000. Shift gears. Put someone responsible in charge.

2. *Don't Issue Negative Reports.*   You have no obligation to either the customer or recipient to issue a credit report, so what do you stand to gain with a negative report. Look at it logically. If your customer anticipated a negative report he wouldn't have listed you as a credit reference. Why say good-bye to a customer? Your best policy is to simply refuse *any* credit information. Credit managers may disagree, stating it's counterproductive to the flow of credit information, but you're in the business to sell to customers; you're not a credit-rating bureau.

3. *Don't Do Favors.*   You may be tempted to do a customer a favor by issuing an unjustifiably glowing credit report. Some suppliers do it to cement goodwill. Others hope the new credit line with another supplier will free up the cash flow to allow for payment on their own overdue bill. More than one supplier enters into a conspiracy to furnish a bogus report in return for payment. One supplier, in exchange for payment on a one-year-old $1,200 balance, issued an excellent report on behalf of its customer, allowing it to flimflam $80,000 in additional credit from unsuspecting suppliers.

You know the legal ramifications. Even if the burned recipients decide not to chase you, they'll certainly remember you when you call for a credit reference. Credit is a reputation business.

4. *Stay with the Facts.*   A customer is not a "slow pay," "fast pay," or anything in between. The words mean different things to different people. Your customer has a track record based on hard numbers alone. Tell the recipient only: the credit line, unpaid balance, aging, and any other factual data. The best procedure is to send out a photocopy of the ledger card. It tells the whole story. Why interpret it?

5. *Avoid Recommendations.*   You're in no position to recommend or not recommend credit. You can't be certain the customer will pay your next bill, so how can you judge what he will do with a new supplier? The struggling company may land a bank loan tomorrow and clean up its creditors. A healthy company may suddenly find itself in trouble. Put away your crystal ball.

6. *Put It in Writing.* The credit report should be reduced to writing for several reasons. It avoids a contest as to what was said. Remember the bank in the cannery case? Perhaps its verbal report wasn't exactly as the angry supplier remembered it. It will be a battle of memory and credibility. Accurate written reports not only protect you, but recipients appreciate it more because *it is* inclined to be accurate.

7. *Carry Insurance.* Few business people think of the risk associated with credit references. You can obtain insurance coverage to protect you from claims of negligent reporting. It won't help you for intentionally deceptive reports; however, most claims are based on negligence rather than deceit. And the cost for this type insurance is surprisingly low. If you don't presently carry coverage, put it high on your agenda.

HOW THE ANTITRUST LAWS CAN SNARE YOU

Discriminatory credit practices are prohibited under the Robinson-Patman Act, one of the several antitrust laws. Violations of the law can be particularly costly because a customer incurring discriminatory treatment has the right to collect triple the amount of its actual damages plus attorneys' fees. Moreover, this same customer may initiate a class action on behalf of other customers discriminated against.

Robinson-Patman violations are increasingly used by debtors as a defense in collection cases. In a good number of these cases the customer establishes a claim against the creditor well in excess of the creditor's claim.

Uniformity is the key to compliance under the Robinson-Patman Act. The law does not interfere with your established policy provided it's equally applied to all customers. Its intent is to avoid one or more customers being singled out for preferential treatment, or conversely certain customers not receiving equality of treatment with the others.

Check your compliance with the Robinson-Patman Act:

1. *Interest Charges.*   They must be uniform. If your interest rate is 1.5% per month for accounts over 30 days, then this policy must be in effect for all customers. You can't charge select customers more or less, or impose differing accrual periods. There is one exception. If you convert an overdue open account balance to a promissory note, then you may charge a different rate, and it appears that the rate on promissory notes may differ between customers in this category.

2. *Cash Discounts.*   This is more likely to be a trouble spot. Again, uniformity is required. You're prevented from granting some customers a 2% cash discount and others a 5% cash discount. Time for payment to qualify for the discount must also be uniform. Don't require some customers to pay in 10 days and allow others to pay in 15 days to receive the discount. In a technical sense, acceptance of a discounted payment beyond the due date is a discriminatory policy, but as a practical matter, it's of minor consequence if it's an exception to your policy and the exceptions are evenly handled.

3. *Trade Discounts and Pricing.*   It's in this area that you're likely to run into the most serious danger. Prices, trade discounts, concessions, brokerage, advertising, and service discounts must be equal. You may however, reduce prices to larger buyers to pass through the actual cost savings by selling in larger quantities. For example, if you grant customers buying $5,000 a month a 10% discount, the same discount should be extended to all customers buying in comparable amounts. Customers buying $10,000 a month may qualify for a 15% discount if the extra 5% approximates your savings.

This basic provision of the law dovetails with credit policy. Commonly, a supplier will penalize an overdue account by dropping discounts or allowances extended to current accounts. This is an illegal practice. Many suppliers do it on the assumption that the delinquent account is a "captive account" and is in no position to complain because he is delinquent. It's faulty thinking. Eventually that same customer may seek to reclaim triple the lost discounts or excess price.

The right way to handle the situation is to grant the overdue customer the same prices and discounts as others buying in comparable quantities . You may credit earned discounts to the overdue balance, but always reflect that discount on the invoice and how it's applied.

You do have the right to define credit limits on an account-by-account basis. For example, you may place some accounts on COD and grant others 15-day terms and still others 30-day or extended terms, provided cash discounts and interest are uniform.

Review your own credit and pricing policy and look out for variations between customers. Have your attorney review these situations before they are spotted by a smart but disgruntled customer not receiving equal treatment.

Another caution under the antitrust laws: Set your own credit policy. Don't collaborate with competitors and run afoul of the Sherman Act. Most businesspeople know they can't enter into price-fixing agreements with competitors, and yet these same creditors will think nothing of a collective credit policy—equally illegal under the law.

The prohibition against collective agreement extends to any trade practice. Joint agreements on interest rates, cash discounts, return goods policy, and other credit terms are all outlawed. Don't even discuss it with competitors. There's a fine line between discussion and agreement, and the former can easily be construed for the latter.

It was only a few years ago that several leading light-fixture wholesalers banded together and agreed to cut credit terms from 30 to 15 days and place a 20% handling cost on return goods. Between stiff fines and punitive damages payable to their retail accounts, it cost them a bundle. That's why I give you the advice to get up and walk out whenever your competitors begin to talk terms.

Boycotts are another illegal activity. Typically two or more suppliers will share their agony over a particular customer and agree to adopt an even credit approach toward the customer. Some suppliers mistakenly believe that it's only an illegal boycott to collectively agree not to do business with a particular customer. Not so. Collective restrictions on credit are equally illegal.

It all comes down to one axiom: Decide your own policy; it's the only safe policy.

CONSUMER CREDIT: MOVE WITH CAUTION

While this book focuses on commercial credit—business-to-business transactions—you'll need more than this chapter, and indeed an entire book, if you want to check the laws of *consumer* credit.

During the 1970s, consumer credit laws mushroomed. The government made consumer credit too risky and complicated for a small business owner. If you want to venture into the "no-win" world of consumer credit, hire yourself a lawyer experienced with the maze of regulations. And these laws and regulations are ungodly complex and technical. For example, the truth-in-lending law—in itself a good-sized book—prescribes exact words you must use to state interest charges even down to the required typeface. It makes even the Internal Revenue Code simple by comparison. These same protective rules extend through every stage of the credit process, even to the point of trying to collect, should you have the courage or audacity to even try.

Should you engage in consumer credit, the place to start is by writing to the *Federal Trade Commission* for some descriptive brochures:

1. The *Truth-in-Lending Act* contains all the provisions for computing and stating interest rates.

2. The *Equal Credit Opportunity Act* is designed to assure females equal access to credit regardless of marital status.

3. The *Fair Credit Billing Act* tells you how to handle customer complaints on billings.

4. The *Fair Debt Collection Practices Act* restricts the techniques you can use to collect from people who do not pay you.

5. The *Fair Credit Reporting Act* gives consumers the right to see their credit files and correct any erroneous information.

Bear in mind, these laws only apply to consumer credit. However, if you want to bolster your bookshelf with other additional information on the laws of commercial credit, order the *Credit Manual of Commercial Laws* (National Association of Credit Management, 1983). It's the best book on a very important subject.

11

QUESTIONS
AND ANSWERS

Although considerable information is contained in the preceeding chapter, some points require amplification and explanation in context to a specific situation. So let's stop here and deal with questions frequently asked by creditors. The questions and answers are based on real situations; however, the identity of the participants has been disguised to preserve confidentiality.

1. Q: Our flower distributorship has many overdue accounts. We try to have them catch up the balance by issuing a series of postdated checks, but many of the checks subsequently bounce. Can we file a criminal complaint based on the returned checks?

A: Probably not, however, you should review state law. Most state laws provide a bad check is not a criminal offense unless it's for a COD shipment. Payments on antecedent or back bills don't count.

Nevertheless, accepting a pay-out by a series of checks can be effective. Psychologically, customers tend to honor them as committed expenditures in juggling their cash flow. In fact, checks returned are far less common than missed payments on an installment note. As with a promissory note, the issuance of the checks is good evidence of the validity of the obligation should it become necessary to sue for the balance.

If the series of checks is for an extended time payment, say 3 to 4 months, you should have the customer acknowledge in writing your rights to pursue the entire balance without delay upon the return of any one check. Without this provision, some courts would hold you bound to the agreed time for payment and only allow you to proceed on the checks actually returned.

There are two other approaches to follow:

Postdated checks should be apportioned in weekly, rather than monthly installments. Smaller checks have a much greater chance of clearing.

Have the customer (if a corporation) issue the check to the principal, and have the principal endorse it over to you. By obtaining the owner's endorsement, you'll have him on the hook if the corporation goes under while checks remain outstanding.

2. Q: As distributors of a vitamin line to drugstores and health and beauty aid shops, many of our customers offer to settle the account with return merchandise. Although we can put the goods back into inventory for resale, we prefer the cash instead. How do we handle it?

A: Of course you prefer the cash. Who doesn't? Start with the premise that you'll only accept goods if you believe there's a 60% chance or less of receiving a cash settlement. That's about all you'd end up with if you have to turn the claim over for collection.

If you do decide to accept returns on this basis, then negotiate a handling charge of 25 to 35%. Surprisingly, many customers will pay this small amount to square away the bill and allow you to accept the return goods at their discounted amount.

Going after returns in lieu of a questionable collectible is good strategy, but it has one danger. Word gets around you will accept returns and even your solvent customers begin to consider it policy rather than the exception. Therefore, return goods should be accepted, sparingly only, as a final but practical alternative.

3. Q: What are the limitations of a consolidated financial statement? We sell promotional merchandise to a subsidiary corporation, with a parent and three other operating subsidiaries.

A: The consolidated financial statement has very little value because you can't determine the financial strength of the particular subsidiary responsible for your debt.

In many cases a subsidiary will try to propose its credit strength instead on the basis of its internal financial statement. The points to watch for are intercompany assets and liabilities. For example, debt owed by the subsidiary to another subsidiary or to the parent should be subordinated to your debt if you'll be a substantial creditor.

A better approach is to demand a guarantee from the parent and the other subsidiaries. Many creditors know enough to request a parent company guarantee but overlook the fact that the parent may "spin-off" its other subsidiaries, leaving you without the total corporate strength you're bargaining for. That's why I suggest you also look for co-subsidiary guarantees.

Don't forget the fact that you'll need a certified resolution from the Board of Directors of each corporation issuing the guarantee to validate authority.

4. Q: Our paint firm is owed $4,000 by a paint store operated as a partnership. The partnership shows among the liabilities $100,000 owing to general creditors and $40,000 owing partners. Do the partners have the same pro-rated claim against the assets of the business as general creditors?

A: No. Arm's-length creditors stand first in line. Only upon full payment to other creditors can the partners make claim for the balance from the sale of assets.

It's more complicated with a corporation. Non-stockholder officers and directors who loan money to their corporation can share pro-rata with other creditors. They cannot, however, give themselves a preference over creditors by taking a security interest on assets.

Stockholders represent another problem. Bankruptcy cases have held that stockholder debt should be subordinated to other debt. In effect, the loans become a contribution to equity and are last paid.

In your particular situation you should block participation by the partners until you are fully paid. If the business assets don't fully satisfy your claim, you can sue each and all of the partners personally for the balance due.

5. Q: As a manufacturer of specialized furniture we are thinking of switching our credit policy from 2/10 net 30 to COD. We know we'll have some customer resistance but believe we can offset it by offering lower prices. What other problems can we expect with COD?

A: Theoretically you'll eliminate credit risks, but COD never totally solves your problems. Even COD offers these problems to cope with:

1. Bad checks.
2. Refused acceptance.
3. Cancellation before delivery.
4. Nondelivery for a variety of customer-created reasons.

The problem of bad checks can be minimized by a quick bank reference check before you accept the order. If you question the check's value, change the terms to cash or certified check on delivery. Provide immediate notification of the change of terms and confirmation received before you start manufacture.

If the bank's reference is so shaky for this type customer, you'll be smarter to demand payment *before* manufacture to protect yourself in the case the customer fails before delivery.

Refused acceptance, cancellation, and other customer-induced reasons for noncompletion are ordinarily more of a nuisance than financial risk. When goods are made to order, however, you can't readily resell upon buyer default. Therefore, I'd suggest you always request a deposit to cover any anticipated loss in the event of cancellation or nonacceptance. Include return shipping and storage costs in calculating the necessary deposit.

Many large rated accounts have been known to cancel orders made to specification. They remain liable for the difference between contract price and resale price of the product—or your lost profits—whichever is greater, but they still cancel with regularity and leave it to you to chase. For this reason your deposit requirements should be applied uniformly even to the rated accounts.

6. Q: We operate a small subcontracting firm and engage in doing concrete foundations for general contractors. A large job came up involving $100,000 in concrete work. As a small concern we can't afford the loss that could result from this job. The contractor tells us he's bonded, so we shouldn't worry. Is the bond sufficient protection?

A: No. You have to know what type bond the contractor is talking about. Chances are it's a *performance* bond that only protects the landowner from losses in the event of contractor-default. And the financial criteria for obtaining this type bond are far different than the credit criteria you have to consider.

What you want is a *payment* bond, which is essentially a guarantee from the bonding company to the subcontractors that they will be paid.

Even with a payment bond you have the problem of cash flow in the event of contractor-default. It may take you a year or two to collect from the bonding company. If you have considerable money invested in the job, you could be out of business before you have a chance to collect. There's only one solution: Your contract should provide for partial or interim payments to parallel your work progress. As an addition to the payment bond, it will minimize risk and maintain cash flow. An added caution: The contract should also state your right to terminate further work in the event an installment payment is not timely made.

Contracts and bonds between contractor and subcontractor should always be reviewed by counsel. Construction is a high-risk business, and most subcontractors fail when they overreach and end up in a cash-strangling legal problem with their contractors.

7. Q: Upon our request for financial statements, a prospective customer mailed us the balance sheet but not the profit and loss statement. How can we quickly detect profitability from the balance sheet alone?

A: The only possibilities are to look for two balance sheet indicators:

1. Earned surplus (retained earnings) which is equivalent to the prior accrued profits retained within the company. Its weakness is that it doesn't show the profit trend.

2. Tax refunds due, as a current asset, is an indication the company probably operated at a loss during the prior year.

Since current profitability is a primary factor in assessing credit risk, you shouldn't ship unless the balance sheet is exceptionally strong and there's a logical reason for the missing P & L Statement.

8. Q: Our wholesale firm is redesigning financial statements to be completed by new accounts. What specific contingent liabilities should we ask about?

    A: There are three to keep your eyes open for:

1. Outstanding guarantees: I recall one company with only $100,000 in assets who had over $90,000 in outstanding third-party guarantees. Without disclosure of the guarantees, the balance sheet looked healthy. As you might expect, it eventually was hit for one $72,000 guarantee, eliminating the company and many surprised creditors.

2. Pending lawsuits: Get the facts and have it reviewed by your attorney to obtain an idea of its significance.

3. Tax audits pending: A major audit can put a formidable creditor ahead of you.

4. Other governmental audits: For example, firms in defense work can undergo retroactive audits to prove costs. Pharmacies, nursing homes, and other health care providers may be subject to Medicaid audits.

At any given time I'd say that about 40% of my small business clients have substantial contingent liabilities pending. Some are quite healthy today but won't be around in a year or two.

It's wise to ask pinpointed questions about contingent liabilities. Many businesspeople conveniently forget to list such claims as a financial statement footnote, or under a broad question.

9. Q: How effective are humorous collection letters compared to the "straight" or serious letter?

A: Humorous letter have their limitation and are used far too often. A truly humorous and personalized letter or card can take the place of a first reminder. But it should only be used when creditor–debtor relationships are on a personal basis.

Some firms think they're in the comic book business and send out a whole series of humor-oriented notices. You send letters to collect not entertain. If the first one doesn't do it, the second, third, and fourth may keep your customer laughing, but the big question is: At who?

10. Q: Personalized collection letters are supposed to be more effective than form letters. But does it justify the investment in a word processor to create the personalized letters?

A: It's a matter of economics. Personalized letters are about twice as effective as form letters. As a rule of thumb a word processor is cost-justified if you send out 25 or more collection letters a month.

Why more collection agencies and attorneys with their high volume of collection correspondence don't wisely use word processors still remains a mystery. However, it's clear most debtors are conditioned to ignore form letters and attach greater importance to the personalized.

11. Q: Our lighting-fixture-supply firm was promised a $4,000 check from a retail customer on a 90-day-old bill. On the strength of his promise we shipped a second order for $2,000, which is still in transit. Needless to say, his first check never arrived. Can we stop the goods in transit?

A: You can, unless the customer has a negotiable bill of lading.

The right to stop goods in transit exists when it's discovered the customer is insolvent during the transport period. But the word "insolvent" in this case takes a subjective test and does not necessarily mean insolvent in a bankrupt sense. The fact the customer not only held out on his first payment but never followed through on his payment promise should be sufficient grounds to put a hold on the goods.

Some quick steps to take: Notify the carrier immediately and have them confirm in writing the goods have been stopped and returned. Sometimes carriers have their own communication problems and ignore a seller's instructions. You want recourse against the carrier should it happen to you.

Your second step is to notify the customer you stopped the goods, and why. Put it in writing; always protect the file.

A practical solution is to have the customer wire $4,000 (although you may now want to hold out for the entire $6,000) directly to your bank. This facilitated payment will allow you to release the goods for continued transit without going through the added reshipping expense.

12. Q: One of our customers owes our trucking firm over $2,000 in unpaid bills. This particular customer is a first-class deadbeat who stiffed other trucking firms and quite a few other creditors. I'm about to tell him that unless we get our check, pronto, we will notify every other trucking company in the area. Do you think it will work?

A: Not if your customer has any smarts. He'll be quick to point out your liability if you do.

There's a fine line between the qualified privilege a creditor has to share credit information *when solicited*, as opposed to an active campaign to disclose a credit program.

I think your customer would have a good claim for libel should you go ahead and carry out your threat. Maybe you had in mind the threat without actually carrying it out, in hopes the customer would scrounge up your $2,000.

But even the threat can cause legal problems. The threat alone may constitute a deceptive trade practice, although it cannot be libelous since it wasn't communicated to a third party. That's the real problem. Suppose the customer suddenly finds increased credit problems. He'll assume you carried through with your threat and may institute suit.

A better way to handle it is to say to the account, you receive many requests for a credit reference on him. So far you have declined comment. Unless the check is received you'll disclose the sorry facts. It's the right way to use the credit reference weapon.

13. Q: What day of the week is best for our salespeople to hit customers up for overdue payments? We extensively use sales personnel to make personal collection calls on these accounts.

A: You didn't indicate the nature of your customer's business, but here's a good rule-of-thumb. Businesses that are open on weekends (retail stores, restaurants, etc.) have the best checkbook balances on Monday. They have the weekend receipts and payrolls don't usually roll around until Friday or Saturday.

Wednesday is best for the five-day business. They have three days' receipts and two days to go before they make payroll.

It's not so much the day of the week you approach the customer as the day the check can clear the bank. The best approach is to encourage your sales reps to work with the customer and postdate the check ahead a few days when the cash is expected to be in the bank. Follow up is all important. Either deposit the check so it's timed to arrive at the customer's bank on the precise due date or have it certified by the bank if it's convenient. Make every day a collection day, and don't let your salespeople be put off with the "I don't have the money right now" excuse.

14. Q: Our physical therapy clinic is owed over $8,000 from the U.S. Department of Labor for services rendered governmental employees this agency insures. It's been over a year and all we get are bureaucratic bumblings. Can we tack interest on to the bill? Can we make it retroactive?

A: When it comes to getting paid from the government—at least on time—it takes more than magic or miracles. However, you can't charge the federal government (or most states) interest on their overdue bills. Unlike the IRS, who will pay interest on tax credits, the federal government is exempt from any interest or service charge unless specifically agreed to by contract.

As I write this book, legislation is pending to require the government to pay interest on overdue bills. Perhaps, by the time this book is published it will be law—but I doubt it.

15. Q: Most of our accounts are either well rated or have a good credit history with us. How often should we do a credit review on these "automatic" shipment accounts?

A: Do a new credit analysis at least once a year. Financial pictures can change very rapidly. Even when your account has a solid track record, it may suddenly run up a whopping bill and hit you with a surprise problem.

The best way to handle it is to have them issue new financial statements. Timing is what's important. Coordinate your request with the month new financial statements are ready, which would be the due date for filing tax returns.

A simple approach is to find out the account's fiscal year when you open it on credit. Your request should go out annually, 90 days after the close of each fiscal year thereafter.

16. Q: I recently heard an economist say bad debts increase with an economic recovery. This statement doesn't make any sense to me. What's the basis for it?

A: The statement is absolutely true. Most people flunk the test on this one, but it does make sense when you consider the dynamics of the marketplace.

During bad times, suppliers are sales-oriented. They will be lenient creditors to keep the flow of goods going and the plant humming, even at the expense of increased credit losses.

During good times, however, suppliers and banks become selective. With high sales activity they become credit-oriented. Once the economy turns up, they tend to drop the high-risk or marginal account and turn the screws on their accounts to collect the high liabilities created during the depressed market. The very worst time for collections is when the economy is about at the halfway mark to full recovery.

As a debtor's lawyer, I've seen it happen in practice. When the economy is down-turned, everybody thinks we're the busiest. They're wrong. That's when my clients, like squirrels, are out collecting the nuts. Payday comes later, when the suppliers are again back in the driver's seat.

Remember one more point. What's a depressed economy for one industry may be a high-rolling economy for another. Look at the economy only as it relates to your industry.

17. Q: Our printing supply firm maintains its customer lists on computer for up to ten years after we conclude doing business with the firm. It helps us check up on "new accounts" who may have stiffed us five or six years earlier. How else can we index the computer to crossreference back to prior accounts?

A: It's easy for a shrewd customer to slip by you, unless you crossreference by:

Corporate name.

Trade or business name.

Address.

Principal officer's name.

Let me show you why each is important.

I recall one case when a young chap opened a greeting card shop, we'll call it the XYZ Corporation. He ordered $3,000 in goods from a supplier and burned him. A year later he placed another order for $3,700, but this time he used the corporate trade name, we'll call "The Lemon Tree Shop." Of course the supplier had no account under "The Lemon Tree Shop," so again they shipped, and with predictability took it on the chin a second time. Nine months later the XYZ Corporation went bankrupt, but this deadbeat entrepreneur bought the assets back at auction under his new corporate name—ABC, Inc. So this same supplier, not having the location programmed, gave clearance for $4,200 to ABC, Inc. Another loss. Finally, this deadbeat turned bust-out artist, opened two more stores, under separate corporations, and took this same supplier for still another $12,000.

I see it frequently, when credit runs out, debtors set up "paper" divisions, buying subsidiaries, or affiliates, to become that "new account." Plenty of creditors fall for it, and end up chasing the very same person for 12 orders shipped to 9 different companies at 6 locations.

Plug in your computer. Program it to effectively crossreference, so you *know* who you're doing business with.

18. Q: Is there any accepted method for handling the customer who takes an unearned discount? We have one clown who always sends his check in two or three weeks after the discount date, and marks the discounted check "payment in full." To add to it, the check is always dated one or two days *before* the discount date.

A: I don't think there's any one right answer to this perennial problem. But assuming you're dealing with only an average account, the most common policy is to let one unearned discount go through each year. Also, let checks arriving within three days of the due date go through. Beyond that the discount date should be enforced by returning the check and asking for payment of the gross amount.

Checks without a release endorsement may be deposited, and you can charge back the discount to the customer. Since your check has the "payment in full" endorsement, cashing would constitute acceptance in full. Continued acceptance is not the right way to handle this customer. Arrange to "swap" checks and put him on notice your discount policy will be enforced.

19. Q: We are setting up a plant to manufacture vacuum cleaner and carpet cleaning accessories. Some of our people think we should distribute on a consignment basis to decrease sales resistance at the retail level and to protect ourselves from credit losses. Do you see any disadvantages?

A: Earlier in this book I outlined how consignment sales can accomplish the two objectives you mention. But there are also several drawback:

1.   Retailers don't "push" a consigned line as aggressively as merchandise purchased on outright sale. The reason should be obvious. When a retailer buys the merchandise he's in a hurry to liquidate it and recoup his investment. Why "push" consigned inventory when they don't have money tied up in the stock. One way to overcome passive selling of consigned merchandise is to allow the retailer a greater percentile profit than he would earn on merchandise acquired on outright sale. An added 10% may do it. Now the retailer is motivated by the *profit*, not *return on investment*.

2.   The one big disadvantage to a consignment sale is its impact on your own cash flow and capitalization requirements. You'll need considerably more capital for a consignment plan, unless you believe the merchandise will turn over as rapidly as the due date on a net billing. For example, if you place $240,000 in merchandise on consignment, and expect it to sell through over one year, then at the end of

60 days you'll still have approximately $200,000 outstanding. Assuming an outright sale with total collections within 60 days, you'll have your entire $240,000 back within the same 60 days. This shouldn't discourage you, but it does signal the need for very careful cash flow planning so you don't strip your working capital.

3. Consignment sales do not eliminate the need for credit investigations, although risk is less than on an outright sale. The retailer is still a debtor to the extent of sold merchandise on which payment is due.

Why not consider a split approach. Go consignment for marginal accounts and for accounts who will only take the merchandise on a consignment basis. But use consignment as a backup, shooting instead for outright sales to well-rated accounts who offer no sales resistance. It's the best way to balance the advantages and disadvantages of each method.

20. Q: Franchisors as creditors of their own franchised outlets routinely perform the accounting function for their franchisees; so they always know how their individual franchisees are making out. Do you think it's feasible for a major wholesaler to offer accounting services to its retailers on a group-rate basis? The retailer would benefit by the lower group rate and our financial counseling; and we would benefit by staying on top of our customers' financial condition.

A: It's an excellent idea, but it's not a new one. Some examples:

A large drug wholesaler in the Chicago area lined up a General Business Service firm (a financial bookkeeping firm) to provide accounting work for its participating drugstore accounts. I understand over 50 pharmacies signed up for the service, since they were obtaining the service at a 20% reduced group rate, and at considerably lower fees than charged by independent accountants. The wholesaler used the service as a sales tool to attract new accounts and it was smart because it was a service without cost to the wholesaler.

As this wholesaler discovered, you have to go further to make it work as a credit tool. To obtain access to the customers' financial information you have to tie the program in with a voluntary financial counseling program, or a mandatory disclosure approach as used by franchisors.

Voluntary financial counseling can work for an arm's-length major supplier. Retailers, particularly, need counseling and a wholesaler with a strong financial advisor available can provide a valuable service to both the retailer heading for trouble and the wholesaler who would be victimized by the loss.

There's a final ingredient for its success: Objectivity. Don't set up the program if it's only a self-serving method to spy on your retailers. You have to be sincere in wanting to help them, consistent with your own credit goals—clearly a tightrope not easily walked.

21. Q: Analyzing the collection rate for our stationery supply firm we find that only 20% of our retailers pay within the discount period; while most take 30 to 60 days to pay. This is surprising considering our 5%–10-day discount. How can we increase the percentage of discounted payments?

A: Hit them hard with reminders—and put it in *dollar* terms not *percentage* terms. People understand dollars.

When a $200 statement goes out, stamp across its face in large letters, "You save $10, if paid before the tenth of the month."

Follow up with a card mailed about the 7th or 8th of the month again reminding them to "Mail the check today and save $10."

It's not time-consuming but it is effective. I've seen one supplier triple the number of discounted payments with just that approach and he offered only a 2% discount. Unless you're dealing with too many marginal accounts, you should do appreciably better with a strong 5% discount.

22. Q: Can a guaranty be revoked by its guarantor? Our guaranty form says nothing about termination of the guaranty, but a principal who signed the guaranty for his company sent us a certified letter he'll no longer be liable for future bills under the guaranty. Isn't he bound?

A: Not for future credit. A guarantor can always rescind his guaranty for *future* indebtedness. He cannot, of course, rescind his obligations for prior credit.

Some guarantees contain language that termination may only be by certified or registered mail (to prove delivery) and will not take effect until 30 days after receipt. This gives the creditor opportunity to stop goods in transit or put a hold on orders in process. When goods are made to specification or special order, the guaranty should also state the guaranty termination does not affect orders previously accepted but unshipped.

Why is the guaranty being rescinded? That's an important question in determining future credit. In many cases it's due to a sale of the business. The new owners should, of course, be approached for their guaranty. In every instance, however, a guaranty rescission should be followed up by a new credit analysis.

23. Q: Whenever a retail account for our wholesale tobacco firm gets behind by 45 days or more, we immediately put him on COD shipments and expect a partial payment with each shipment toward the back bill. What oftentimes happens is that the customer switches to another tobacco jobber who extends one or two weeks credit. While we are generally paid down, we find CODs a poor way to retain customers. Any solutions?

A: You're right. COD is the easiest way to lose a customer. It's the only alternative for the customer who won't cooperate or are destined for an early bankruptcy, but COD is used far too often. There are better ways, if retaining the customer's business is important.

Customers resent COD for a variety of reasons. The most common complaint is that COD is difficult to handle as the check must be processed to coincide with delivery. Admittedly, it's an inconvenience at best for an absentee owner or one busy with his own customers.

The best solution is to put the account either on one-week payment or order-to-order payment, coupled with a pay-down on the old balance. Consider what little you have to lose and how much you stand to gain.

I'm reminded of a typical case involving one of my own clients who owed a wholesaler $14,000 on a 60-day bill. At the time my client, a small bakery, was buying about $7,000 a month from this wholesale supplier. With one phone call from its credit manager, the bakery was on COD. So my client switched to a competing wholesaler who extended one week's credit. Look at the economics. For additional credit of about $1,500 (one week's purchases), the old wholesaler could have retained an $80,000 to $90,000-a-year account. Moreover, it would have retained a supplier relationship with the bakery, making it easier to work out a pay-down of the past bill.

The new wholesaler was the big winner. For a $1,500 to $2,000 credit line, it won an account who will add $10,000 to $15,000 to profits. COD victimizes the creditor more than the customer. Look for a way to give the account a very short credit leash, and use COD only as a last resort.

24. Q: At what point will a request for financial information insult a credit applicant? We try to obtain financial data on all new accounts, but some large firms refuse, and a few have even canceled their orders.

A: It's hard to predict who you will insult and who you won't. The insult usually comes when you're asking a triple-A-rated conglomerate for its financials to back up a $500 order. Use commonsense.

The tack to follow is to tell the customer you want the financials to establish the best possible credit line. Notice, you didn't say a thing about it being a requirement to ship the $500 order, and who would resent submitting financials to establish its best credit line. It's all in the wording.

Tact is important. Credit managers playing by the book can kill a sale quicker than 10 salespeople can make them.

Here's a classic story and it involved me as the insulted customer. Several years ago I wrote a book for a major publisher. Over the years I ordered a few additional copies of my book, and always paid the invoice within 30 days. Wanting a few additional copies, I recently put in an order for 10 more books ($125) and received back a letter from the credit department that they can't ship on credit without my completing financial statements, even though I am the author. And this very same publisher (not John Wiley) has two other books of mine ready for publication! Some people don't use their heads.

25. Q: Our credit department is always at war with sales. We want to run a tight credit ship, but the salespeople say we're too tough. Shouldn't credit have the final say?

A: No. Neither should sales. When an account is turned down by the credit department over the objections of sales, it should be reviewed and resolved by an executive with overall profit responsibility. He or she can look at the account with greater objectivity than either sales or credit.

26. Q: Our new credit manager insists that new marginal accounts be put on a COD basis to start—with the possibility of credit after three to six months. What does this accomplish?

A: Very little. Let's suppose the customer does buy COD for six months. What does it prove? Only that he needed the product. It's not an indication of credit worthiness.

I've seen one wholesaler use that very same policy. For six months an account paid COD and then obtained 30 days' credit. During the 30 days' credit he ran up an $18,000 bill and another $12,000 between 30 and 45 days when the credit manager finally cut him off. This wholesaler never did get paid.

Credit should be based on a very gradual turning of the spigot. Start with an order-to-order credit line, limited both as to amount and time for payment. Once the account performs, credit can be increased. Another approach is to split the order; 50% COD and 50% credit. Not all credit people agree. One credit manager justifies starting an account out COD on a "loss recoupment" basis. He reasons that if a customer buys $30,000 in product on a COD basis, and burns him for $5,000 once credit is open, the profits on the $30,000 will cover the loss. It's another viewpoint.

27. Q: Our lumber supply firm is a $200,000 general creditor of a contractor under Chapter 11 reorganization under the Bankruptcy Code. We know they can't pay our back bills during the Chapter 11, but why should they be allowed to continue payments to their bank?

A: Because the bank probably holds a mortgage (security interest). A secured creditor, unlike a general creditor, not only can be paid under a Chapter 11, but frequently the court insists, particularly if there's a question about the adequacy of collateral to protect the secured creditor.

That's another reason why a trade creditor should fight for a security interest, even if the customer is already mortgaged to the hilt. Those checks for pre-Chapter 11 bills can keep on rolling in while other creditors are on hold.

28. Q: Whenever I phone an account for payment, I usually find myself on the phone with a secretary, clerk, or bookkeeper instead. Everyone but the Indian chief who I really want to talk to. Can I disclose the nature of the call to these people without running afoul of the libel laws?

A: Of course. Find out the person's capacity with the firm. If the person has either the responsibility to communicate messages to the boss or plays a clerical/bookkeeping role, then dealing with creditors is part of their job.

The trick is to confine your comments to the issue, not the character of the boss. I recall one case where an angered creditor phoned and told a secretary "her boss was a damned deadbeat who stiffs everybody and she should quit before her own reputation goes up in smoke." It cost this creditor $12,000 to settle a nasty libel suit.

In another unusual case, an imaginative creditor who didn't understand his legal limitations thought it would be a good idea to appeal to the employees. Printing leaflets that read "Your company owed me $19,000 for six months. Would you wait that long for your wages?" The creditor handed the leaflets to workers leaving the plant for the day. The court ruled it an improper communication because these workers had no managerial responsibility and the obvious intent of the leaflets was to coerce and embarrass.

29. Q: Our contracting firm is chasing a subcontractor who absconded with a $100,000 work deposit. A lawsuit is underway, but recovery looks doubtful since our attorneys tell us the subcontractor has few assets left. When should we charge the debt off as a loss or bad debt?

A: Immediately. If you figure taxable profits on the accrual method of accounting you should deduct the $100,000 as a reserve for a bad debt. Assuming your company is in the 30% tax bracket, an early writeoff would save you $30,000 in taxes. The interest earned on this $30,000 at even 12% would produce $3,600 a year. Now let's assume the lawsuit drags on for five years and you end up without a dime, you will have earned $18,000 in interest from the earliest possible tax writeoff. Should you recover, you would take the income in the year received.

To satisfy your early reserve for bad debt, have your attorney issue an opinion letter outlining the basis for determining the likelihood of loss, and run it by your accountants to make certain it will stand up as a justified early reserve.

If you report income on the cash method of accounting, credit losses are of no taxable consequence as you never reported the unrealized income from the sale.

30. Q: Our beverage firm uses our delivery people to pick up COD payments from customers. Some of our customers pay by cash instead of check by choice, and others are on a *cash*-only delivery basis because their checks aren't acceptable. Now our problem. We learned one of our route salespeople absconded with over $18,000 in cash collected over the prior month. Who bears the loss?

A: Your company—rather than the customer—bears the loss resulting from employee dishonesty.

Here are some pointers to help reduce future losses:

1. Delivery people who handle cash on delivery should go through a thorough security check before they are hired.

2. Bonding is the next step. Have each delivery person bonded for the maximum amount of cash they can be expected to handle. If an employee can't be bonded, he or she can't be hired.

3. Carry insurance for theft of cash in transit. Sometimes a delivery vehicle is robbed or burglarized, and since this doesn't involve employee theft it isn't covered by the bond and may not be covered by your regular business insurance. You'll probably need special insurance to cover it.

4. Encourage payments by check rather than cash for accounts whose checks are acceptable. Don't invite temptation or needless loss by allowing excess cash transactions.

5. Require duplicate receipts. One for the customer and the original for the company.

6. Make it policy that all funds be turned in at the end of the day. Delivery people should not be allowed to hold funds overnight as this opens still other security and insurance problems.

7. Consider shorter billing cycles, particularly for COD customers. If you send out weekly (or biweekly) statements instead of monthly invoices, both you and your customer can detect embezzlement faster without letting it go for an entire month.

COD pickups involve many problems. Security is only one. Lost time and reduced delivery efficiency is another. In fact one company reports that CODs slow down deliveries by 30% for his firm.

You may do better to go order-to-order instead of COD. If there's a week or more lag between deliveries, remittance can be by mail.

Take a page from the book of a similar firm with the same problem. A dry cleaning plant made several deliveries a week to its small retail dry cleaning customers. The average daily cash pickup per customer per day was about $200. It solved its problems by placing the better credit risks on one-week terms. The weaker accounts prepaid each week. For example, an account with average weekly billings of $1,000 would pay $1,000 by Friday of the preceding week to cover the following week's deliveries. "We gave these accounts an extra cash discount to make it worthwhile," reports Harry Blackman, its owner, "but it kept our people out of the collection business and increased delivery efficiency.

31. Q: When we receive bad checks we advise our customer that unless it's made "good" we'll file criminal charges. Our lawyer says this is extortion. Is he right?

A: Yes. You can never threaten an account with criminal action as an alternative to payment. The only exception is when the state statute compels notice of intended criminal proceedings as a final warning on bad checks.

There was a case of a supplier who suspected a customer of "back dooring" merchandise to a friend's business. This supplier threatened to report the fraudulent activity to the U.S. Attorney unless he paid up. This was a classic case of extortion and the supplier ended up in hotter water than the customer who proved his honesty.

You can commence criminal prosecution if you believe you have the grounds. Just avoid the prior threat. But even here follow a word of caution. Make certain there's a reasonable basis for believing a criminal act occurred. If you proceed without sufficient investigation or belief, you can be liable to your customer for malicious prosecution if the charges prove totally unfounded or brought for improper purposes.

You can always threaten a civil lawsuit to collect. Extortion only applies to criminal actions. The words "legal action" are acceptable as it implies civil proceedings, although it does not necessarily preclude criminal.

32. Q: Does the federal *Truth-in-Lending* law apply to business, or trade credit?

A: No. The law is consumer-oriented. It covers credit primarily for personal, family, household, or agricultural purposes. Even if a principal of the firm guarantees the debt, the law doesn't apply as the transaction is for business reasons.

33. Q: We routinely ship on COD terms, but one of our common carriers refuses to deliver unless it's handed cash, certified check, money order, or bank cashier's check. We're willing to accept a customer's regular check until it proves unreliable. How do we get around it?

A: Your common carrier is absolutely right in its position. In fact common carriers should decline a regular check unless instructed to the contrary. Too many carriers ignore this requirement.

Here's how to handle your situation. Endorse the bill of lading and shipping order with the statement "Consignee's check acceptable for COD amount."

If you are afraid of your customer's check and want cash or a certified check you have a right to insist on it for a COD shipment. Customers don't always understand this and have to refuse delivery because they're not prepared. Drop them a card in advance of delivery so they are ready. It can save a sale.

34. Q: Our book publishing firm charges overdue accounts 1.5% per month interest on bills overdue 30 days. The courts in our state impose an interest charge of only 8% on pending lawsuits. Assume a case takes three years to reach trial. Are we entitled to our stated 18%, the 8%, or the combined interest of 26%.

A: In most states you'll collect only what the court allows, 8% in your case. That's one problem with lawsuits; time favors the defendant, as they can play with your money at a substantially reduced interest rate, since most courts are far behind the times in increasing interest during litigation to a commercially reasonable amount.

35. Q: Our furniture plant relies primarily on Dun and Bradstreet reference reports. Do you think we'll have better luck with a specialized reporting agency?

A: It's not a matter of doing better. You want to cover all the bases. D & B may provide information a specialized reporting agency may omit.

The advantages of a specialized reporting agency are their greater familiarity with your industry and their ability to obain credit information from other creditors in the trade.

I also believe a specialized reporting agency offers more current information as they have only their one industry to focus on.

36. Q: Most credit books say credit standards should be stringent where profit margins are slender. Is this really the determining factor in setting credit standards?

A: Only in textbooks. The theory remains theory, as it crumbles away in the face of more practical considerations.

Competition is the key factor. I have seen industries where margins were high go for tight credit terms and just the opposite. Tobacco distribution is a very low-margin industry. Yet, in the

Boston market they extend 30- to 60-day terms, not because it's *margin* justified but because it's *competitively* required.

37. Q: I know credit interchange clubs and associations meet for purposes of exchanging credit information on accounts, but why can't they get together to draw up tighter credit restrictions for their industry? Wouldn't that solve the problem of competitors fighting with more lenient credit terms?

   A: There are two problems. One is legal and the second is practical.

   Suppliers cannot meet for purposes of agreeing on a credit policy. It's an anticompetitive practice and violates the Sherman Act, one of the more vigorously enforced antitrust laws. In fact, competitors cannot meet and agree on any trade practice. A few years ago, area drug wholesalers allegedly met and agreed to refuse return goods from their customers. It's a wonder they didn't go to jail. All a credit interchange group can do is swap information and nothing further. Even an agreement to put an account on COD (or restrict credit) may be considered an unlawful boycott under the Sherman Act. You, of course, have a right to decide how you'll handle an account provided it's not based on a reciprocal agreement or understanding with competitors.

   Even if you could legally agree on credit terms, how effective would it be? There will always be a maverick in the crowd who won't go along with it and move in on your customers with a more aggressive policy.

38. Q: Our phone bill is astronomical. Telephone collections are expensive for our importing firm, as we have to call customers all over the country. How practical are "collect" calls?

   A: Telephone costs can eat up profits on small orders. Many firms report success with the "collect" call, at least for the first phone call. Of course, if you can get through, you have passed the cost on to the customer. If your customer refuses to accept you still pushed the message through. Your customers know why you're calling.

One giftware supplier informed me that it received about a 28% success rate with the "collect" call. In most cases the call was refused, but the check was received a few days later.

If the "collect" call produces neither acceptance of the call nor the check, try it several times more over a one- or two-week period. Getting paid is knowing how to be a pain in the neck, using your customer's "nickel."

Spread the joy of your collect calls around. If accounts payable won't bite for it, perhaps the comptroller or treasurer will. Don't call the same person twice. Even if you get through but don't get paid the advice fits. It's time to work your way up the corporate ladder a rung at a time until you get results.

39. Q: Our wholesale firm has several major area competitors. One of the major wholesalers recently filed bankruptcy, and as you'd expect the rest of us are in hot competition to pick up its 800 retail accounts. Competition is so fierce that we have suspended the exchange of credit information. How do we know which retailers have the best credit history with this bankrupt wholesaler?

A: Don't rely on the direct approach by asking the retailer. They may lie through their teeth. You need written documentation. Ask the prospective account for his accounts payable file with this wholesaler. Scan the invoices and billings and you'll quickly see the credit picture.

Even this should be backed up with verification. Why not hire one or two salespeople from the defunct firm. It's your best strategy. They not only know the accounts from a credit standpoint but have the customer relations to swing the better accounts your way.

40. Q: What's the best way of asking for "cash in advance"? Our specialty firm receives 50 to 60 orders a week in the $200 to $300 range and we don't want to be bothered with credit checks for such small amounts.

A: Your best approach is to notify the customer you don't want to delay shipment pending a credit check and, therefore, request prepayment on the initial order.

For accounts that refuse, try a split approach, asking for 50% prepayment. It's no assurance of credit worthiness; however, it does cut losses.

If this doesn't do the trick, review the D & B rating to at least obtain a quick fix on the company. That's how most firms handle the first small order, and considering the labor intensity of a complete credit investigation, it's a reasonable indicator to go on.

41. Q: We have a retail account who's in to our housewares firm for $40,000. We now have it on COD, but we doubt if we'll ever be fully paid. Here's the question. We extend a 10% trade discount to customers buying in his volume. Can we drop the discount for this customer?

A: Absolutely not. The Robinson-Patman Act prevents discriminatory trade (or cash) discounts between customers buying on equally proportionate terms. So this customer is equally entitled to the 10% discount. But here's how to make it work for you. Have the account agree to apply the discount to the back bill. That's legal since the customer is obtaining his full credit.

Don't stop there. See if you can arrange a small additional payment with each order (or month) toward the back bill. Work out a cash-flow statement and agree on a mutually satisfactory amount.

Finally, see if you can obtain a security interest or collateral for the debt. Become a secured creditor; don't hang out as a general creditor.

What can you offer as an incentive? Offer a long-term promissory note at a slightly lower interest rate than what you charge overdue accounts. Order-to-order payments, instead of COD is also a reasonable incentive once the customer puts a good dent in the $40,000 owed.

There's a wide mix of possibilities. The problem should nevertheless be resolved through an agreement to:

1. Secure the money owed.
2. A systematic pay-down.

Aside from the illegality of canceling the 10% discount, it's doubtful the account will stay with you long; instead it will go hunting for a competing supplier who will grant the concession. That's counterproductive to both your profits and chances for collection.

We once handled a case remarkably similar to yours. Our client, a small variety store, owed a school supply jobber $12,000. The jobber promptly cut off the 8% trade discount. A year later the supplier sued for his $12,000. Since our client lost $2,400 on discounts over the prior year, based on his $30,000 in COD purchases, he counterclaimed under the Robinson-Patman Act for treble (triple) damages. The court said we were right and deducted $7,200 from the $12,000 owed. But we were also able to tack on our legal fees which conveniently equaled the balance of $4,800. The supplier never saw a dime. Had the practice continued for longer, the supplier would have owed my client money. Don't play around with discriminatory discounts. It's expensive.

42. Q: Based on your extensive experience in representing debtors, how many actually go into business with the objective of "busting it out" by not paying creditors?

A: It's rare. I don't think I ever met such a character. It happens, of course, but less often then creditors think. Most people bring to an enterprise a certain sincerity in widely varying degrees.

What oftentimes does happen is that at some point in time, a debtor realizes he or she is in over their head with debt, or the business isn't working out for a variety of reasons and a soul-and-cash-saving sale isn't in the cards. That's when they become creative with creditors—trying to land trade credit to pay-down a bank (holding their guarantee) or to recoup their own investment in the business. The sorry facts are that many businesspeople buy goods knowing they'll never pay. It's all a matter of perception. Theirs is survival.

43. Q: We are concerned about $200,000 in officers' loans on the books of one of our retail sporting goods customers. This account wants us to open a $100,000 credit line, and despite the $150,000 net worth of the firm, I think the officers should subordinate their debt to ours. Is this an unreasonable request?

A: No request designed to improve your chances of collecting is unreasonable. At the very least, the officers should agree to subordination. Push for an even better position—a security interest on business assets and/or stockholder guarantees. The objective should be to stand first in line ahead of *all* creditors, including the officers.

If the officers refuse security or total subordination, try some alternatives:

1. Will the officers agree to a compromise, perhaps a *partial* subordination for $100,000?

2. How about having the officers *assign* their debt to you as security for the debt owed you?

3. Can you at least reach agreement that the officers will subordinate *future* loans to the business?

4. Are the officers inclined to *defer* repayment of their debt, while money is owed you?

As you can see, the possibilities are endless. The true purpose of subordination is not necessarily to protect you—as few subordinations actually accomplish this in financial terms. Its real value is to determine the officers' own confidence in the business by allowing your interests to come ahead of theirs.

44. Q: A few months ago we found ourselves in the awkward position of borrowing money at 22% for which we charged accounts 18% on overdue receivables. Fortunately, the prime lending rate came down so now we are borrowing at 17 to 18% and not losing interest. Should the prime rate increase again, can we increase the interest rate to our customers?

A: Your question requires a two-part answer:

On existing debt, the customer is only obligated to pay the interest rate stated at the time of purchase. If the invoice announced interest at 18% (1.5% per month), then you'll have to live with that interest charge.

It's another story for future debt. Any interest is legal provided it doesn't violate state usury statutes and is stated (usually on the invoice) at the time of sale. Compliance with usury laws are the bigger problem. For example, your state may allow 24% interest, but you may be bound by the usury laws in the state where the customer operates its business. If the customer's state prohibits interest in excess of 18%, your 24% interest may not be enforceable.

And it's even more complicated. Some usury laws provide only *excess* interest will be forfeited. Other laws say *all* interest is forfeited. And some states with a punitive twist allow forfeiture of *both* interest and the underlying debt.

If you have customers in diverse states you have some investigating to do. However, if you only deal with customers in your own state, or one or two adjoining states, it won't take your attorney long to find the maximum permissible interest for each.

45. Q: Since we started our sheet metal fabrication plant several years ago, we had several credit losses. A few centered on disputes over quality or delivery scheduling. One case for $60,000 has been tied up in court for two years already and we still can't get a trial date. Should we use an arbitration clause in future contracts?

A: Arbitration instead of litigation has its advantages and disadvantages.
The advantages of arbitration are:

1.   *It's faster.*   In most areas you can obtain a hearing before the American Arbitration Association within 4 to 5 months. Courts measure time in terms of years.

2.   *It's less costly.*   Since arbitration is less formal and faster than litigation, legal fees and related costs can be substantially less.

3.   *It provides expertise.*   Arbitration cases are generally heard by a panel of arbitrators knowledgeable in the field. This is particularly useful in technical cases involving problems a court or jury may not easily grasp.

The one disadvantage with arbitration is that you cannot seek the pretrial remedies a court provides. And this is an important consideration. Courts, for example, may grant injunctions and attachments in advance of trial if it appears the creditor has a strong case. These pretrial remedies can go a long way in protecting and enforcing collections.

For this reason arbitration lends itself best to complicated, fact-riddled cases. Construction and service firms generally favor arbitration. Firms providing a general product usually favor litigation and the pretrial powers of a court.

You cannot compel arbitration unless both you and your customer agree to it at the time of contract. If your terms are silent on arbitration, both you and your customer can later agree to it.

It comes down to collection strategy—and it should be reviewed by your attorney who can assess the pro's and con's of each to your firm and the nature of its dealings.

46. Q: We have one account who has been promising us payment for five years on his overdue $1,200 balance. He has made token payments over the years, but now I find the account is over the four-year statute of limitations imposed in our state. Are we out of luck?

A: I don't think so. Three actions by a debtor can extend the statute of limitations, namely: The making of partial payment, written acknowledgment of the debt, or a new promise to pay.

It looks like you can still go after your customer for four years from the date of his last payment or promise to pay as either starts the four-year time period anew.

47. Q: One of our smaller accounts owes us $400 for hardware sold to his appliance distributorship. A few days ago we received a five-page tale of woe outlining his poor financial condition. With it came a composition agreement asking us (and all other creditors) to accept a 20% payment in full discharge of our $400 debt. Should we accept?

A: Without further information it's difficult to say, but generally small creditors (under $300 to $500) should hold out when faced with a composition agreement.

The reason is in its strategy. Rather than allow small creditors to wreck a well-conceived composition agreement by holding out and coercing the debtor for full payment, large creditors usually pitch in and pay the small dissenters. It's not charity. The larger creditors in such a case realize the composition is in their best interests and want it to be successful. Small nuisance creditors, like yourself, stand in the way of that success.

There's one important exception to the rule. If you see the customer as a future source of profitable business then support the composition if it's reasonable. You're no longer fighting to save your $400 but the goodwill of the customer.

I recall a creditor who foolishly played tough. As a supplier
to a small nursing home he refused to go along with a general
creditor settlement (composition) on his $600 bill. The customer
paid him in full and this creditor declared himself the winner.
It was a short-lived victory, however. This nursing home operator
now runs a chain of twenty nursing homes. For the sake of $600
our creditor friend lost a customer who would now be able to
buy over $300,000 a year from him.

Never think in nickel-and-dime terms unless you are sure those
are the only nickels and dimes you'll ever see from the customer.
Otherwise gamble and go for tomorrow's bigger sales dollars.

48. Q: We are having a battle with one of our collection agencies.
We forwarded to them a $3,000 claim against a clothing chain.
The customer wants to settle by returning $3,000 in merchandise,
which is fine with us. That's where our problem comes in. The
collection agency wants their full commission on the $3,000. We
say they're entitled to nothing since we received no cash in settlement. What's the standard practice?

A: The standard rule is to pay a one-half commission. For
example, if the agency charged 25% fee on cash recovery, it
would be entitled to $750 had you received cash. Here the com-
mission would be $375. Chances are your agency has a commission
rate list and you may be bound by it.

I don't agree with this policy. I think collection agencies and
attorneys should be allowed their *full* commission on return
goods. Stop shaking your head. I know return merchandise isn't
the same as cash in your economic terms, but consider it in terms
of motivating an agency and attorney to go after possible returns,
instead of impossible cash.

I see the problem at work every day. Our firm is always going
to war against a large law firm representing creditors. We routinely
offer to return merchandise. They routinely refuse. My clients
routinely go bankrupt. Their clients routinely end up with nothing.
It's one big nonsense routine. They admitted their reason for
discouraging return goods settlements. It cuts their fee. I don't
think it's objective representation for their client. If they were
assured their full fee, I'm sure it would motivate them to look

in *every* direction for payment. And it's not a unique situation. It's an industry-wide problem ready for a new solution.

49. Q: How accurate are financial statements completed by small business firms? We always send them to new customers for completion and two months after the "healthy" customer sends back his glowing financial statement the account goes "belly-up."

A: You answered your own question. Customer-completed financial statements are hardly worth the paper they're written on. It reminds me of the old song "Accentuate the positive, eliminate the negative."

Some creditors try to keep accounts honest in reporting financial information by having them sign under the penalties of perjury. It never stops the cockeyed optimist who believes what he writes down.

If you want financial information, look to the financials prepared by the accountant. At least use them as a backup for comparison purposes.

50. Q: Should we check into insurance coverage as a condition for credit? Once or twice a customer's business was destroyed by fire and we received no payment due to inadequate insurance coverage.

A: A major supplier certainly should. It's not a major item for a small creditor.

There are several problems with insurance:

1. The policy can be canceled without creditor notification. A secured creditor should be named as a loss-payee and would receive both notice of cancellation and payment in the event of loss.

2. The insurance, regardless of coverage, cannot exceed the value of assets. This may be considerably less than total liabilities.

3. Small businesses frequently let their insurance lapse once they become insolvent or run into serious cash-flow problems. They reason that it's foolish to spend valuable cash-flow dollars on insurance, only to protect the interests of creditors.

51. Q: How can we sharpen up the skills of our credit people? They need some new ideas.

A: Hopefully this book helped. But I have an even better idea. Send them down the hall to spend a few days at accounts payable. They'll see the other side of the coin, and they'll see what your own creditors are up to in shaking money loose from your firm.

Every company has its offensive team (credit) and its defensive team (accounts payable). As with football, each team must learn certain tricks from the other if it's to improve their own performance.

Let them sit behind the desk, handle a few heated phone calls, and invent some tall stories. They'll have a better idea of what *getting paid* is all about.

52. Q: Under what situations is it advisable for creditors to petition a business into bankruptcy after it has made an assignment for the benefit of creditors?

A: The only time it's recommended is when you suspect the debtor of fraud, or when there is a voidable preference that could be set aside under a bankruptcy but could not be recovered under an assignment.

You also want to watch out for "friendly" assignments where the assignee is not "arm's length" from the debtor. The assignees should preferably be an attorney with no prior affiliation with the debtor, and it certainly shouldn't be its attorney as the assignee is now representing the interests of creditors.

The bankruptcy should be instituted within four months of the assignment; otherwise the assignee may be able to continue with the administration of the estate. A bankruptcy court also has the right to abstain in a post-assignment bankruptcy if it believes the interests of creditors are adeqately protected under the assignment and no advantage would be gained by proceeding as a bankruptcy case.

In most cases creditors dump an assignment into bankruptcy to retaliate against the debtor. The vindictive reason is far more common than the expectancy of any greater creditor recovery. Once the firm is in bankruptcy, the debtor is obligated to go through the proceedings, prepare schedules, and incur legal fees avoided under the less complex assignment. But creditors may pay some price for this, including a smaller dividend due to higher expenses of administration and a much longer time delay in receiving dividends.

53. Q: We experience a problem collecting from accounts who we have under an extension agreement. Most of these customers do pay, but usually the payments are 30 to 60 days late and seldom consistent. How can we improve the payment performance without renegotiating the payments?

A: Every extension agreement should be secured by assets. It puts you in a much better position to enforce payments.

What I try to do when negotiating an extension agreement is to offer an incentive for timely payments. For example, if the interest rate is 18%, you may offer to reduce interest to 15% if all payments are made within the due date. The interest rebate could be repaid once all payments have been made, or it can be applied to the final payments.

The reduced interest incentive isn't enough for the seriously troubled firm, and that's why you should try to obtain security as your primary objective.

54. Q: What practical purpose does a security interest on assets have if the assets are already overencumbered? A retail clothing store customer has a secured SBA loan against the business in the amount of $60,000, but if the business were to liquidate its assets wouldn't bring more than $20,000 to $30,000. Still, our area credit supervisor has been pushing me to obtain a security interest from this customer to secure our $9,000 overdue balance.

A: I agree with your credit supervisor. It's true. The business doesn't presently offer a chance to bail out your debt if it went into liquidation, but the security interest still has a value.

Its major value is as a "club" to enforce payment. If the account does not pay, you can threaten foreclosure. It won't put any money in your pocket, but your customer faces the loss of its business.

A second reason for the security is that you never know how much will be owed the SBA when the business does go into

liquidation. Many SBA loans are also secured by real estate mortgages, and in more than one instance I have seen the SBA paid
down from the real estate, leaving the business assets free for
subordinate lien holders.

Security is no criterion for credit with the overencumbered
firm. But it can be an effective "back up" for credit based on
other yardsticks. Obtaining security once the debt exists is a
greater problem. What are you offering the customer in return?
The most common incentive is a lenient pay-out period. I have
seen many debtors agree to a security interest and a one- or two-
year pay-out in exchange for less collection pressure.

55. Q: We have a problem with a manufacturer who claims
$10,000 in delivered fabric is defective. The total shipment was
over $60,000 and now he's holding up payment on the entire
balance. What approach can we use to collect?

A: Any time there is a dispute over part of a debt but the
remainder is uncontested, your best alternative is to try for payment
on the uncontested portion. See if the account will pay the $50,000,
leaving open the question of liability for the $10,000.

A shrewd customer won't fall for this, as he loses his bargaining
leverage. After all, he may be able to prove damages in excess of
the $10,000 due to inability to fulfill contracts and lost profits.
Even if he can't, his defense on the $10,000 may hold up the
entire claim once it goes into litigation. So time is on his side.

56. Q: Our merchants association offers a service of providing
collection letters with the association imprint. We prepare the
letters; however, to the customer it appears to be sent by the
association. The threat behind the letter is the impression that
nonpayment will result in dissemination of the customer's name
to other interchange members. How effective are these third-party
association letters?

A: They are slightly more effective than direct creditor correspondence. Generally, debtors attach the same importance to
them as collection agency letters.

Usually these letters are the third in a series of collection
letters, following the reminder and request-for-payment notice,
but prior to the demand letter.

57. Q: Should we send our customers advance notice of our intent to send a sight draft to its bank, or ignore a letter and just go ahead with the draft.

A: Send the letter first. The letter is more important than the sight draft. Understand that the bank can't honor the sight draft without the debtor's approval or signature. Most collection people think a sight draft is effective because it embarrasses the debtor with its bank. That's not my experience. I think the value of a sight draft is that the average small businessperson doesn't know what a sight draft is and may *think* you can draw down on his account. And this type letter can certainly create that impression.

Gentlemen:

Your account balance of $957 is now four months in arrears, and you have not responded to our prior communications.

We do not feel we can carry your account any longer. Unless we hear from you by September 15, we will assume we have your permission to draw a draft on your bank for this amount. It will be drawn through the First National Bank of Suffolk.

We hope that you will want to avoid this inconvenient method of payment and prefer to call us to make other arrangements.

Very truly,

Many of my clients do call when receiving this advance notice and do make payment arrangements without realizing the bank can't honor the sight draft under any circumstances without their signature.

58. Q: We mailed a customer a letter advising that we granted it a $10,000 credit limit. The account has always paid us on time and presently owes us no balance, but wants to place a $6,000 order. We learned the customer is in default of its bank loans and the bank is threatening to foreclose. Our problem is that we won't ship on credit under the circumstances, and the customer is claiming we are breaching the terms of our credit letter. Can we be liable?

A: In many states a letter that grants credit is treated as a contract. As a practical matter you still shouldn't ship if you believe the customer is a serious credit risk. If the customer were to sue, it would have difficulty proving damages, but on the other hand, you certainly would suffer a loss if the customer could not pay.

Since you can be bound by what you do—and do not say—in a letter granting credit, use some protective language. The letter should provide you the right to terminate or reduce credit at any time.

The purpose of the credit-granting letter should not be to create a contractually binding contract. Then it only favors the customer. What the customer is interested in is the present credit you will grant, with it implied he will maintain credit worthiness.

59. Q: How accurate are financial ratios that use net worth in the calculation?

A: I think they are the least accurate ratios. Since net worth is the difference between assets and liabilities, its accuracy can be no better than either of these. Assets, of course, include fixtures, equipment, and real estate which may be depreciated down to a low book value, while they really have a sizable value; licenses, patents, and trademarks may also be understated.

Certain fixed assets may also be overstated. This is true when a customer recently buys a business and allocates a high percentage of the price to tangible assets to recover depreciation.

Rather than look to net worth as a decisive credit indicator, look to the retained earnings. It can be a much more accurate indicator of financial condition.

60. Q: Some firms maintain a record of their customer's banks. What purpose does it serve?

A: Aside from it being useful in tracing uncredited payments, knowing a customer's bank can help you collect in two ways.

One reason to know the customer's banking affiliation is so you can present a sight draft. Your attorney may also have a use for it. It many states the courts routinely grant a prejudgment attachment over a debtor's bank account. Since this attachment is without notice, your attorney can only find out the name of the bank from you.

Although your credit applications disclose your customer's original bank, record any new or recent banking affiliations so you always know the *present* bank. And be on the lookout for the customer who constantly changes banks. Usually it's because of a history of overdrafts or bounced checks.

61. Q: How important is "Highest Recent Credit" on a credit agency report?

A: "Highest Recent Credit" is a widely misunderstood term. It can easily be mistaken for the credit line established by the creditor. In actuality it only represents the highest balance recently outstanding. And this balance may be in excess of the approval credit line.

What you want to look for is "Highest Credit Against Amount Owing." This indicates whether the subject of the report is using the maximum credit line reported by its creditors.

"Amount Past Due" also requires some examination. A report showing little indebtedness, when checked as to paying record, often indicates a lack of creditor confidence.

62. Q: What is the best way to determine the efficiency of our collection program?

A: There are three common methods:

1. Accounts receivable aging.
2. Days sales outstanding.
3. Receivable turnover.

Aging of Receivables is the basic method. The aging shows you who owes you money, how much, and for how long. The advantage of this analysis is that it provides an individual account analysis. Obviously, you should focus on the accounts with the highest balances outstanding the longest.

Most accounts receivable aging breaks the receivables down by category percentile. For example, the percentage of customers in the 30- to 60-day category will be shown. This helps see any shift of percentages to the older categories and can signal either increasing credit leniency or decreasing collection effectiveness.

Days Sales Outstanding measures overall credit efficiency by dividing the closing accounts receivable balance by the average daily credit billings. For example

$$\frac{\text{Closing Accounts Receivable}}{\text{Average Daily Billings}} = \text{D.S.O.}$$

The D.S.O. should parallel your terms of sale. If your terms are 30 days, then the D.S.O. should approximate those terms. A D.S.O. appreciably in excess of the terms of sale shows too lenient a credit and collection policy.

Receivable Turnover is sometimes referred to as the average collection period. The calculation shows you how long it takes to collect an "average account." It essentially shows you the same as a D.S.O., so the difference is more in terminology than function.

When receiving the D.S.O. (or average collection period), compare it to industry averages *and* your prior figures. A constantly increasing D.S.O. or collection period shows a weakening credit picture.

63. Q: Our firm has bad debts in excess of 3%. We are thinking about credit insurance to protect us from further losses. How does credit insurance work?

A: You can write to one of two companies who offer commercial credit insurance: (1) London Guarantee and Accident Company, and (2) American Credit Indemnity Company.

Credit insurance is only available for commercial rather than consumer credit. The policy amount is based on the policyholders sales volume and size of credit business. For example, a business with sales of $10 million may have a policy equal to 5% of sales, or $500,000.

The policies also have a deductibility feature, expressed as a percentage of sales. If the deductable is 0.5% on sales, the deductible would be $50,000 on sales of $10 million, but increase to $60,000 should sales increase to $12 million.

Insurance limits per customer is based on its credit rating. Usually Dun and Bradstreet is used as a reference. For example, a firm rated 3A or better may qualify for $100,000 in coverage, whereas a FF account may have a $5,000 ceiling. Nonrated firms are subject to insurer's approval.

Insurance costs are based on sales volume and account risk. Since insurance costs can approach 1% of sales, and do not necessarily cover marginal accounts, many firms do not believe insurance is cost-justified. Many of the firms that do have it are required to have it to satisfy borrowing conditions.

64. Q: One of our larger customers is in Chapter 11 proceedings and has been for three months. Our concern is that inventories are decreasing, providing us with less recovery if the business fails. What steps can we take to protect ourselves.

A: The first step is to review the debtor's financial reports. Under bankruptcy procedure, a Chapter 11 firm must submit biweekly statements showing income and expenses. Since these are really cash-flow statements, you can't measure profitability.

Tracking losses should be the function of the creditors. But any creditor can ask the court to require the debtor to post indemnity for any future losses. For example, if the business is losing $3,000 a week, the owners of the business may have to pledge a cash bond equal to this amount (or the continuing losses) as a condition for continuing the business.

It's common for a debtor to go into Chapter 11 without either plans for rehabilitation or any reasonable chance for it happening. In the meantime the business is slowly drained of assets. The legal safeguards are there for creditors, but they have to use those safeguards.

GLOSSARY

ACCEPTANCE. An agreeing, either expressly or by conduct, to the act or offer of another so that a contract is concluded and the parties are bound.

ACCORD AND SATISFACTION. The full settlement of some disputed claim by the performance of some different action.

ACCOMMODATION INDORSER. One who endorses a note without receiving compensation, so that another person may raise money or obtain credit thereby.

ACKNOWLEDGMENT. The act of one by whom an instrument has been executed in declaring before a competent court or officer that it is his act or signature.

ACTION. A legal proceeding by which one demands or enforces one's right in a court of justice.

ACTIONABLE. Subject to, or affording ground for, an action or suit at law.

ADMINISTRATOR. A person who is legally vested with the right of administration of an estate, especially of one belonging to someone judged incapable or the estate of a deceased person.

AFFIDAVIT. A written statement signed and sworn to before an authorized officer.

AFTER-ACQUIRED PROPERTY. This term applies to mortgages or other indebtedness acquired by a debtor and which secures the indebtedness.

AGENT. One who acts on behalf of another person.

AMICUS CURAE. A Friend of the Court. An outsider who introduces evidence or argument in a case for the court's assistance.

ARBITRATION. Submission of a disputed matter to a disinterested third person for consideration.

ARRANGEMENT. An agreement between a debtor and his creditors modifying his obligations to them by a composition or extension.

ASSIGNMENT. Written transfer of title or interest; a transfer of property; a grant.

ASSUMPSIT. An action on contract to recover damages for a breach of contract.

ATTACHMENT. The method by which a debtor's personal or real property is placed in the custody of the law pending the outcome of a creditor's suit.

ATTESTATION. The act of witnessing any act or event. Used with reference to signing or executing a document. As applied to wills, it is a clause at the foot of the instrument declaring it was signed in compliance with statutory requirements.

ATTORNEY-IN-FACT. A person appointed by another to act in his place. This power is given by an instrument called power of attorney.

BAILMENT. A contract by which goods are delivered by one person (bailor) to another person (bailee) for a certain purpose, upon an expressed or implied promise by the bailee to return them to the bailor after the purpose has been fulfilled.

BILL OF EXCHANGE. Also known as a draft. It is a negotiable instrument which is drawn by one person, ordering a second person to pay a definite sum of money to a third person on sight or at some definite future time.

BILL OF LADING. A document given by a common carrier, representing both a receipt for goods shipped and a contract for the shipment.

BILL OF SALE. A written agreement transferring or assigning personal property, goods, and chattels.

BLANK INDORSEMENT. Writing one's name on the back of a negotiable instrument making it payable to bearer.

BLUE SKY LAWS. Law pertaining to punishment of persons who sell illegal stock; provide jurisdiction over investment companies.

BONA FIDE. In good faith. Honestly, without fraud or collusion or participation in wrongdoing.

BONA FIDE PURCHASER. A purchaser in good faith, that is, without notice of any defect and for a valuable consideration.

BULK TRANSFER. Movement of inventory or a portion thereof outside of regular course of business.

CAVEAT EMPTOR. Let the buyer beware. Unless a warranty is offered the buyer buys at his own risk.

CERTIORARI. Writ issued by a superior court directing an inferior court to send to former court the record of a certain case.

CHATTEL. Any kind of movable personal property.

CHATTEL MORTGAGE. A mortgage on personal property.

CHOSE. Personal property; a thing.

COLLATERAL SECURITY. Given in addition to principal security; that is, if a person borrows money on a mortgage (principal security), he may deposit additional bonds or stock with lender as collateral security.

COMMON CARRIER. A person or firm in business of transporting goods or persons.

CONSIDERATION. The act or promise or price for which an agreement is entered into.

CONSIGNMENT. Sending of goods to another to be sold for the former's account.

CONVEYANCE. A means by which property is transferred from one person to another by a written instrument and other formalities.

COPYRIGHT. The grant, by the government, of an exclusive privilege to print and dispose of designated writing.

COUNTERCLAIM. A cause of action, set up by the defendant, which is to be tried at the same time as the cause of the action alleged by the plaintiff.

COVENANT. An agreement between two or more parties. A promise in writing and under seal.

DEVISE. A gift of land or other realty by a will.

DISHONOR. To refuse to pay a negotiable instrument when due.

DRAFT. An instrument used in the collection of a debt. Also a bill of exchange.

DRAWEE. The one on whom a check or a draft is drawn, usually the bank.

DRAWER. The one by whom a check or draft is issued and signed.

EASEMENT. The right of a landowner to use the land of another for a specified purpose.

EMINENT DOMAIN. The right of a government to obtain private property for public use.

EQUITY OF REDEMPTION. The right, which is enforced by equity, of a mortgagor to redeem the mortgaged land by payment of the principal and interest.

ESCROW. Delivery, to a third person, of a deed or other instrument to be held until the perfomance of some act or the happening of some event.

ESTOPPEL. A rule of law barring a person from asserting certain facts because of his previous act or statement inconsistent therewith.

FACTOR. One who transacts business for another.

FEE SIMPLE. Complete and clear title to real property.

FIXTURE. Something which has been added to real estate and may not be removed without damage to the property.

FORECLOSURE. A deprival of rights of property because a mortgagor fails to pay off the mortgage debt.

FRANCHISE. A privilege; a grant from a sovereign authority; a right given by a corporation to another to sell a certain product or service in a given area.

GARNISHMENT. Attachment on money or wages to be paid to a defendant, requiring the withholding of payment because of a creditor's claim on it.

GUARANTY. A collateral promise to answer for the debt, default, or nonpayment of another.

INCHOATE. Begun but not completed; as a contract not executed by all the parties; or a wife's interest in her living husband's lands called her "inchoate right of dower."

INDEMNITY. A collateral contract or security to prevent a person from being harmed by an act or forebearance which he does at the request of another.

INDORESMENT. The signature, on the back of a check or other negotiable paper, of the one transferring it.

INSURABLE INTEREST. Monetary interest in property or in the life of another person, which is necessary in order to insure property or take out life insurance.

INTESTATE. One who dies without leaving a valid will.

JOINT LIABILITY. An obligation or liability incurred, either under contract or otherwise, by two or more parties.

JOINT TENANCY. Ownership of land by two or more persons, with the survivors taking the whole interest in the property.

L.S. Initials used following a signature in place of a seal.

LATCHES. A lack of activity; procrastination by a person in enforcement of a legal right.

LIEN. A right by which a person can claim a charge against the property of a debtor as security for the payment of a debt or performance of a duty.

LIQUIDATED DAMAGES. Pertains to agreement included in some contracts indicating that, if the contract is broken, the one breaking it will pay a given amount to the other party. This amount must be equal to the proximate value of the loss or an agreed upon amount that is to be paid in the event of breach of contract.

LIS PENDENS. A notice of a pending suit or action on real property.

MINOR. A person under legal age.

MORTGAGE. A pledge or security of property, or interest in property, for repayment of a debt or performance of some obligation.

NEGLIGENCE. Want of proper care or diligence in doing something or in omitting to do something which creates an injury or wrong.

NEGOTIABLE. A form in which an instrument is transferable and can be delivered with the rights originally created by it.

NISI PRIUS. Unless before. Used for certain causes, writs, actions, or trials.

NOMINAL DAMAGES. If little damage or loss has been sustained, the award is called nominal damages.

NOTARY PUBLIC. A public official who witnesses a deed or any other written statement to establish its authenticity.

PER CURIAM. By the court, decisions or opinions of more than one judge.

PER STIRPES. Used to designate that mode of reckoning the rights or liabilities of descendants in which children of any one descendant have or take only the share which their parent would have taken if living.

PERJURY.   A false statement made by a witness under oath in a judicial proceeding.

PERSONAL PROPERTY.   Property which is movable, but not land or that which is permanently attached to land.

PLEDGE.   A bailment of a chattel or object of personal property as security for the satisfaction of a debt or other obligation.

PREFERENCE.   Priority in the right to demand and receive satisfaction of an obligation.

PRIMA FACIE.   At the first view; on the face of it. Evidence sufficient to establish a fact.

PROBATE.   Processing of a will to prove its authenticity.

RATIFICATION.   Confirmation of an act or contract entered into by another party; which when so ratified takes effect as if originally made by the person himself; this validates a voidable contract.

REAL PROPERTY.   Property, such as buildings, land, mineral deposits, and trees, that is generally permanent and not easily moved.

RECEIVER.   A person appointed by the court to realize the assets or protect the property until legal rights of parties have been ascertained or established.

RECLAMATION.   A demand by a state to which a person or thing belongs that he or it be delivered up by those who have acquired control irregularly.

REPLEVIN.   An action to return goods, which have been unlawfully removed, to the original possessor.

RESCISSION.   The cancellation or breaking of a contract by either court action or agreement by the parties concerned.

RES ADJUDICATA (OR RES JUDICATA).   A judicial decision on a question which is conclusive until reversed; a matter which has been adjudged previously.

SATISFACTION.   The exhaustion of an obligation by performance or some act equivalent to performance. Thus, where a debt is due by one person to another, payment by the debtor produces satisfaction of the debt.

SEAL.   An impression or mark usually made on the lower-left corner of a legal instrument.

SET-OFF.   A cross-claim for money by defendant for which he might maintain an action against the plaintiff and which has the effect of reducing the plaintiff's claim by that amount.

STATUTE OF FRAUDS. A law requiring that certain contracts be written and contain the signatures of both parties.

STATUTE OF LIMITATIONS. A law regulating the period of time during which debts may be collected.

SUBROGATION. The right of one person to substitute for another as a creditor.

SUMMONS. An action, in writing, served upon a person to appear at a certain place on a given date.

SURETY. A party who legally binds himself to pay a specific sum if a debtor does not do so on a specific date, or to perform a given act if another person does not do it in accordance with a written agreement.

TENANCY IN COMMON. The tenancy of those who hold lands or other property in common.

TENANCY BY THE ENTIRETY. A tenancy in which husband and wife are seized of the whole but without power of severing, thus differing from joint tenancy.

TESTATOR. A person who makes a will.

TORT. A violation of the legal rights of another by negligence, assault, battery, slander, or libel.

TORTIOUS. Wrongful; of the nature of or implying tort or injury.

TURNOVER PROCEEDING. A proceeding authorized under the Bankruptcy Act which requires property of a bankrupt to be turned over to receiver for administration.

ULTRA VIRES. Acts of corporation which are beyond powers originally authorized.

UNDERWRITER. A person who joins with others in entering into a policy of insurance as the insurer.

USURY. An excessive or inordinate premium for the use of borrowed money.

VENUE. In criminal procedure, the venue is a note in the margin of an indictment, giving the name of the county or district within which the court in which the indictment is preferred has jurisdiction. In common law practice, the venue is the part of the declaration in an action which designates the county in which the action is to be tried.

WAIVER.   Giving up a legal right.

WARRANTY.   A guaranty or undertaking forming part of a sale or other transaction. It can be either expressed or implied.

WRIT.   A document in the name and under the seal of the government, a court, or an officer of the government, commanding the person to whom it is addressed to do, or forebear from doing, some act.

INDEX